CROWDED HOUSE

Gill Books

Hume Avenue

Park West

Dublin 12

www.gillbooks.ie

Gill Books is an imprint of M.H. Gill and Co.

© Frank Greaney 2020

978 07171 90263

Edited by Jane Rogers

Proofread by Djinn von Noorden

Printed by CPI Group (UK) Ltd, Croydon, CR0 4YY

This book is typeset in 12.75 on 19.5pt Garamond Pro

The paper used in this book comes from the wood pulp
of managed forests. For every tree felled, at least one
tree is planted, thereby renewing natural resources.

The author and publisher have made every effort
to trace all copyright holders, but if any have been
inadvertently overlooked we would be pleased to make
the necessary arrangement at the first opportunity.

A CIP catalogue record for this book is available from
the British Library.

5 4 3 2 1

CROWDED HOUSE

THE DEFINITIVE STORY BEHIND THE
GRUESOME MURDER OF PATRICIA O'CONNOR

FRANK GREANEY

GILL BOOKS

For Pops

CONTENTS

AUTHOR'S NOTE

Given my work previously as a crime reporter with 98FM and my current role as Courts Correspondent for Newstalk and Today FM, it's safe to say I'm no stranger to gruesome tales. Throughout my career, I have covered some of the most distressing and harrowing criminal cases to come before the courts, including the Belfast rape trial, the murder of Elaine O'Hara by Graham Dwyer, the 'Mr. Moonlight' murder trial and, more recently, the Ana Kriégel murder trial. Over the years, I have been approached on a number of occasions to write true crime books about the stories I've covered, but nothing ever felt right. You see, I didn't want to just retell a horror story for the sake of it. It felt wrong to dredge up all that trauma for the families without good reason. There had to be more – a greater purpose.

What appealed to me about this story was that it presented the opportunity to set the record straight about the victim. Murder victims don't have a voice. All a jury is ever concerned about are the events leading up to a person's death, how they died and who was responsible. More often than not, you don't get a feel for who the person was, what kind of life they led, their hopes and dreams. That makes sense, of course. Cold, hard evidence is all a jury needs for their deliberations. However, in this case, the jurors learned a lot about Patricia O'Connor. Through the words of those squashed together in the dock, she was portrayed as a violent bully who used to terrorise everyone in the house. *Her* house. Wild allegations were made about her. She was even accused of trying to kill her husband and of beating and harassing her own grandchildren.

I like to approach every case with the widest of open minds, but the depiction of Patricia O'Connor during the trial didn't sit well with me. During the proceedings I became familiar with her wider family. Some of her brothers and sisters would take the train from Kilkenny every day to be there. They were there to support their beloved Trisha. They struck me as the salt of the earth. They grew up in Windgap, Co. Kilkenny, a place that reminded me of my own hometown in Co. Galway. Her son Richard is a decent, kind and hard-working family man. I heard only great things about him. So I wondered how could this woman, who was being depicted as a monster by some of those closest to her, including her own daughter, be of the same stock? It didn't make sense to me. Unsurprisingly, I quickly learned that the picture being portrayed by the accused persons was a web of self-serving lies, told in the hope of furthering their own warped versions of what happened.

The initial research for the book proved difficult because the trial was still live, and there was a reluctance on behalf of those closest to her to speak with me. Totally understandable, of course. Then Covid-19 hit. That proved to be the greatest challenge of all, particularly in the early stages when it was impossible to travel to locations or meet people in person. The key to a successful interview involves building a good rapport with whoever you're interviewing. Personally, I feel that's something that can only truly be achieved through face-to-face meetings. However, that wasn't possible due to travel restrictions during lockdown. The most important thing for me was to convince the people who mattered that I was writing the book for all the right reasons. Patricia's family and friends were devastated at how her name was blackened in court, and I wanted to give them a platform to tell her story. Numerous conversations were held over the phone before a single question was asked. For me, it was all about developing a mutual trust. I wanted them to know that I would be the greatest custodian of their cherished memories. Once that trust was established, the key then was to ask the right questions at the right time to extract as much about her as possible, while also being extremely mindful of the sensitive nature of what we were talking about. I preferred to conduct interviews in stages, to allow everyone a breather. This also proved fruitful in relation to drawing more historic memories to the fore. I left my door open throughout the whole process too, and some contributors came back to me weeks, even months, later, having just remembered something they felt was important.

Without being able to visit the various crime scenes, I initially had to draw from those closest to the case, such as gardaí, members of the search team, neighbours, and residents of Windgap. When I was eventually in a position to travel safely to the various locations relevant to the book, I was then able to add more detail, but it was vital for me to have a good idea of what each place looked like in my mind's eye before I ever put pen to paper.

Colour pieces have no place in day-to-day court reporting. There are strict rules surrounding what can and, more important, what *can't* be said during a criminal trial in order to protect the rights of an accused person. As a rule, court reporting during a live trial must be a 'fair and accurate' portrayal of the day's proceedings, with no room for opinion. That said, I found it useful to jot down my own observations throughout the case. It was great to be able to look back and see how somebody in the dock reacted to a particular piece of testimony, for example.

What was absolutely crucial for me, was to tell this story in a way that didn't make it read like a series of news reports. As often as I could, I told the story through the eyes of Patricia's loved ones, Rita and Breda in particular. I felt it added more of a human element to the story, and made it read more like a novel in places. I also chose to introduce the chapters about Patricia early on so readers would have a better idea of who she was and where she came from before they got to the horrible lies that were told about her.

I found the writing process challenging, but in the best possible way. I had to adopt a completely different mindset. As a broadcast journalist, I'm trained to say more with less words. People want quick updates while sitting in the car or having their dinner. Even the longer updates with Pat Kenny (Newstalk) in the mornings and Matt Cooper (Today FM) in the evenings were no more than ten minutes long. The spoken word is a very different animal to its written counterpart, so it felt like learning to write all over again. I thoroughly enjoyed the process, though. I'm a perfectionist, almost to a fault. Almost! I like to plan and love nothing more than when a good plan comes together. The deadline was tight, so I found myself at my desk researching from 5 a.m. most mornings. After plotting out my day, I found it useful to then go for a run to allow everything to distill in my mind. By the time I had breakfast, I then had a clear picture of how to approach a particular part of the story. When it came to writing, I found I was most productive late at night, when it felt like the whole world was sleeping. I used to carry a notebook with me at all times too. I would scribble down ideas or turns of phrase in it as they came to me during my day. I used to leave the same notebook on my bedside locker while I slept, and would often wake during the night with some inspiration that needed to be jotted down immediately for fear it would be lost by morning.

Something else I found useful during the whole process was to keep the project to myself. Aside from the team at Gill Books, my business partner and one other special person in my life, I didn't tell a soul what I was up to. I really didn't want a fuss made, but more than that, I didn't want the added pressure of being constantly asked about progress, especially when days in front of the computer were not as fruitful as I would have liked – a common anguish for fellow writers, I'm sure. At least now, those closest to me know why I went off the grid during lockdown!

The world was robbed of a kind soul when Patricia O'Connor was brutally murdered by Kieran Greene in May 2017. He stole her dignity too when he disrespected her body afterwards. To add insult to injury, he also tried to rob her of her good name. I hope this book goes some way to restoring that, and I really hope it offers a little comfort to those who valued it most.

1.

A GRIM DISCOVERY

F or as long as she can remember, Christine Murphy and her family have picnicked in the Wicklow Mountains every summer. It's a tradition, and the summer of 2017 was no different. Her father was home from England, and the annual outing was set for 10 June to coincide with his visit.

On a sunny Saturday afternoon, fourteen members of her family travelled in convoy towards the Sally Gap along one of the narrow, twisting roads that carve up the vast, wild landscape. As they approached the iconic crossroads, they drank in the spectacular views of the mountains and surrounding blanket of bog. It was a great day to be alive.

The Sally Gap is one of two east–west passes across the mountain range. It leads you north to Dublin, west to Blessington, south to Glendalough or east to Roundwood. The Great Military Road, which leads to the Sally Gap, was built by the British army in the years after the Irish rebellion of 1798. The lack of access to the mountains caused a headache for the Crown forces during the uprising. There were four roads crossing the mountains from east to west, but nothing connecting them from north to south. Rebel leader Michael Dwyer was born in the mountains, and he knew them like the back of his hand. He also had a band of followers there to help him. The British army built the road to allow troops to quickly traverse the rugged landscape, but also to keep a close eye on the rebels in the hills and help them put down insurgents who were hiding there.

Today, it's still an important and well-worn north–south route across the spine of the mountains, with breathtaking views along the way. Places like the Glencree Valley, the dark waters of Lough Tay, the Kippure Mountains and Glenmacnass Waterfall attract hordes of strollers, hikers and sightseers all year round. Dublin city and its sprawling suburbs south of the River Liffey are just a short spin away, and it's easy to see why it's such an attractive draw for those looking to get away from the hustle and bustle of city life.

The bloody uprising in the late eighteenth century isn't the only link to military combat in the area. Located in a landscape quarry next to the Glencree Centre for Peace and Reconciliation is the Glencree German War Cemetery, and therein lie the graves of 134 German soldiers, mainly Luftwaffe and Kriegsmarine World War II personnel. Many of those interred at the cemetery washed up on Ireland's beaches or fell from the skies in crashed aircraft. A German spy called Major Hermann Görtz was moved there under cover of darkness in 1974 by a group of former German army soldiers, who exhumed his remains from Deansgrange and re-interred them alongside his fellow combatants. A grisly yet appropriate tribute to their fallen comrade.

Christine and her family parked near the Sally Gap and basked in the warm sunshine while enjoying something to eat together. Later that evening, they drove to the Old Boley on the edge of Glencree Woods, not far from the eventual resting place of Major Görtz.

The road to this popular hiking destination gradually rises to reveal the might of the valley below in spectacular fashion. In the distance, the peaked summit of the Sugarloaf Mountain can be seen on a fine day. When the weather turns, its misty veil makes it even more powerful and alluring, as minds wander to thoughts of what lurks beyond the fog.

After their second picnic of the day, Christine and her sister-in-law left the party to get some baby wipes from her brother's car. The cars were parked along the side of the road, not far from where they had set up camp. After fetching the wipes, Christine went looking for somewhere discreet to answer nature's call. She wandered down a slight hill just off the road, and was no more than a few metres from the road when she spotted something in the ditch that stopped her in her tracks. When later asked to describe what she saw, she said, with a nervous giggle, that it looked like a 'piece of a pig'.

Christine didn't go near it. Instead, she walked back down to the spot near the river where her family were still gathered. They stayed there for another half hour or so, catching up on everyone's busy lives and enjoying the dying embers of the balmy evening. When it was time to go, they gathered up their belongings and made their way back to the cars.

On returning to where they had parked, they noticed that one of the car windows had been smashed and a handbag was missing. The family spread out and began searching for it along the bank. They hoped that the thief had discarded it after pocketing its contents.

Christine's aunt Breda Kenny was busy checking the verges just off Military Road when she saw what she thought were animal remains lying in the ditch. She initially discounted it, and the search continued. When Christine stumbled upon the same remains again, she called her brother Jonathan over.

Jonathan moved down into the ditch for a closer look and recoiled when he realised the remains were not of an animal. He had a sinking feeling that this was a far more sinister discovery. As he crouched down and inspected what lay beneath his feet, he was sure he was looking at the upper torso of a human being. He figured it was the part that runs from the ribcage up to the neck. He was right.

2.

TRISHA

Patricia Cooke was born in Windgap, County Kilkenny on 19 March 1956. When she came along, there were already six children in the nest. Six more joined them later, making her the middle child of the family. John was the eldest and Rita was the baby of the family. Tragically, another child died in early infancy.

Patricia's parents, Patrick and Helen, settled in the countryside, a half-hour drive from Kilkenny city. Several lush fields separated them from their nearest neighbours. Windgap is a typical Irish village with a great sense of community. Everybody knows everybody and they all look out for one another.

It has experienced somewhat of a resurgence in recent years, thanks to the hard work of its proud locals who refused to allow their home place to follow in the footsteps of so many others, whose youngsters left in search of work during the recession and never came back. The community rallied together to give people a reason to visit and, more important, to give their own a reason to stay.

After years of detailed planning and dedication, it's now one of the finest villages in Ireland and it attracts people from all over the country and further afield. Local businesses have been revived in recent times and the heart of the community is beating even stronger than ever with the renovation of the community hall and the opening of a new playground. Aside from the people and its local offerings, the real draw to Windgap lies in its natural beauty and historical importance.

Its rich soil has unearthed some significant treasures down through the years. Many of the hidden gems that made their way back into the light have since found a home in Dublin. Just up the road in Killamery, a silver pin brooch from the Viking Age was found by a labourer digging in a field in the 1850s. Legend has it that, not realising what lay beneath his boots, he accidentally broke the pin with a blow from his spade. It can now be seen in the National Museum of Ireland.

Ogham stones can also be found scattered around Windgap. Ogham, often referred to as the 'Celtic Tree Alphabet', is the earliest form of writing in Ireland. It is made up of a series of strokes along or across a line and was usually carved on standing stones to commemorate someone.

One of the few remaining League Houses in Ireland is also found in Windgap. It was built by the Irish National Land League in 1881 to house a farming family evicted from their own lands.

It is a testament to the people who live in Windgap that they've found a way to make their village an attractive and viable place to live in the here and now, while both casting an eye to the future and giving a respectful nod to the past.

It's a far cry from the quiet village Patricia and her siblings grew up in. When she was a child, there were a few shops, two pubs and a post office on the main street, and that was that. Simpler times, perhaps, but she had a very happy childhood.

Her parents were well known and very well respected in the area. They were hard workers. Patrick Cooke worked in forestry and Helen was a homemaker. Helen was christened Helena, but everyone knew her as Helen. Those closest to her called her Nelly.

Helen was extremely house-proud. It was a busy house, but she kept it spick and span with a little help from those living under her roof. Everyone pulled their weight. They had to. Helen hated laziness and instilled a great work ethic in her children from a young age.

When Patricia was small, she and her sisters used to go down to the local well to fetch buckets of water for the house. They had no running water, so Helen would send them down before dinner every day. The well was at the end of a nearby glen, and they would fill their bellies with fresh spring water before they dunked their buckets. She used to go to a local farmer every evening too, for a pint of milk 'for the baby'. She'd be sent down later in the week with a half-crown as payment.

At Easter, they used to go hunting for eggs. Patricia would knock on neighbours' doors looking for any spare ones; her siblings did the same. After bringing their haul back to the homestead, Patrick would tell them they could have as many eggs as they wanted on Easter Sunday. Boiled eggs didn't taste quite as nice as their chocolate equivalent, but the kids left that minor detail out when regaling their classmates about how many eggs they had eaten over the holiday.

The Cookes had their own hens out the back, too. One day, when Rita was very small, she dashed inside with a freshly laid egg cupped in the palm of her hand. She was so proud of her discovery and couldn't wait to tell her father. She ran straight over to him. 'Dada, look!' she squealed as she revealed her treasure.

'What's this, Babby?' he asked.

'I saw the egg come out of the hen's *hole*,' she replied.

Despite his best efforts, Patrick couldn't hide his amusement. The others didn't even try. They roared laughing.

They didn't have much growing up, but the Cooke family home was a happy home, and there was always food on the table. They prayed the Rosary every night before cramming into bunk beds together. There were bodies everywhere. The house got particularly cold during the winter months, so Helen would throw heavy coats over the children after putting them to bed. She used to knit everything for them, including bed sheets, which she made out of flour sacks.

The kitchen was the heart and soul of the house. Helen loved to cook and there was always something in the oven. Visitors were often greeted by the warm and welcoming whiff of a freshly baked loaf of bread. The sweet aroma of hot jam bubbling on the stove tickled the nostrils of summertime guests.

Like all Irish mammies, Helen could turn her hand to pretty much anything. She grew fruit in the garden for the homemade jam. The kids helped her pick the berries when they ripened. When the jam was nearly ready, they'd crowd around her in the kitchen waiting for it to cool. One would slap a label on the jar, while another scribbled down what type of jam it was.

If the kitchen was the heart and soul of the house, the garden was the engine room. Vegetables were grown there all year round. Plucking mucky potatoes and carrots straight out of the ground for dinner was another chore delegated to little hands.

As they got older, the kids were all expected to go out and get jobs. Everyone had to earn their keep. When she was a teenager, Patricia used to babysit for a few families around the village. Her services were always in high demand. She loved minding kids, and people would say she had a motherly way about her that belied her age. Her younger siblings, or 'the little ones' as she called them, looked up to her as more of a mother figure than an older sister. The kids she babysat adored her. They got very excited when they saw her wild red hair bouncing past the window. Trisha, as her family and friends called her, was always so jolly and full of life. She had a great sense of fun, and people saw her as a bit of a free spirit. They were easily drawn to her.

In 1972, when she was sixteen, Patricia moved to Dublin for work. Some of her older siblings were already living there. Back then, most young people left Windgap for 'The Big Smoke' as soon as they were old enough to get a proper job. Kathleen, her eldest sister, was working in a hotel near Harcourt Street at the time. It was just a short stroll from St Stephen's Green. She was living in the city centre and was more than happy to take her little sister under her wing when she arrived.

Dublin city centre was less than 150 kilometres from home for Patricia, but it felt more like a million miles away. Some visitors to the city in the early 1970s saw it as a poor and dirty town with little to offer apart from noisy, smoke-filled bars lined with patrons in cheap, ill-fitting suits.

The year she arrived was the bloodiest year of the Troubles. The sectarian conflict claimed just under five hundred lives in 1972, and Dublin wasn't immune from the violence. The British Embassy on Merrion Square was burned down a few days after British soldiers opened fire during a protest march in the Bogside area of Derry on a day that became known as 'Bloody Sunday'. Thirteen people died on the day itself and another man died from his injuries five months later.

Despite the underlying tension in the city at the time, Patricia was happy in Dublin. She saw it as a very cosmopolitan city and an exciting place to live. Busy men clutching briefcases bustled about; others, sporting wild beards and dodgy tartan flares, moved at a far slower pace. Patricia loved fashion and she had a good eye for it too. Green was her favourite colour. She thought redheads should always dress in green.

Dublin's two main shopping streets, Henry Street and Grafton Street, were always awash with stylish women in colourful dresses hidden away behind trendy raincoats. Dublin Corporation, or 'the Corpo', as it was known back in the day, trialled the pedestrian-isation of Grafton Street the year before Patricia moved there, but it would take another decade before traffic was permanently banned from the street.

O'Connell Street was a blurry rainbow of Ford Escorts and Morris Minors drifting between huge double-decker buses. It was noisy, it smelt funny and it was a far cry from the idyllic homestead Patricia had left behind. But she loved every inch of it.

Patricia settled into city life quickly, but she was very family-oriented and never forgot her roots. She went home to Kilkenny as often as she could. Christmas was a particularly special time because it was the one time of the year when everyone would get together. The house was always full and Helen wasn't afraid to put her prodigal sons and daughters to work when they returned for the holidays. They all had their chores – fetching vegetables from the garden, prepping the dinner, cooking, washing up. Everyone had a job to do, just like when they were kids.

Patricia's first job in Dublin was as a cleaner in a hotel just off Grafton Street. Not long afterwards, she met her future husband, Augustine O'Connor, on a night out at the Crystal Ballroom on South Anne Street. In the 1950s and 1960s, the venue played host to the best jazz and swing orchestra bands in town. The great Johnny Cash played there in 1963. It was later renamed McGonagles, but many locals still referred to it by its original name. Inspired by their early days in Dublin, U2 later immortalised the Crystal Ballroom with a song of the same name.

When Bono first introduced the song to a crowd of fans in Chicago in June 2015, he told them the iconic venue held a special place in his heart. Not only had it helped a fresh-faced U2 make a name for themselves in Dublin in the late 1970s, his parents used to socialise there back in the day. Many matches were made there, and Patricia and Augustine's love also blossomed underneath the chandelier at the Crystal Ballroom. He was ten years older than her, but they had an instant connection. Patricia became pregnant not long afterwards, and they got married.

Augustine, or Gus for short, was a hard worker too. He left school when he was fourteen and became a bike mechanic for the Raleigh Bicycle Company. He was made redundant in his forties and then worked as a porter in various hotels around Dublin. In later years, he took up a job at the Department of Transport, where he remained until he retired, aged 68. From the start, Kathleen approved of her younger sister's suitor. She found him to be kind and very easy-going. She also knew he adored Patricia, so Kathleen had no doubt he'd take great care of her. She used to visit them regularly, and there was always a bit of dinner in the pot for her when she called over on Sundays. Bacon and cabbage was usually on the menu when Gus (or Gussie, as Kathleen used to call him) was on cooking duty.

Their life together started out in a dingy, detached house on Dorset Street. The walls were so damp, you couldn't even hang wallpaper on them. Their first child, Richard, was born in May 1973. The house was no longer fit for purpose, but they were on the council housing list, and were eventually offered a four-bedroom terraced house in Rathfarnham: 66 Mountain View Park.

It wasn't much to look at from the outside. A battered section of redbrick wall lined the footpath leading up to its narrow drive-way. Six concrete steps paved the way to the front door, which was surrounded by grim pebbledash walls. But there was so much space inside and, much to Patricia's delight, it had a long back garden. Her fingers were still green from her days tending to the Cooke family garden in Windgap. The garden at Mountain View Park was maybe fifteen metres or so in length, so there was also plenty of scope to extend to the rear if they ever needed to.

The living room, just off the entrance hall, led to a bright kitchen with access to the rear garden. You could also get to the garden from the front by walking down a gated alleyway to the side of the house. There was a shed out the back too. Upstairs, there were two large double bedrooms and two single bedrooms. The only bathroom was downstairs. It was small. The floor was tiled, and the walls were part-tiled. It had a wall-mounted sink and a shower.

The house was within walking distance of various shops and other amenities in the area and it was well serviced by public transport. There were also some excellent schools nearby. Patricia and Gus wanted to have more children, so that was important. As the name suggests, Mountain View Park is set in the foothills of the stunning Dublin and Wicklow Mountains. Patricia enjoyed living in the big city, but she was a country mouse at heart, so it was comforting to know the mountains were just a stone's throw away. Rathfarnham is actually the start of the 60km-long Military Road, and the village itself was the scene of some skirmishes during the Irish Rebellion of 1798.

Just before Christmas 1978, Patricia and Gus welcomed a second child into their lives, a little sister for Richard. Louise had red hair, just like her mother. When they were small, Patricia used to bring them down to Kilkenny to visit her family during the summer holidays. She would arrive in Windgap weighed down with bags of clothes for whoever wanted them. Her kids loved it there. They would spend all day running around and playing outside in the fresh air with their country cousins.

The door of 66 Mountain View Park was always open, and Patricia welcomed her younger siblings up to Dublin every year during their summer holidays. Helen used to make the trip with Rita, the youngest of her thirteen children. They would spend weeks there and Rita loved every second of it. Louise was a few years younger than her, but Richard was roughly the same age and they got on like a house on fire. Rita really looked forward to her trips to Dublin. It was a world away from where she lived in Windgap and she loved spending time with her big sister, who spoiled her rotten and treated her as if she were one of her own. It was a happy house, and Rita never remembered anyone giving out or being cross. There was always a lovely atmosphere there. Patricia had made it a proper home.

Patricia loved having Rita around, buying clothes for her and cooking her favourite meals. Baking was a hobby of hers and the smell of freshly baked goodies was a lovely reminder of the home sweet home that Helen had made for them in Windgap. When it was time for Rita to return to reality at the end of August, Patricia would take her shopping for new school clothes. She even bought her a fancy new school bag that caught her eye when they were out shopping one day. Rita was so proud of it she couldn't wait to go back to school to show it to her friends. She thought of her big sister every time she threw its straps over her small shoulders. Its sentimental value was far greater than the heavy books and copybooks stuffed inside.

Rita wasn't the only sibling to avail of Patricia's kindness and hospitality. Her older sisters Kathleen and Helen stayed with her for a while at various times too, and she also took in Colette, the second youngest. Colette became pregnant when she was sixteen years old. At the time, having a child out of wedlock in Ireland was bad enough, but to have one outside of marriage and at such a tender age was unthinkable. Her parents were furious. She was told she was bringing shame on the family and was no longer welcome in their home.

Without hesitation, Patricia came to her rescue. She told her parents not to worry, that Colette could stay with her in Dublin. Colette gave birth to a beautiful baby girl and they both lived there, on top of Patricia's own family, until they found their own home nearby. Colette never forgot her sister's act of kindness. Looking back now, she struggles to think what she would have done if Patricia hadn't offered her somewhere to stay. Her own mother didn't want her under her roof, but Patricia welcomed her into her home with open arms. It was already a busy house with her own children, who were very young at the time. The addition of a screaming baby raised the noise levels even more, but Patricia never complained. Not once did she lose her temper. She was so easy-going and did everything she could to help her little sister in her time of need.

Patricia knew what it was like to be a young mother – she wasn't much older than Colette when she had Richard. She was a young bride too and over time, she and Gus started to drift apart. The age gap between them seemed to get wider and wider as the years went by. Patricia was adventurous and full of life, while he was a placid, contented man. She affectionately referred to him as 'the auld fella'. Gus was devastated when they broke up. He felt he'd been a kind and loving husband throughout their marriage. He described her as the 'perfect wife' and he was still very much in love with her when they went their separate ways. Patricia stayed in the family home for a time afterwards, but in her mind the marital flame had gone out and she wasn't interested in reigniting it. She'd find love again and she hoped Gus would too.

3.

THE SEARCH

At 7.43 p.m. on 10 June 2017, Garda Gráinne Warren received a 999 call from a distressed member of the public. The caller identified herself as Breda Kenny. She and her family had just discovered what they believed to be human remains in the Wicklow Mountains, and they didn't know what to do. Breda gave her location and was asked to stay where she was until gardaí arrived. Garda Warren then dispatched a patrol car to investigate.

The grisly discovery just off Military Road drew Breda's nieces and nephews in for a closer look. There were young children among them, and some were looking down into the ditch. Everyone was horrified by what they'd just found.

It took about an hour for Garda Paul Lacey and Garda Joseph Keenan to get there from Enniskerry Garda Station in County Wicklow. That hour felt like an eternity, especially with restless children to entertain after a long day in the sun.

Garda Keenan spoke with the family before taking a look in the ditch. What lay there did appear to be a human torso, but he couldn't be sure. It was over the bank, just off the road, as the family had directed him. His colleague Garda Lacey also thought it looked like human remains. He noticed several sets of footprints in the ditch, so the quick-thinking Garda photographed the soles of everyone's shoes, and they preserved the scene.

Detective Sergeant Brendan Maher was next to arrive. He had travelled there on his own in an unmarked garda car. The body was just ten metres away from a nearby woodland. That didn't make sense. He wouldn't have expected it to be out in the open like that, especially with the cover of dense forestry so close by. The neck portion of the remains was facing him as he looked down from above. He figured the body part was about two metres below where he was standing at the top of the ditch. There wasn't a strong smell off it, which led him to believe it hadn't been there for very long. Something else that struck him was the colour of the grass beneath it. From where he was standing, it didn't appear as if it had been deprived of sunlight for a prolonged period. He guessed the body part had been dropped there in the last 24 hours or so. The grass leading down to it was also freshly flattened, which suggested the torso had been tossed from a height and had then slid down to where it now lay. Sergeant Maher called his superior, Superintendent Pat Ward, who was based in Bray Garda Station. A doctor attended the scene later that night to formally identify the remains as human and pronounce death.

On that same day, Noel Ruane had gone for a drive with his partner. They drove through the Dublin suburb of Rathfarnham en route to the mountains from the Marlay Park side. It was a glorious drive. They stopped at Glenmacnass, 'the Glen of the Hollow of the Waterfall', and decided to go for a walk. They were in no rush, and gulped in the fresh mountain air as they strolled towards the 80m-high waterfall that sits at the top of the valley. It's a stunning location and a popular selfie stop for visitors. The waterfall itself is a sight and sound to behold, especially when in heavy flow. Noel couldn't make out its smooth granite bedrock on this occasion, though – the water was unusually discoloured. As the couple walked along an embankment near a stream, they noticed what they thought were the organs of an animal strewn across a rock. They dismissed it and went on their way.

A news report on the radio the next day gave Noel pause for thought:

'An investigation is under way following the discovery of human remains in Enniskerry, County Wicklow,' the newsreader announced.

Surely not, thought Noel. He turned up the radio.

'They were discovered off Military Road near Glencree yesterday evening.'

Noel's day of rest had just turned into anything but. He couldn't stop thinking about what they'd seen the day before, and he struggled to shake off the feeling that it had something to do with the gruesome discovery near the cemetery.

It wasn't clear at that point whether the remains belonged to a man or a woman, and the newsreader appealed for anyone with information that might assist the investigation to contact gardaí.

Noel thought about calling them, but he didn't want to waste their time. What if he was wrong? What if the remains were gone?

He would hate to bring them all the way out there for a false alarm. They have enough to be doing, he thought. Instead, he decided to go back up and take another look.

He was relieved when he saw that the remains were still there, and he waited where he was until gardaí responded to his call. His suspicions were later confirmed. An analysis of his discovery revealed it to be the lower torso of a human body. The news report was soon updated.

Experienced detectives approach each case with great caution, especially in the early stages of an investigation, when an open mind is one of the most valuable tools at their disposal. Unsurprisingly, the investigation team, led by Superintendent Pat Ward from the Bray district, suspected this second body part was linked to the one found the day before, but they couldn't say for sure, and so nothing was taken for granted.

At this point, investigators didn't have much to work with. They had no clue who the remains belonged to, and they couldn't even tell what gender they were. One striking feature that the two discoveries had in common, though, was that no effort had been made to conceal them. They were totally exposed, just left out in plain view. The investigators hoped the rugged landscape would throw up some more clues.

It was time to start looking.

• • •

The Wicklow Mountains sit in the heart of County Wicklow and stretch outside its borders into Counties Dublin, Wexford and Carlow. They are an incredible vista on Dublin's doorstep, and where they creep into parts of the capital city, locals refer to them as the Dublin Mountains. Whatever you choose to call them, one thing is certain; their towering presence fills those living in their shadows with as much dread as it does wonder.

The rolling hills, with their many streams, lakes, bogs and wooded landscapes with dense foliage and vast terrains, make them a popular dumping ground for those looking to bury dark secrets. But dark secrets don't always stay buried forever, and over the past fifty years many of those secrets have made their way back into the light.

Phyllis Murphy, a 23-year-old woman from Kildare town, went missing three days before Christmas 1979. She was last seen making her way to a bus stop after spending the day buying gifts for her brother's children. Over the next few days, her boots, cardigan, mittens and coat belt were found in the Curragh area of County Kildare, a 22 km-square flat open plain renowned for racehorse breeding. Phyllis's body was found in a woodland in the Wicklow Gap almost a month later. She had been raped and strangled. It took another twenty-three years for her killer to be brought to justice.

On 11 July 1987, David Bowie brought his Glass Spider tour to Ireland when he played at Slane Castle in County Meath. Antoinette Smith, a 27-year-old woman with two young daughters, was lucky enough to get a ticket to see him. Sadly, that was one of the last things she did. She left a nightclub in Dublin city at 2.15 a.m. that night, but never returned home. Her body was found the following Easter Monday in a drain on Glendoo Mountain, just outside Enniskerry, County Wicklow. She too had been raped and strangled before her body was buried in the bog. Her killer has yet to be caught.

Marioara Rostas was just shy of her nineteenth birthday when she was abducted by a Dublin criminal on a Sunday afternoon in January 2008. She had been out begging with her younger brother when she was enticed into a car and driven to a house in Dublin city centre. She was held captive there for a time before she was shot four times in the head. Her body lay hidden in a shallow grave deep in a forest between Manor Kilbride and the Sally Gap in County Wicklow. It had been wrapped and buried beneath the soil over a kilometre from the nearest road, and there it remained for almost five years. A man stood trial for her murder in 2014, but he was acquitted by a jury at the Central Criminal Court. To date, nobody else has been charged with her murder.

• • •

A thorough search of the Wicklow Mountains is no easy task. Sergeant Pat Carroll was assigned to head up the operation, and he decided to refine the initial search to within a 30km radius of where the first body parts were found, between the Featherbeds and Laragh. He knew that the dense forestry and woodlands would make the operation a difficult one.

Hundreds of gardaí and army personnel from three battalions were brought in to comb the area on Monday, 12 June 2017. Members of the Irish Civil Defence, a volunteer-based organisation that supports frontline emergency services, also offered to help.

The search zone was a buzz of activity from first light. Sergeant Carroll and his team pored over detailed maps of the area, and assigned each unit a specific grid to search. Every square inch was accounted for, and no stone was to be left unturned.

The operation also required the services of the Garda Water Unit, and specialist divers splashed into the Glenmacnass River that day, not far from the waterfall where the lower torso was discovered over the weekend. Visibility was poor, but Garda Gerard O'Dea's highly trained eye spotted the next grim piece of the puzzle through the murky waters. It was hard to make out underwater, but it turned out to be part of a human leg. At a glance, he figured it was about twelve inches in length, and it appeared to have been cut just above the ankle. It was taken away for further analysis.

Back on dry land, Corporal Barry Hannon from Cathal Brugha Barracks was searching an area between the waterfall and the Sally Gap when something caught his eye. It was about 4 p.m. He shouted 'Stop!' As per protocol, the others in his search team froze to their spot. He approached with care. Clumsy footwork can compromise a crime scene, so every step was carefully considered. To his left, he saw three pieces of what looked like butchered meat. There were two large pieces and one smaller piece. They were not attached to one another and they were lying just six feet from the road, right out in the open. Another army corporal thought it looked like 'pork lying under a bush'. He later described it as 'meat, with bone protruding from it', and said the third piece looked like a bent elbow. They shouted 'Find!' and gardaí took over. A post-mortem later revealed these 'pieces of meat' to be the upper right arm, the right thigh and knee, which had been cut downwards from the front of the thigh, and the right upper elbow and forearm.

Given the scale of the search and the nature of what the investigators were looking for, it came as no surprise that the operation attracted a lot of media attention. News crews assembled and flocked to the mountains to cover the story. The Garda Press Office was flooded with requests for updates.

The public was horrified when news of the discoveries reached them over the weekend, and the vacuum of information after the search got under way was leading to all sorts of speculation and hysteria. Many wondered if it had something to do with a bloody gangland feud raging in Dublin at the time, or perhaps it was a crazed serial killer still on the loose. The best guess of bar-stool detectives was that the remains belonged to one of the six women who had gone missing from the Leinster area in the 1990s.

Deirdre Jacob, Fiona Pender, Jo Jo Dullard, Fiona Sinnott, Ciara Breen and American woman Annie McCarrick all disappeared on various dates between 1993 and 1998. All are presumed murdered. These high-profile cases are still being treated as live investigations, and all intelligence and new leads are pursued with vigour by the Garda Serious Crime Review Team through Operation Trace.

Were the mountains about to spew another dark secret from the past back into the light? The pressure was on. People wanted answers, and while there were more questions than answers at this early stage, it was time to address the media.

A press briefing, led by Superintendent Pat Ward, was arranged for the following afternoon. Reporters, photographers and TV crews were advised to approach the Garda cordon at the Sally Gap from the east.

Before fielding questions from the gathered journalists, Superintendent Ward first appealed to members of the public who had been in the general area of Military Road/Laragh, County Wicklow in the recent past and who may have seen anything suspicious or unusual. By now, an incident room had been set up at Bray Garda Station, and anyone with information was asked to contact it directly, or to call the Garda Confidential Line if they wished to remain anonymous.

He then said it appeared that the body parts had been thrown from a moving vehicle, and no effort had been made to conceal them.

'From Glencree right down to Glenmacnass, the pattern seems to be the body parts were dispersed on the side of the road, from a moving vehicle; a van or something like that,' he said.

'It seems a vehicle travelled from north to south on Military Road, or the opposite way. And as that car travelled along it seems the body parts were discarded in this cruel manner.'

No post-mortem results were available at this point, so a murder investigation was not yet officially under way, but Superintendent Ward assured the media it was being treated as such. He said they were satisfied the victim had met a violent end. The highly experienced police officer refused to add fuel to any of the theories being lobbed from the floor. It was simply too early to tell what they were dealing with, and he wasn't going to be drawn into wild speculation.

'This could be the result of anything. It could have been an argument, it could be a domestic situation, it could be anything,' he said, with the widest of open minds.

Unlike the clues scattered in plain sight across the mountainside, information was thin on the ground, but gardaí did at least have some clue as to what they were dealing with. Initial examinations of the first body parts found by members of the public over the weekend revealed they belonged to a young man, most likely in his twenties.

Back up the mountains, the words 'Stop! Stop! Find!' once again filled the valleys. A human foot had been found, again just a few feet from the road, reinforcing Superintendent Ward's suspicion that someone had just tossed the body parts out of the side of a moving vehicle.

4.

KEEP SMILING

In 1987, Patricia joined the catering department at Beaumont Hospital, where she saw out the rest of her working days. She made friends for life there. The shifts were long and hard, but she used to come into work singing and whistling every day. She didn't have much of a back catalogue: 'Always Look on the Bright Side of Life' was her go-to, much to the annoyance of some of the chefs. That said, it didn't take long to win them over. Her good mood was infectious. She gave everyone a lift, especially when it was busy around mealtimes.

'You'd be at the height of it, flying up to big wards, and she'd just be whistling away like a mad yoke,' remembers her friend and former colleague Sandra Flynn. 'I told her to shut up one day. I was in bad form myself, and she just turned to me with her big smile and sang, "be happy, keep smiling". It was hard not to then.'

She used to adopt the same approach with management, espe-cially when work relations within the hospital were delicate. 'Don't ever let them think you're in bad form,' she used to advise the others. She'd tell them to just keep smiling, no matter what. 'They won't know what to think,' she'd say.

Everyone started in the kitchen. The shifts varied, but Patricia mostly did the earlies, from 7 a.m. to 4 p.m. Breakfast is served at eight, so it's all hands on deck from the moment you walk in the door. Patricia would begin her day by putting trays of food together on the 'belt'. Everything would have to be laid out perfectly; then the trays would be loaded onto trolleys and whisked up to the wards. With over eight hundred mouths to feed, mealtimes at Beaumont Hospital are like a military operation, and if one person is late the whole system breaks down. Patricia was always on time for her shift and she worked hard.

After a while, she was assigned to look after St Anne's ward, the hospital's ear, nose and throat department. The patients adored her. Unsurprisingly, she was most drawn to the younger ones. She could sense they were anxious and afraid, and she went out of her way to comfort them. The sound of her trolley rattling into their ward would often be followed by her loud singing. The staff at the nurses' station used to get a right laugh out of her because more often than not she'd make up the words as she went along. She didn't care. All she cared about was brightening up someone's day. She would play with the younger patients, and if she wasn't dead on her feet, she'd even treat them to a jig, again making up the moves as she went along. Sometimes their food would go cold before she moved on. They didn't care, though. They just hoped she would be the one bringing them their next meal.

Outside the walls of the wards, Patricia used to refer to them as *her* patients. On admission, they'd be asked about their dietary needs, and she was always very careful when it came to that aspect of her job. She knew them all by name and didn't have to ask them twice how they took their tea. The little things mattered to her. She received countless letters down through the years from discharged patients, thanking her for her kindness. Parents would get in touch too, to thank her for lifting their child's spirits as well as their own. Her attention to detail was always noted in the letters and cards she received. The staff used to hang them up on the noticeboard for all to see.

Patricia may have been a joker, but she took great pride in her work – and it showed. She expected the others to pull their weight too. The only time anyone ever saw her lose her cool at work was when dirty trays were left behind on her ward. She'd race downstairs to the kitchen looking for the culprit. Patricia didn't mind giving someone a hand if they were under pressure, but she simply couldn't tolerate laziness and she hated cleaning up after others. It wasn't her job.

As soon as the breakfast trolleys were wheeled away, at about 9.30 a.m., the women would take a short break before turning their attention to the lunch service. Break time was always great craic with Patricia around. Josie Dunne worked in the kitchen, but she always remembered the girls from her ward coming back from their break in high spirits.

'Trisha was very funny. She'd have everyone in stitches. She could be serious when she wanted to be, but she was just full of fun and made everyone laugh all the time.'

Patricia was in good company at Beaumont Hospital. The catering department was full of characters like her. During a break one day, one of the girls shared a story about her husband having a heart attack. The others all gathered round to sympathise with her. They were a tight bunch. They looked after each other. Stone-faced, she continued her story. Some of the girls held her hand as she told them she went home after getting the call and took all her black clothes out of her wardrobe. She said she spent hours scrubbing them and freshening them up, only to find out that 'the bastard didn't die'. She was devastated after all her effort to get ready for his funeral. The hospital corridors filled with laughter. Patricia's booming laugh rose above it all. It could be heard on every ward.

Everyone at Beaumont Hospital adored Patricia. All the doctors and nurses knew her by name, and she took a real shine to one junior doctor in particular. Everyone did. He always had time for a chat, and, like Patricia, he knew everyone's name, and he was genuinely interested in what was going on people's lives. There was a real buzz about him when he walked into the room. People were drawn to him. He was tall, dark and handsome with a friendly, soft-spoken manner. Patricia used to tell everyone he was in the wrong job. 'He's a born politician,' she'd say. She used to love watching him working his way down the wards. He was only in training, but everyone knew he'd do well.

'Howya, Leo!' Patricia shouted at him one day as he passed by. 'It's Dr Varadkar,' he replied with a playful grin. 'Ah, sure I can't pronounce that,' she quipped back. They both laughed.

She made a beeline for him one day as he stepped out of the lift just before his time at the hospital was up. She wanted to say farewell while she had the chance. She wished him all the best for the future and left him with some curious parting words: 'You'll be Taoiseach one day, Dr Leo,' she said.

Over the years, Patricia became very close to one of the hospital's chefs, Breda Wosser. She used to drop her into town after work; and while Breda was grateful of the lift after a long day in the kitchen, it came at a price. Patricia loved old musicals and had all her favourites on CDs in the car. Breda would barely have the seatbelt wrapped across her when she'd hear one being sucked into the CD player. She often thought about rolling out and taking the bus, but Patricia would screech out of the car park before she got a chance, music blaring and singing her heart out. She knew all the words to the songs, and she'd often ask Breda what she thought of her singing. Breda couldn't help but laugh. They used to get funny looks when they were stopped at traffic lights. Breda was mortified. People would stare in the window of Trisha's beloved Toyota Corolla, wondering if she was off her head. Patricia didn't drink, though; she didn't need to. She was high on life.

Before Patricia had her own car, she wanted to buy a motorbike. She was very nervous about applying for a loan, so Breda agreed to go to the bank with her as moral support. The two friends got off the bus at O'Connell Street. Patricia's nerves were completely shot as they approached the bank. She really wanted a motorbike, but she wasn't a bit confident about getting a loan for one.

A van was slowly making its way up O'Connell Street as the women prepared to cross. And as soon as they stepped out onto the road, it seemed to speed up. Poor Breda got caught in its path. Patricia, who had stepped back onto the footpath just in the nick of time, watched on as her friend held on to the side of the van for dear life. Patricia tried to catch up, but the van was going too fast. Eventually, it started to slow down and Breda seized her opportunity to get off. She let go and tried to jump onto the island dividing the street. It didn't quite work out according to plan, though. After taking her leap of faith, she took a tumble and bounced off another car. She was in shock, but unhurt. She got back on her feet, dusted herself off and walked back to where Patricia was now standing open-mouthed. As she approached her friend, Breda noticed a small crowd lining the street. She wondered why they were all staring at her. Patricia was speechless. Breda stood beside her, leaned in and whispered:

'What's up with all those people, Trisha? What's going on?'

Patricia let out a roar. 'You should be dead!' she screamed, laughing her head off. The crowd dispersed and off they went to the bank.

Undeterred by witnessing Breda's near-death experience, Patricia marched straight up to the counter and demanded to see the bank manager. She announced to everyone within earshot that her friend had just been knocked down and she wanted a loan to 'sort her out'. A short time later, they spilled out of the bank in fits of laughter. Patricia got her loan and they raced off for a cup of tea to celebrate. She had her heart set on a motorbike but opted for a car in the end. That way, she could listen to her music and sing along to her heart's content.

• • •

After splitting up with Gus, Patricia did find love again, this time in the arms of a woman. They met at work and began seeing each other a few years after Patricia started in Beaumont. She often told her friends that she wasn't interested in women before Jane (not her real name) came into her life, and she used to joke that she turned her gay.

Being gay in Ireland in the 1980s wasn't easy. Sexual activity between two men, even in the privacy of their own home, was illegal, while lesbian sex wasn't even recognised under Irish law. In the early 1980s, gay men would meet on Saturday afternoons in a pub just off Grafton Street. It was a secret society and a place of refuge for those who just wanted to socialise in peace.

That said, it was also an exciting time for the gay community. The country's first ever Gay Pride festival was held in Dublin in March 1983, the same year Patricia moved out of Mountain View Park. It was a very different event from the festival celebrated nowadays. For starters, it was organised as a protest march in response to suspended sentences handed down to five so-called 'queer-bashers' who had beaten a young gay man, Declan Flynn, to death the year before. Their fully suspended sentences triggered a movement towards equality. It would take another ten years for homosexuality to be decriminalised, but the march in 1983 was seen as a pivotal moment in the struggle for equal rights.

While many gay people at the time hid their true sexual identity, Patricia was very open about hers. She was a private person, but she was happy for people to know about her new relationship. Inevitably, people at work started talking about it. She grew tired of the hushed whispers and sideways glances when she walked into the room, so she just announced one day that she preferred women, and that was that.

'This is life,' she said to the girls. 'This is what it's all about. Sure, look it, I'm not hurting anyone.'

She used to joke that she just wasn't interested in 'auld fellas' anymore. 'Isn't that what I ended up marrying?' she'd say.

After a while, the two women moved into a rented apartment in Rathmines. Life was good and they were very happy together. Until another woman, whom they both worked with at the hospital, arrived on the scene. She used to join them for dinner and would visit them in their apartment. She started spending more and more time with the couple and an intimate relationship eventually developed between her and Jane.

Patricia was heartbroken. Word quickly spread through the hospital. She was tough, but the break-up floored her. Seeing her ex with her new partner at work every day made it even more difficult for her. They were now living together, too, and Patricia was on her own in the flat in Rathmines. It was a particularly tough time for Patricia, but the girls all rallied round – they hated seeing their friend so down. On days when she was particularly low, they'd comfort her by telling her there were plenty more fish in the sea, but Patricia didn't plan on going 'fishing' again anytime soon.

The girls used to try and lift her spirits by pointing out 'lovely birds' to her on the wards. If someone nice came in, they'd even offer to go over and check if she was gay. Sandra would playfully ask her if she wanted her to go over and 'put a word in'. Patricia would warn her not to. Over time, Patricia's work situation became easier. She wasn't one to hold grudges, and everyone remained friends to a certain degree, but she wasn't disappointed when Jane and her girlfriend eventually moved away from the hospital. Things soon went back to normal for her. The singing and whistling returned.

Despite the lunch ladies' best efforts, Patricia didn't find love again. She just wasn't interested. After the break-up, she couldn't afford to pay full rent and bills for the apartment in Rathmines on top of the mortgage she was still paying off for the house in Rathfarnham, so she soon found herself with no choice but to return to 66 Mountain View Park. It didn't bother her. After all, it was her house and she was entitled to move back in if she wanted to. She made that clear to Gus before she moved out. The girls used to slag her about going back to the 'auld fella', but she assured them it wasn't like that. They slept in separate rooms.

As she got older, she just wanted to focus on her family. Despite living away from the house for years, she had maintained a relationship with her kids, Richard in particular. Patricia was known for her unique taste in clothes, and on Richard's wedding day in 2012 she wore a chain-print camisole top with hardware detail on the shoulder. She painted her nails bright red, just like her hair. She looked great and she was bursting with pride as she posed for photographs with her son. He looked so handsome, she thought. She had invited a few of the girls from work too, and they danced and laughed the night away. The next few days in the staff canteen were spent talking about what a great wedding it was. The mother of the groom was delighted that everyone had had such a lovely time.

Aside from their fiery red hair, Louise didn't have much in common with her mother, and their relationship wasn't as tight as the one enjoyed by mother and son. She was a difficult child. She hated school and left in her teens.

The relationship between Patricia and Gus was amicable after the separation, which made things easier for everyone. Gus quietly hoped Patricia's return to the house would rekindle their relationship. He still loved her and was delighted to have her back. He missed her big smile around the house. It lit up every room she walked into. They were happily married once, after all, and he thought perhaps they could be happy together once again. It wasn't to be, though – that ship had long sailed for Patricia. When the girls slagged her about being back in Gus's bed, she'd laugh it off and say, 'Sure what would I be doing with that auld fella. Amn't I gay?'

Two years after Patricia's return to the house, Louise started seeing a young man called Keith Johnston. She was seventeen at the time. Keith, who was two years older than her, grew up in a housing estate in nearby Tallaght. Like Louise, he wasn't very academic, and he also had left school at a young age. He was fifteen when he dropped out. Keith was a hard worker and could turn his hand to any odd job, but he was a particularly skilled tiler, so he pursued that as a trade until a work accident derailed his training. He began taking drugs and his life soon started to spiral out of control, but he overcame his addiction, and his life was back on track by the time he met Louise. She became pregnant the following year and Stephanie was born in 1997. The arrival of a baby into the house brought great joy but also heaped even more pressure on her parents' already fractured relationship. It was a stressful time. Louise was still not much more than a child herself and Patricia had her work cut out for her between looking after the baby and holding down a demanding full-time job. To make matters worse, it wasn't long before a second came along. It wasn't Keith's child, but he treated her as if she were his own flesh and blood.

Patricia and Gus often spoke about doing up the house when the kids had flown the nest, but their plans for the future were put on hold while they helped Louise raise her children. Richard moved out in 2005, but his younger sister showed no signs of following suit. In fact, she moved Keith in around the same time he left. One out, one in.

Patricia slept in one of the double bedrooms upstairs. She had a lock installed to try to maintain some privacy in the busy house. Gus had his own room and the other two rooms were shared between Louise, her children and Keith. Patricia's return had added to an already overcrowded situation, but she didn't care. Why should she? It was her house. If they didn't like it, they could move out. In fact, Keith did move out that year, when he and Louise broke up. It didn't take long for her to meet someone else, and that someone else soon took Keith's place in the house too. One out, one in.

Kieran Greene was 22 years old when he met Louise. She was six years older than him and held the title of his first-ever girlfriend. He also grew up in Tallaght, less than ten kilometres from Rathfarnham. When he was seven years old, an assessment in his primary school found him to be two and a half years behind his classmates. He was taken out of class for a lot of subjects and given one-to-one tuition from one of his teachers. Kieran wasn't wise to the ways of the world – he had lived a rather sheltered life. He had never lived away from home before, but within months of Keith's departure, Louise asked him to move in. It didn't take long for her to become pregnant again, and over the next few years, they had three children together.

Patricia took an immediate dislike to him. There was just something about him. She couldn't quite put her finger on it, but she thought he was bad news, and a mother's intuition is rarely wrong.

Patricia's main concern was for her grandchildren. She never stopped talking about them at work. They came into the conversation every single day, especially Stephanie, whom Patricia took everywhere with her. She didn't think Kieran was giving the children a good life, so she made sure they had enough and were never left wanting. She used to leave her bank card on the kitchen table when she went to work so that Kieran and Louise could buy groceries for the kids. She didn't care about Kieran, and Louise was old enough to look after herself. Her main priority was to make sure her grandchildren were comfortable and had food in their bellies.

She and her older sister Kathleen used to go on holidays together. They loved the sun, and Lanzarote was a frequent destination. She used to take Louise and all her grandkids to the Canary Islands too. She spoiled them rotten, always buying them bits and pieces. It was only in later years that she started to treat herself. She had worked hard her entire life and felt she deserved it. She got laser treatment for her eyes, so that she no longer needed to wear glasses, and later went through hell to get her teeth done. It was purely cosmetic – she just wanted a nice set of teeth. She had always been self-conscious about her teeth, and now that she had the money to fix them, she just thought why not?

'Look after yourself, girl', she said to Breda one day, 'because nobody else will. That's why I'm getting my teeth done. I worked hard all my life. I did all the overtime. Leave nothing to anybody.'

The extra workload at home was really beginning to take its toll on Patricia. She was exhausted all the time. She'd get up early, put in a full day's work at the hospital and then have to tidy the house from top to bottom when she got home after her shift. She dreaded her days off; she just couldn't relax in her own home. Towards the end of her time at Beaumont Hospital, she started doing longer shifts, from 7.30 a.m. to 7.30 p.m. As the only breadwinner in the house, she needed the extra money. She also didn't want to be at home, so she was happy to stay on. Funnily enough, she used to feel sorry for 'the auld fella' at home with the others while she was at work. The lunch ladies thought she was mad to feel sorry for Gus. They felt that since he was the man of the house, he should be sorting them all out. But they didn't know him. Gus avoided confrontation at all costs, and Louise and Kieran walked all over him.

Inevitably, the situation at home led to rows. The last few years before Patricia retired were particularly testing. Kieran was causing all sorts of problems in the house. She used to tell the girls at work that he was giving Louise a 'pig's life'. She desperately wanted him out of the house, but she couldn't put her 'young one' and grand-kids out on the street. She didn't know what to do. Gus didn't get involved. If anything, he took Louise and Kieran's side, so she was outnumbered.

The girls were worried about Patricia. One of them remem-bered getting a lift with her a few months before she finished up at the hospital. Patricia told her she'd drop her into town, but she needed to make a quick detour first. They drove to a housing estate in Ballymun. She pulled up, switched off the engine and started whistling and tapping the steering wheel. She appeared to be waiting for someone. A few minutes later, a young man on a bike cycled over to the driver's side of the car. When she saw him,

Patricia rolled down the window and discreetly handed him some cash. In return, he passed a small package through the window. Patricia had started smoking cannabis at home. She told her friend she just needed something to get her through the situation in the house. She dreaded going back to it every evening. It was that bad.

Patricia told her colleagues that Kieran thought of himself as 'the boss' of the house. *Her* house. She said he had some sort of hold over everyone living under her roof. She couldn't get anything out of him; he didn't work and he didn't lift a finger around the house. He and Louise fleeced her too, often abusing her generosity by treating themselves with the bank card she left out for groceries for the kids.

Louise had her father wrapped around her little finger. He described her as a 'very demanding person'. Looking back years later, he said that he felt he was taken advantage of. Louise controlled the house as far as he was concerned. She took Patricia's phone, so her brother Richard found it difficult to get hold of his mother to arrange a visit. It was a toxic environment, and Gus felt particularly vulnerable when Patricia wasn't around. He later went as far as to say he felt he was the victim of elder abuse, both financial and psychological.

Patricia was a strong woman. Nothing fazed her. Her friends were amazed by how she bounced back after her break-up with Jane. She took whatever came her way in her stride after that. If anything, it made her even stronger than before. But the girls noticed a change in her mood when it came to Kieran. He had really got under her skin. She wasn't afraid of anyone – if she had a problem with someone, she would say it straight out to their face – but she was afraid of Kieran. One day, she told one of the girls at work that he was the type of person you wouldn't mess with. 'He'd cut you up,' she said.

Patricia didn't think Kieran was a good father. She often told him she'd come back and haunt him if he ever did anything to her grandkids. She really didn't like having him around the house. She wanted him out and made no bones about it. She didn't trust him and often told him he shouldn't be bringing up his family in her house, but Louise stood up for him and would tell her mother that he was entitled to be there as the father of her kids. Gus was no use. Her hands were tied. It was a horrible situation.

She often referred to Louise as a 'stupid bitch' for putting up with Kieran. Patricia knew from the start there was 'big trouble' there, and she just couldn't understand why her daughter was so blind to it all. Despite everything, she worried about her too. She felt so helpless. Her sisters would often talk about coming up for a visit, but she'd put them off. She didn't want them to see what was going on. Richard would have helped her – he often told Louise to find her own place – but Patricia was a proud lady and didn't want her son to know the full extent of what was going on in the house. She didn't want to burden anyone with her problems. She'd find a way. She always did.

• • •

Patricia always said she'd retire when she turned sixty, no matter what, and she stayed true to her word. She had lots of plans for her retirement too. She was going to do up her back garden. The girls at work thought it was going to be a mansion the way she went on about it every day. She got it levelled at one point, and she was proud as punch showing them photos of the progress. It was her pride and joy. None of her friends had ever been to her house, but Patricia hoped to have them over when her garden was finished. She spoke about taking her grandkids on another holiday too. The mortgage on the house was almost paid off and she knew she was due a few quid from the hospital to mark her thirty-two years of service.

Breda and the girls threw her a big retirement party at the hospital. Everyone signed a card and they did a whip-round for her too. They also bought her two massive baskets, which they filled with wellies and garden ornaments, and gave her as a retirement gift. Patricia was chuffed, but they could tell she didn't want to be there. As far as they were concerned, she had checked out months ago and couldn't wait to get home to 'sort everyone out', as she put it herself. She didn't even want a party and just seemed to blend into the background on the night before making her early exit. Her mind was elsewhere. She had lots of plans for her retirement, but her main aim was to sort the family out. She felt it was high time for Louise and Kieran to find their own home to raise their family. She wanted them out.

By May 2017, there were nine people living in the house at Mountain View Park: Gus, Patricia, Louise, Kieran and Louise's five children. They also had four budgies, a dog called Sammy and two cats they named after David Bowie's glam alter egos: Ziggy and Stardust. The place was a zoo and it was bursting at the seams. Stephanie was nineteen now, and the three youngest were all aged under ten.

Patricia had a special bond with Stephanie, perhaps because she was her first grandchild. She loved the bones of her. She gave her money all the time; sometimes Stephanie asked her for a fiver and Nana, as she affectionately called her, would give her €20 instead.

Stephanie used to dye her own hair and her colour choices always tickled her grandmother, who preferred a more natural look. All the colours of the rainbow would wash down the drain when she was finished. Green, red, orange, blue. Sometimes pink and purple too. She loved Japanese animation, or anime, and would spend hours watching it on her laptop whenever she could. The hand drawings and computer-generated characters inspired her boldest and brightest hairstyles. It was easy to feel lost in the house with so many people crammed into such a small space, but Stephanie certainly stood out from the crowd.

As the eldest of Louise's five children, she was also expected to take care of her younger siblings at times. Patricia knew how that felt, and it strengthened their relationship even more. Stephanie was shy and quite introverted as a child. She was creative, and expressed herself through her appearance and animations as she got older. Like her grandmother, she didn't really take a drink. She didn't even raise a glass on her eighteenth birthday. While most people her age were out drinking at the weekends, Stephanie preferred to go to things like the Dublin Comic Con, a huge event held in the Convention Centre every year for fans of anime, gaming, comics and movies. Some event-goers go to great lengths to unleash their inner fan by dressing up and mimicking their favourite superhero or gaming character. In many ways, Stephanie was still a kid at heart. She struck up an unlikely friendship with an autistic boy on her street, who was much younger than her. She used to call around every day to play with him. She would colour in with his sister too. They adored her, and so did their mother. She described Stephanie as 'one of the kindest and most caring souls' she had ever met.

Now that Patricia had retired and was spending more time at the house, she and Louise clashed almost every day. Housework wasn't one of her daughter's strengths, and it certainly wasn't something she instilled in her children, like Helen Cooke had in hers. Gus didn't lift a finger either – the mess didn't seem to bother him. Kieran did a bit just to appease her when she was around, but his standard of cleanliness left a lot to be desired, and more often than not he would actually leave a space dirtier than he found it. Patricia wondered if he did it on purpose. Being around them every day was a real eye-opener. She had drastically underestimated how lazy they actually were. She wouldn't stand for it.

The house was always packed. Kieran and Louise rarely went out. Louise often complained of not having a life outside the house, but with five kids to look after and no job to go to, it was hard to sympathise with her lack of a social life. She used to just sit around all day smoking cigarettes and watching TV in her pyjamas. Keith came over a few times a week too. After a rocky start, he and Kieran struck up an unlikely friendship. If Louise had a type, it was hard to pinpoint exactly what she looked for in a man, because these two were worlds apart. In fairness to Keith, he brought something to the table: he was good with his hands and did a lot of odd jobs in the house over the years. He did up the downstairs bathroom around the same time Patricia returned. Kieran was the opposite – he could barely change a lightbulb.

Patricia was determined to sort out the situation in the house, but she didn't know where to start. Nobody listened to her. She used to threaten to throw them all out, but her threats fell on deaf ears. It really upset her. After all, they had no claim on the house. She paid the mortgage and all the bills. Was it too much to ask those living there rent-free to obey some basic house rules? All she wanted was for people to be more respectful of the house and to tidy up after themselves, but more often than not she just ended up doing it herself.

Louise had been diagnosed with an immune system disorder a few years earlier. In Graves' disease, the immune system attacks the thyroid gland, causing it to make more thyroid hormones than the body actually needs. It can affect sleep and cause fatigue. Louise had lost a lot of weight as a result. Her gaunt face and bony fingers made her look far older than her years. Her eyes appeared to bulge too, another symptom of the disease. It was hard to tell if her condition caused her to be easily annoyed too, but she was constantly locking horns with her mother.

Louise was now thirty-eight, and Patricia felt it was time for her daughter to find her own place. Louise, like her mother before her, had been on the council's housing list for years. She was offered a house in Dún Laoghaire at one point but, unlike her mother before her, she turned it down. It just wasn't good enough for her, apparently; she claimed it was too far away from the kids' school and wasn't big enough. Tensions between mother and daughter escalated even further and often led to heated rows. It was particularly frustrating for Patricia to know that Louise had turned down a perfectly fine house. She wanted them out, but she didn't want to throw them out on the street, so this would have been the perfect solution. Aside from her own understandable self-interest in clearing a few bodies out of the rooms, she also wanted the best for her daughter and grandchildren. She wanted Louise to get on with her life, to build a home for herself and her family somewhere.

Patricia was sixty-one years old and supposed to be enjoying her retirement after working hard all her life. She still had family in Dublin – her sisters Valerie, Breda and Kathleen all lived there – but the others, including her youngest sister Rita, whom she doted on as a child, were all back home in Windgap. She often spoke about seeing out her retirement in the countryside. On countless occasions, she told her friends that she'd sell up and move home if Gus died before her.

Whatever about her future, she felt it was time for Louise to start planning out the rest of her life. She didn't like being told to find her own house, but Patricia didn't care. She wasn't a child anymore. Louise would either ignore her or fly off the handle when she brought it up, and Gus would side with his daughter, which certainly didn't help matters.

Richard was married with two kids and had a place of his own. Why couldn't his sister follow suit? She had lived at Mountain View Park her entire life, and now had five kids and her partner living under the same roof. She couldn't live at home forever, so what was she waiting for?

5.

THE CONFESSION

At 7.15 p.m. on the first day of the full search up the mountains, Garda Patrick Foley noticed a shifty-looking man sitting on his own in the public waiting area of Rathfarnham Garda Station.

The public desk attracts all sorts, but there was something about this visitor that caught Garda Foley's attention. He seemed very nervous and kept rubbing his face with his hands. It was obvious he was mentally preparing himself to make the short walk to the hatch. He eventually rose from his creaky wooden seat and crossed the tiles to place his request.

'I'd like to speak to someone in charge,' he said.

Garda Foley, turned gatekeeper, asked him why.

'That body up the mountains is Patricia O'Connor,' he replied.

He went on to say that he had pushed her and hit her with a hurley during a struggle in the house they shared, just over 2km from the station. He had Garda Foley's full attention now as he cocked his forearm and brought it down 'like a hatchet' to demonstrate what he claimed to have done to her. He said it had happened outside the bathroom.

'She fell backwards. There was blood everywhere,' he said. She was unresponsive, so, he said, he took her up the mountains. Garda Foley had heard enough. He fetched his superior.

Detective Sergeant Lucy Myles was the member in charge at Rathfarnham Garda Station that day. She had been on duty since 7 a.m. Garda Foley told her there was a man at the hatch looking to speak to her. She met him at a side door and asked him what he wanted. He told her he had done 'something terrible'. She took out her notebook.

'The stuff up the mountains was me,' he said.

'What stuff?' she asked.

'The body parts that were scattered around the Dublin Mountains. I cut them up and threw them all over the place up there. I blacked out, and don't know what happened. I just threw them all over the mountains.'

She asked him his name.

'Kieran Greene,' he replied.

She closed her notebook and cautioned him. He wasn't under arrest, but he needed to know his rights.

'Kieran Greene, you are not obliged to say anything unless you wish to do so, but whatever you say will be taken down in writing and may be given in evidence.'

Detective Sergeant Myles had her reservations about what he was saying. She was aware that human remains had been found up the mountains, but as far as she knew, they belonged to an unidentified man in his twenties. Could this be a waste of her time? After all, it's not unusual for people to come forward with bogus claims when a high-profile murder investigation is under way. It had been a long day, and she'd been on duty for over twelve hours, but there was something in his manner and the way he spoke that led her to believe this wasn't just some crackpot looking for attention. She had a feeling, so she probed further.

'Who did you cut up, Kieran?' she asked.

'My mother-in-law. Well, she isn't my mother-in-law officially,' he explained. 'I've been with her daughter for the past ten or eleven years. We have three children together.'

He gave her name as Patricia O'Connor. The name rang a bell. A 61-year-old woman called Patricia O'Connor had been reported missing earlier in the month. Detective Sergeant Myles scribbled the name down. She'd look into it.

Kieran then handed her a set of keys to a Toyota Corolla and gave her permission to search it.

'That's the car I used to bring the body away,' he said.

'Why did you kill her?' she asked.

'Well, I was getting out of the shower when she came in, shouting and screaming. She picked up a kid's hurl outside the door and started hitting me with it. I grabbed it and hit her back. All I remember then is coming round, and she was lying on the ground with blood everywhere.'

He told her he put her body in the boot of the car and drove to County Wexford, where he buried her in a shallow grave.

'I panicked and dug her up a few days later,' he said. 'I cut her up and scattered her around the mountains.'

They moved to an interview room in the belly of the station.

Detective Sergeant Myles left the room briefly to speak privately with her colleague, Detective Garda David Connolly. He was also aware that a woman called Patricia O'Connor had been reported missing.

Kieran was very upset when she returned to the room, and during their early exchanges she found him 'fidgety, but coherent' as he added more details to the harrowing story he'd just shared with her. Detective Sergeant Myles was still a bit sceptical, so she let him lead the interview. Her experience had taught her the best course of action in these situations was to allow a suspect to feel like they're the one driving the conversation. Her initial input was minimal. Less is often more in these situations. Skilled journalists and lawyers do the same, especially with tricky customers. Ask a question, and let them do the work. Once they've run out of gas, the trick is to wait a moment before responding or asking a follow-up question. That moment of silence will feel like a lifetime under the heat of the spotlight and if you're lucky, they'll go off-script and fill the void with what you're really looking for. Detective Sergeant Myles did ask probing questions, but for the most part, she just let him tell his story in his own words.

He began by telling her he felt 'terrible' about what had happened. He said there had been a fight over a cat earlier in the day, and everyone went to the park. When they came back, he said, she came downstairs and started another fight. He then claimed she stormed out of the house. Her husband Gus went to bed early, according to Kieran. So did Louise and the kids.

He said he was in the bathroom when Patricia returned just after midnight and claimed she opened the bathroom door armed with a hurl and kept telling him to get out as she lashed him with it. He eventually grabbed it from her, and couldn't recall what happened next. He said he just woke up on the bathroom floor some time later, and saw blood everywhere.

He told Detective Sergeant Myles he panicked and carried her upstairs to her bedroom. He brought her back down an hour or so later, and bundled her into the boot of her own car, a 2008 Toyota Corolla. He had placed blankets on the floor of the boot, and just started driving.

He said he drove all over the place before eventually stopping on a narrow road. There was a farmhouse to his right, and 'a little alcove thing'. He said he walked through the gate, carrying a shovel, and just stared digging. He couldn't dig very deep, maybe a foot or so. He then covered her with clay before turning for home.

Detective Sergeant Myles conducted this interview alone. She asked a few questions, but mostly observed and listened while writing his answers down in her notebook as fast as she could. She was later criticised for not asking a colleague to join her in the interview room, but this was a voluntary statement. Kieran Greene was in the driving seat, and he hadn't been forced to take the wheel, so she was happy to hear what he had to say on her own. Given her experience as a senior police officer, she felt confident in her own capabilities.

There are rules for taking such statements. The so-called Judges' Rules were first drawn up over a century ago to ensure that suspects are treated fairly. Detective Sergeant Myles was aware of her obligations, and she made sure everything was above board.

At one point during the interview, a big fat drop of sweat could be seen clinging to the base of Kieran's chin. Judging by its track, it had made its descent from his clammy forehead, where many more were waiting for their turn to jump. He became more and more upset as the interview went on. He was fidgety and kept rubbing his hands. His demeanour worsened as he recalled what happened next.

A few days after he claimed to have killed Patricia and dumped her body, he said, he panicked and returned to the shallow grave with a hacksaw and some gloves. He said he couldn't move her, so he cut up her arms, legs, torso and head, put the pieces in bags, and scattered them up the mountains, along with the hacksaw and his clothes.

'It was so dark', he said, 'I thought I was off road at times.' He said he went home afterwards.

The interview room went quiet, and the bulging drop of sweat finally dropped from his chin and splashed onto the table below. The others soon followed, but he cut them off at the pass with a quick swipe of his forearm.

Detective Sergeant Myles brought the interview to an end.

6.
MISSING

Richard O'Connor thought it odd when he didn't hear from his mother on 30 May 2017. It was his birthday, and she always got in touch to wish him a happy birthday.

He called his sister Louise the following day. She hadn't wished him a happy birthday either, but he would have been more surprised if she had. Patricia didn't have a mobile phone, so he used to call Louise when he wanted to get hold of her.

Louise told him she had stormed out of the house the night before and hadn't returned. She said she was in the bathroom when she heard her mother running off after some sort of argument. She told her brother the row was about car insurance. Louise's partner, Kieran Greene, was insured to drive their mother's silver Toyota Corolla, and there had been a crash of some sort. She didn't see her leave, but she described her as angry when she left, and told him she heard her shouting, 'I'll be back when that auld fella pops his clogs.' She figured she was talking about their father, Gus, who seemed happy enough for everyone to be living under the same roof.

He certainly didn't have it in him to turf them out.

It just didn't make sense to Richard. Sure, his mother could be a bit of a hothead, and there was no denying that she was a sharp-shooter who didn't mince her words, but she wouldn't forget his birthday. It just didn't sit well with him. Sleep didn't come easy that night.

The next day, he decided to call over to the house at Mountain View Park in Rathfarnham. He hadn't lived there in about ten years, but Louise, who was thirty-eight at the time, had spent her whole life there. Richard was always giving his sister advice, and he often found himself the middleman in the many domestic dis-putes between mother and daughter. He was blue in the face telling Louise to give up her dream of getting a free house off the council. She had been on the housing list for years, and had even turned down a perfectly fine house because it was too far from her kids' school. She was always locking horns with her mother, and Richard thought the best thing for her to do was to get out of the house and rent her own place. He had no doubt their fractious relationship would improve if she did, but she didn't listen to him.

She could be very stubborn and that, coupled with her adversity to housework, led to most of the friction between the two women of the house. Patricia was very house-proud, Louise wasn't, and it was the cause of many rows between them. Patricia would often come home after putting in a long shift at the hospital to find the house had been turned upside down while she was away. It drove her mad, and Louise didn't lift a finger to help her out. Kieran did a bit, but most of the housework fell on Patricia's shoulders. She wasn't afraid of hard work – her life was defined by it – and she hated laziness, but she was supposed to be enjoying the first year of a well-earned retirement. Cleaning up after everyone wasn't exactly how she'd planned to spend it.

When Richard arrived at the house, his sister and Kieran Greene were both in. His father was there too. Kieran didn't say a word. He rarely did, in fairness. Louise was definitely the one wearing the trousers in their relationship. Richard got on well enough with him. He didn't hold a high opinion of him, but they had an amicable relationship. Apart from his sister, they didn't have much in common. Richard found him a bit plain, to be honest, and once described him as 'something of a fool and a moron'. Richard found it hard to drag a conversation out of him, so more often than not he didn't even bother trying. Kieran rarely made his presence known. Sometimes he'd just stand there, taking everything in, and you'd be forgiven for completely forgetting he was actually in the room.

Patricia was still nowhere to be found, and nobody had heard from her since she stormed out. Richard was worried, but the others didn't seem too bothered. Kieran didn't open his mouth. Again, no surprise there. What did surprise him, though, was that Louise didn't even want to report her as a missing person. She said there was no need to get the guards involved.

Their mother had stormed out of the house in a rage two days ago, and had seemingly vanished into thin air, and she didn't think it appropriate to go to the guards? She wouldn't just run off like that, and it struck him as unusual that his sister didn't seem to care. He was going to the guards, and he'd go alone if he had to. In the end, his father agreed to go with him.

Richard and Gus arrived at Rathfarnham Garda Station just after 6 p.m. Garda Andrew Quinn greeted them at the front desk. They told him they wanted to make a missing person report.

Garda Quinn took down some details and punched them into the Garda computer system. The first 72 hours of a missing person investigation are the most critical. Investigators are essentially working against the clock, and every passing hour diminishes their chances of success. By now Patricia hadn't been seen for two days. Memories fracture and begin to fade after 48 hours. Ask someone what they had for lunch on any given day, and they'll be able to give you a blow-by-blow account of what time they took it at, where they went, what they had, how it tasted, what the weather was like when they went to collect it – minute details can be easily recalled. Ask that same person what they had for lunch two or three days ago, and the details aren't as easily harvested, and they become far less reliable. The fresher the memory, the more accurate the information, and the easier it is to act on. As time goes by, there are fewer breadcrumbs to follow.

Richard gave his sister's phone number to Garda Quinn. Despite her reluctance to even report her mother as a missing person, Louise was to be his point of contact.

Garda Quinn began digging straight away. He called a number of women's refuge centres. None of them had taken in a woman by the name of Patricia O'Connor. He called Louise to see if she could give him a bit of a steer. She told him nobody had heard from Patricia. She said her mother banked with Permanent TSB, so he made contact with the bank to see if there had been any movement on her account since 29 May. It hadn't been touched. That was worrying.

Garda Quinn asked Louise if she could provide him with a recent photo for a public appeal. She said she'd check. He also needed a description of her mother to accompany a press release seeking information about her whereabouts. Patricia took pride in her appearance. She loved her red hair and took great care of it. She was very stylish, and always wore bright, vibrant dresses. She was 61 years old, 5ft 1in in height, and of stocky build.

Kieran Greene handed himself in eleven days after Richard and Gus reported Patricia as a missing person, and while Detective Sergeant Myles listened to his story that evening, Detective Connolly went to check the Missing Persons file. Sure enough, a file for a 'Patricia O'Connor' had been set up on 1 June 2017. He flicked through it. The investigation was still live, and, so far, hadn't thrown up many leads. The trail was cold and there wasn't a breadcrumb in sight. Detective Connolly grabbed his jacket and made the short journey to the house at Mountain View Park.

Louise O'Connor was outside chatting to her neighbours when he arrived. She was crying as she told him that Kieran had just confessed to murdering her mother and disposing of her body parts. On the evening she went missing, she said, she came home with the kids, and Kieran just told her that her mother had left the house after a row. 'Kieran hasn't been himself since,' she added. Next thing she knows, he's confessing to her mother's brutal murder.

Detective Connolly returned to the station with a head full of question marks. He discussed the case with his colleagues. They were all scratching their heads too. The body parts were male. It just didn't make any sense.

It was decided that Detective Connolly and Sergeant Kieron O'Neill would interview Kieran on tape. He still wasn't under arrest, so the ball was very much in his court. He could have walked out the door if he wanted to, but he didn't. He played ball.

It was also decided to take a detailed statement from Louise, who had taken the kids to Kieran's family home in Tallaght. Garda Quinn was sent to take her statement.

Louise began by giving him an outline of the living arrangements at Mountain View Park.

'My partner Kieran lives with us. My five children all live there too. I've lived there my entire life. I've been in a relationship with Kieran for ten years now. He's lived with me most of the time. He's the father of three of my children.'

Then the conversation moved on to Louise's mother. Garda Quinn was somewhat taken aback by her account: she hadn't revealed any of the details she was giving now in their earlier discussions.

'Mum hasn't always lived there. She left when I was five or six, but she moved back to the house after her new relationship ended. She retired from Beaumont Hospital last July, and she has been very hard to live with.'

'Why is that?'

'Well, she was just always irritated. She always seemed to be giving out. Constantly giving out.'

'Tell me more about the day she went missing.'

'She was really bad that day. She was really angry. She was screaming and arguing about stupid things.'

'Like what?'

'I was looking for some receipts for her pension to get Dad a medical card, and she wouldn't give them to me. We also had a row about her car insurance. Kieran had an accident the previous week. She was so angry. She hit me with a teapot, and she was just roaring at him.'

'At Kieran?'

'Yeah, and she was out of weed. She wanted me to go out and get some. I refused, and that annoyed her too. At about seven o'clock, I brought Dad and the kids to the park, just to get out of the house. We were gone for about two hours. When we left, she was in her room. Kieran stayed behind too. He said he wanted to have a shower, and he told me he'd follow us down afterwards.'

'And did he?'

'No. He texted me on the way home about picking up lunches for the kids, which I did. When we got home, he was shaking and really stressed out. He told us Mum got worse after we left, and that she'd been like a raving lunatic while we were gone. He said she walked in on him having a shower. He'd left the door unlocked.'

'And had she calmed down by the time you got home with the kids?'

'No. She stormed downstairs after we got in and just started screaming about how she couldn't even go to the toilet in her own house. She was calling us all pathetic. She was so fired up. She was just storming around the house, banging and making noise. After a while, I heard the front door slam, so I ran outside and I saw her heading up the road towards Nutgrove. She had a bag with her. It was about nine o'clock. Dad came home about half an hour later.'

'Did she say anything before she left the house?'

'Yes, she shouted, "I'll be back to get what's mine when that bastard pops his clogs!" I told Dad what happened. I normally sleep on the couch with my daughter, but I slept upstairs that night. Kieran slept on the couch on his own.'

'What time did you go to bed at?'

'I was wrecked. I went to bed at eleven o'clock. Kieran was lying on the couch playing solitaire when I went upstairs. There were three kids in the room with me.'

'And what time did you wake up at?'

'Seven a.m. The kids had school. Kieran was in the bathroom getting ready to paint it.'

'At seven a.m.?'

'Yeah. He said Mam had been on to him to do it for ages, so he was going to get a few jobs done before she came back. He dropped the kids to school in her car. He then painted the bathroom and did a few other jobs. Keith helped him.'

'Who's Keith?'

'Keith Johnston, my ex. He's the father of my two eldest. They get on well. We were all so annoyed with Mum. She didn't have a phone, and as the week went on, we got worried so Dad and Richard went to the guards.

'Kieran was getting more and more stressed and irritated, and then he just lost it this evening. He was crying and hugging the kids, and he said something like, "If you do something wrong, you have to face up to it."

'He turned to me then, and told me he was sorry he hurt my mum. He said he didn't mean to, and that she'd come at him with a hurl. He told me she was lashing him with it, so he took it off her and next thing he knew they were on the floor. I thought it was some sort of sick joke, but then he went and handed himself in.'

It was also decided to take a witness statement from Louise's daughter Stephanie. Her parents had split up when she was small. She liked Kieran, and held him in high regard for the way he took care of his children. She thought he was a 'great Dad' to them. She was also staying at his parents' house with her mother, and Sergeant Nuala Burke arranged to meet her there to ask her a few questions.

Sergeant Burke began by asking her about the living arrangements at 66 Mountain View Park.

'I've lived there all my life,' she said. 'Nana and Gus sleep in separate rooms. They've never lived as man and wife as far as I can tell. She retired last year, and she rarely goes outside.'

'What was she like to live with, Stephanie?'

'On the good days, she was great. Her bad days were terrible.'

'How so?'

'She made Mam's life terrible. She just sucked the life out of her. She liked to make people unhappy. Like, she used to say she could throw us all out anytime she wanted.'

'What do you remember about the day she went missing?'

'Well, I remember my cat Ziggy got into Nan's room, and she got really angry. By the sound I heard from the landing, I think she literally threw Ziggy out of her room. She kept going on about bed bugs, but that wasn't the cat's fault.'

'And what happened then?'

'I remember comforting Ziggy on the landing, and then we all left the house at maybe twelve o'clock in the afternoon. Nana stayed in the house. Like I said, she rarely left it. Kieran said he'd follow us down. So, we all went down to the park, and we stayed there until it got dark. That's how bad she was. We were glad it didn't rain so we didn't have to go back sooner.'

'Did Kieran eventually catch up with you and the others in the park?'

'Erm, I can't remember if he did or not. When we got home, she was in her room or in the toilet, maybe. I didn't see her. I just went into the living room with the kids. Mam went into the bathroom. She has Graves' disease. It affects her thyroid gland.

'I could hear Nana ranting and shouting about something, and I heard her coming down the stairs then. The hall door opened, and I remember her shouting something before she left.'

'What did she shout?'

'She said something like "I'll be back when he kicks his clogs." I figured she was talking about Gus.'

'Can you remember what time she left at?'

'Not really. It was before 10 p.m. anyway. I think we went to bed then. Kieran stayed on the couch on this own. I think Mam wanted to be with the kids.'

Sergeant Burke was scribbling down her answers. She looked up at this point, and asked if Stephanie had woken up at any stage during the night – had she heard any disturbances while she was in bed? Stephanie said she didn't recall anything waking her up.

'And did you see your grandmother again after she left the house?'

'No. I came downstairs at about 9 or 10 a.m. the next morning, and she wasn't there. I figured she was still in her room, but when she hadn't come down by lunchtime, I began to wonder.

'A few days went by, and there was still no sign of her. Mam was getting worried. Kieran was emotional. I figured it was worry too. They reported her as a missing person and the guards called over.

'Next thing I know, Kieran's telling the boys about owning up when you do bad things. He was red in the face from crying, so I started to suspect he'd done something to her. He told us Nana came back to the house around midnight that night, and hit him with a hurl. He said he took it off her, and before he knew it, she was dead on the floor. He said he took her body and brought her to Wexford. Then he left the house to hand himself in. We all just sat there in shock.'

Sergeant Burke asked her if she wanted to tell her anything else. She didn't, so she closed her notebook and thanked Stephanie for her time.

Stephanie's father, Keith Johnston, also gave a voluntary statement that day, and he didn't have too many kind words to say about his daughter's grandmother.

'She had a foul mouth on her. She said she was raped by a priest, and seemed to have an issue with all men. She used to pick on Gus all the time,' he said.

Keith moved into the house for about a year in 2006. He didn't live there anymore but used to call over regularly, maybe two or three times a week. He was asked if he got along with Kieran.

'I didn't get on with him at first, but we eventually became friendly. Louise started going out with him about a year after I moved out. She got pregnant shortly afterwards.'

Detective Garda David Sheehan asked him what he knew about what happened to Patricia.

'I knew she was missing. Stephanie called me to say she was on the warpath before she left. As far as I was told, there had been a big blow-out between Trisha and Louise. I did a bit of work in the house then.'

'What work did you do?'

'I fixed the shower step in the bathroom and some broken tiles.'

'And what did you use for that?'

'I had to buy some screw heads and drill bits, but I had the grout myself. Kieran helped me a bit by cutting some wood, but he's useless at that kind of stuff. I came back the next day to grout the tiles. The grout was a different colour, so I decided to change it.'

What he said next was very interesting, and it would come into greater focus later in the investigation. He chose his words carefully.

'At one point, I thought I could potentially be cleaning up a crime scene,' he said. 'I just had this nagging thought in the back of my head, so I had a sneaky look around. Kieran was minding the kids and making dinner. He was extra quiet and there was tension in the house. I could tell he wasn't normal.'

Detective Sheehan asked him how he found out that Kieran had killed Patricia.

'It was at the house. The boys were crying. Kieran was crying. He was a blubbering mess, and just started saying that he did it. He was talking in half sentences. I can't exactly remember what he said at all. He said it was to protect the kids. His parents arrived. They fell down on the road when they heard. He told us he was going to hand himself in. Louise was nearly getting sick.'

He finished his statement by saying that he'd never seen Patricia hit anyone. 'It was always her mouth,' he said.

Back at the station, Detective Connolly asked Kieran Greene why he had decided to hand himself in. He said it was because it was 'eating him up'.

'I can't handle the guilt. I just keep looking at my kids. I can't sleep. As soon as I lay my head down at night, I just feel consumed by what I did.'

On the day in question, he said, Patricia was going mad because a cat got into her bedroom. He said she was non-stop giving out, claiming nobody listened to her, and just kept calling them all 'leeches'. He said she then left with her suitcase, and announced she'd be back when Gus popped his clogs. He was going to sleep in the living room that night. He said she came home about midnight, opened the bathroom door and came at him with a hurl. Next thing he remembered was waking up on the ground with her next to him. He thought he saw his dead uncle there too. Patricia was on her back. He figured she must have banged her head on the tiles.

'We were both struggling,' he explained.

He drew a rough sketch of the layout of the bathroom, and scribbled the word 'Trisha' beside the head of a stick figure he used to illustrate where she was lying when he came to.

'How much blood was there?' he was asked.

'Maybe a cup or so. It was coming from her head. I panicked, and brought her upstairs to her bedroom.'

Patricia had her own room. It was the first one on the right at the front of the house.

He started sobbing as he recalled what happened next.

'I was all over the place. I was in panic mode, and didn't know what to do. Everyone was in bed, but I was petrified of someone getting up during the night and seeing the bloody mess. Who could I turn to? Who could help me? Nobody.'

Kieran felt he couldn't tell anyone, but he knew he had to get rid of her, so he brought her back downstairs and into the car.

'I just drove,' he said through ugly tears. At this point, he started to complain of chest pains. Time to call it a night.

Detective Connolly and Sergeant O'Neill took Kieran to his parents' house. Louise was there, and her ex, Keith Johnston, emerged from the kitchen at one point. What was he doing there? That was odd. Louise felt fine about Kieran staying there too. The man had just confessed to murdering and butchering her mother, and she was happy to spend the night under the same roof as him? Another oddity, but then this wasn't a conventional family unit.

Kieran agreed to return to the station the following morning to pick up where they had left off, but he would need a lift. The detectives agreed to collect up at 10 a.m. and made their farewells. They had one more stop that night, though.

It was late, but Gus was still up when they arrived at the house at Mountain View Park. He was happy to let them take a look around. They went straight into the bathroom where Kieran claimed to have murdered Patricia, and got down on their hunkers to inspect the floor. Nothing.

The search of the mountains resumed at first light the next day. Private Dean O'Neill's colleague found something, again just off Military Road, and it dawned on him that most of the pieces had been found just a few feet away from the road. His unit was moving to another location in an army transporter. He was seated up high in the cab of the truck. It was the perfect vantage point, he thought. He told the driver to slow down, and just a few seconds later, he spotted another piece of the torso.

Two kilometres away, in Carrickshock, Private John Curtis was part of a 40-strong search team operating in a skirmish line. Everyone lined out, five metres apart from each other, and moved forward together in a horizontal line. It's a great way of ensuring that a grid is thoroughly searched. Every inch is covered, and it avoids doubling over.

As they were shuffling through their assigned area just after lunch, he walked into what he described as a 'funny smell'. It was pungent. He kept going; until he spotted something that looked like 'rotten meat' covered in a blanket of feasting flies. They flew away when he moved closer. The smell was unbearable, but he battled through it. Its source was the bottom part of a human torso. It included the pelvis, which had some underwear wrapped around it.

Kieran was watching TV when Detective Connolly called for him the morning after he handed himself in. He still wasn't under arrest. As promised, he agreed to go back to the garda station to answer some more questions. This interview would also be recorded. With everyone in place, the sticky record button was pushed. It was 10.37 a.m. on 13 June 2017.

Detective Connolly began by asking him to start from the beginning again.

'Tell us everything. Don't leave anything out,' he said.

With every retelling of his story, Kieran added a bit more detail.

He said his stomach was bothering him that night, and he was sitting on the toilet when Patricia burst in. He never locked the bathroom door. Detective Connolly was pretty sure he had told Sergeant Myles that she walked in on him while he was in the shower. He'd return to it. For now, he just wanted to hear what he had to say.

He told them he couldn't remember how many times he hit her with the hurl after he took it from her, but he said he definitely hit her more than once. He claimed she got the hurl back off him, and they were fighting and wrestling with one another. She stumbled to the ground and hit her head. He said he fell on top of her and blacked out. When he came round, he said, she was lying on the bathroom floor beside him. His story didn't stray too far from the version he had told them the day before, so they pressed him for more detail. They needed to test the consistency of what he was telling them. If this story was rehearsed for some reason, the devil would be in the detail.

'How was she positioned?'

'On her back. I was lying down beside her. There was a pool of blood beside her head.'

'What did you do next?'

'I brought her upstairs.'

'How?'

'Honestly, I don't know. It was a miracle. I don't know where I got the strength from. She was heavier than me. I think my dead uncle gave me the strength.'

'How exactly did you get her upstairs, Kieran?'

'I must have been backwards going up. I'm not a hundred per cent sure. I felt safe at that point. I felt she wasn't going to hurt the kids or pick on them anymore.'

'What do you mean by that?'

'She used to tell my daughters they should be raped, and she'd tell my son he should be a girl. I couldn't let her hurt them anymore. I just wanted to protect them. If I could take it back, I would.'

Kieran sobbed his way through the statement, but really broke down at this point.

'She was very abusive. It was constant. She was always threatening to have us killed. She wanted us gone.'

'Okay, Kieran. Tell us what happened next. What happened after you brought her upstairs?'

'I went to the toilet and threw up. I was panicking at this stage. I stuck the kettle on, and hoped she was just knocked out. She wasn't breathing, but she was still warm. There was blood on the tiles near the shower step where she fell so I mopped it up and cleaned the bathroom. Afterwards, I cleaned out the mop bucket with bleach.'

'Was there any blood in the bedroom?'

'Yes. Her floor was made from wood, and I noticed some on the floorboards so I cleaned that up too. I decided then that I had to move her, so I lifted her up by grabbing her under her arms. I walked backwards. She was facing away from me as I dragged her down the stairs. Her feet just fell off each step on the way down. I left her body by the bathroom door and fetched the car keys.'

'What time was that at, can you remember?'

'Erm, it was after 2 a.m. at least. I got the keys and opened the front door of the car, and then the boot. I then went back into the house for her. I managed to lift her body into the boot, and then I pushed the rest of her in.'

'And where did you take her, Kieran?'

'I just started driving. I was sobbing, and made sure not to speed. I headed south and took exit 23. I parked in a small alcove. There was a broken gate leading into some sort of crop field. I found a spot. I then went back to the car and got her. I dug with my hands and a stick, and placed her in the hole. I covered her up with muck.'

On his way back to the car, Kieran said, he noticed a farmhouse on the land. He hadn't noticed it when he passed by earlier. Shit, he thought. He said he drove home and went to sleep on the couch.

'What did you do with your clothes?'

'I stripped off and put them in a black bag, and then I put that in the boot of the car.'

'And then what happened?'

'I couldn't stop thinking about that farmhouse. It kept playing on my mind. I became convinced that the farmer would find her, so I decided to move her maybe five or seven days later. I returned to the site with black bags and a hacksaw. I couldn't move her, so I chopped her up into smaller pieces. I spewed a few times.'

While he was cutting up his girlfriend's mother, he said, he just kept thinking of his kids. When he was finished, he put her body parts into five or six bags, drove up the mountains, and just started dropping them into ditches. He also dumped the saw, boot liner and his clothes.

Afterwards, he told them, he just sobbed and sobbed. He felt that he was finally free. Free from the torment and pain she had caused him. As the days and weeks went by, it started to kill him. He couldn't sleep. He couldn't look his children in the eye. That's why he decided to hand himself in.

Detective Connolly and Sergeant O'Neill stepped out of the interview room for a chat. They didn't believe him. The information they had at the time was that the remains found up the mountains were male. Sure, Patricia O'Connor was missing, but they just couldn't accept what Kieran was telling them. He was saying he drove over 100km to Wexford with his girlfriend's mother's body in the boot of the car. His children's grandmother, for God's sake. He was claiming he put her there after beating her to death, and then used his bare hands to bury her in a shallow grave. This was the same man who was watching cartoons with his kids on his parents' couch that morning. It just seemed unbelievable. There were also slight inconsistencies in what he was telling them now, compared to what he had told Sergeant Myles previously. They needed more. They returned to the interview room.

'Will you take us to where you buried her, Kieran?

'Of course.'

Blackwater is a small village in County Wexford, about 16km north of Wexford town. It's a quiet spot close to Ballyconnigar beach, a popular amenity for the 300 or so people who live in the area. From Rathfarnham, the drive to Blackwater takes just over an hour if you don't get stuck behind any farm machinery. A drive up the coast road during the summer months is a real treat, especially when the wheat is ready for harvest, with fields of gold as far as the eye can see, and the distant din of combine harvesters chewing up their bullion.

As they escorted Kieran to an unmarked garda car, the only landmarks Detective Connolly and Sergeant O'Neill were concerned about were the ones leading to where he claimed Patricia O'Connor's penultimate resting place was.

There was a little bit of chat as they drove down the M11, but not much. Every now and again, Kieran would pipe up from the back seat with a direction. The narrow country roads looked very different in daylight, and he kept scanning the landscape for landmarks to try to find his bearings.

'Not far now,' he said after passing through Kilmuckridge. They drove past a gateway on the side of a road in Killeagh less than ten minutes later, and he told them to stop.

'We're here,' he said.

The gate led into the cornfield, and with an outstretched arm, Kieran told the two detectives to walk down about 50 feet along the left-hand side of the field.

'That's where I buried her,' he said.

Kieran was told to wait at the gate. If what he was telling them was true, the field could soon be declared a crime scene and the last thing they needed was the number-one suspect potentially contaminating it.

It was still bright and as they walked down the field, they saw some disturbed earth where he told them they'd find the shallow grave. Detective Connolly examined the scene, and thought it was consistent with what Kieran had told them in his voluntary statements. He saw what appeared to be human hair in the grave, maybe light brown in colour. There was also a small piece of fabric on the ground. It was caked with dirt, and it was hard to make out exactly what was on it without potentially contaminating it, but it appeared to have a floral pattern on it.

They dashed back to the gate and within seconds, Kieran Greene was arrested.

7.

IT'S HER

The underwear found wrapped around the pelvis discovered by Private Curtis just after lunch on the afternoon of 13 June 2017 was a woman's thong. That didn't make sense. Investigators thought they were dealing with a male victim.

They were working from the findings of preliminary examinations on the first body parts found by members of the public over the weekend. Bone measurements led to the conclusion that they were dealing with a young man, most likely in his twenties. But the initial analysis wasn't based on DNA testing, and they were wrong. The whole case was about to be turned on its head.

The second day of the search unearthed the most significant clues. The discovery of women's underwear gave the investigation team pause for thought, but what lay inside a black plastic bag dumped just off Military Road stopped them in their tracks.

Inside the bag was a badly decomposed human head. At a quick glance, it was difficult to make out any distinguishing features. There were visible cuts and fractures to the skull, and it had been subjected to a lot of blowfly activity, but one thing was certain: it was female.

A pair of human hands were also found inside the bag. They appeared to have been sawed off at the wrist. The nails were cut short and didn't appear to be broken.

With the head now in their possession, detectives went back to the drawing board. The victim profile was updated, and soon they'd have a better idea of how she had died.

In cases of violent death, the human head is the ultimate oracle. More often than not, it provides the most answers. In fact, it's so important to an investigation that a definitive cause of death can't be established without it.

Elaine O'Hara's family still don't know how she died because her skull has never been recovered. She was murdered in August 2012 by a sadistic architect called Graham Dwyer, who preyed on the childcare worker's vulnerabilities and killed her to satisfy his own warped sexual desires, following a lengthy and cruel pursuit of her in both the online and offline worlds. He was convicted of murder three years later following one of the most notorious and shocking cases to come before an Irish court.

To this day, only two-thirds of Elaine's remains have been recovered. They were found deep inside a wooded area on Killakee Mountain, just over 10km from where the main focus of Sergeant Carroll's search was now taking place.

Dwyer's prosecution relied entirely on circumstantial evidence. Given his penchant for knife play and his insatiable desire to end someone's life while having sex with them, one can only assume Ms O'Hara was stabbed to death. But that wasn't, nor could it be, proved beyond a reasonable doubt at trial because her skull, hands and arms were among the bones never recovered.

Word quickly filtered back to the incident room at Bray Garda Station that a woman's head had been discovered during the afternoon search. Like all the other parts found, it was taken away for a post-mortem examination. Superintendent Ward made it clear that he wanted to know as soon as there were any findings in relation to how this woman died.

A decision was made to address the media for a second time that day. Earlier appeals for information were made in the misguided belief that the victim was male. The record needed to be corrected as soon as possible. Memories fade quickly, and minds needed to be refocused. A press release inviting the media to attend another press briefing was written up and sent to every news desk in the country. Its lack of detail didn't deter news editors in the slightest. If anything, it piqued their interest even more. It was obvious there had been some sort of breakthrough or significant development in the case. Why else would there be a follow-up press briefing so soon after the first one? All eyes and ears were on the Wicklow Mountains. Phones were picked up and news crews were again dispatched to the frontline of the unfolding story.

The second briefing took place outside Bray Garda Station at 8 p.m. Superintendent Ward approached the TV cameras with Superintendent John Ferris from the Garda Press Office in tow. He stopped at the tall microphone stand in front of the press pack.

'Thank you all for coming out at such short notice,' he began. 'I just want to give you an update on the investigation.

'As you know, this has been a very complex investigation for us. It has been unusual in its manner. It has been a very fluid investigation, and has been ongoing since the first discovery on Saturday evening.

'We are now in possession of more information and we have developed a more complete picture.'

A quick-fire volley of shots from the cameras in front of him punctuated his every word. Brightly coloured foam covers on the ends of outstretched microphones bobbed in front of his face, while reporters frantically scratched down the latest developments on battered notepads. He began his address.

'As you know, the area we are searching is very challenging, but we have made significant progress in that area.

'The findings to date reveal that … eh …' He hesitated for a split second. What he was about to say would shock a nation, and cause great upset to the victim's loved ones, whoever they may be.

'I may be a little gruesome in what I say, but I have to say that what we have found today are limbs. We have also found some significant parts of the torso, and we have found the head and hands of the deceased.

'The findings today and the extensive forensic examinations that have been carried out now indicate the body is that of a female, an adult female.'

One reporter gasped at this revelation. Another asked why it had taken so long to establish the victim's gender.

'While earlier indications were that the body was that of a male, the significant and complex investigation that we've undertaken up to this point now indicates that the body is that of an adult female.

'We're satisfied that we've discovered most of the body, and we are also satisfied that we're dealing with one body, and not multiple bodies in the area. This is a significant development from our point of view and we're now in a position to be more definitive in our approach to the case.'

Superintendent Ward told the gathered media that he was confident that this woman had met a violent death sometime in the week or so leading up to the discovery of the first body part by a member of the public the previous Saturday evening. With that in mind, and armed with this new crucial piece of evidence, he then made a fresh appeal to anyone who might be missing a loved one – whether a family member, friend or neighbour – to come forward.

It was too early to put an age on the victim, and Superintendent Ward refused to even hazard a guess. He confirmed the victim was white but sidestepped a question on whether clothing or jewellery had been found on the victim 'for operational reasons'.

The search was ongoing, but most body parts had now been found, and more autopsies were due to take place the next day. Clearly, the examination of the head was of most interest. Every clue would be extracted, and no resource would be spared in the pursuit of this woman's killer.

'Do we know what colour her hair was?' one reporter asked.

'Not yet.'

Superintendent Ferris brought the briefing to an end a short time later, and the reporters retreated to their cars and vans to get the story out as soon as possible. Twitter was the first port of call for most, and videos of this latest update were soon all over social media. The public horror was evident.

Identifying the woman and finding out exactly how she died was now the main focus of the investigation team. All the recovered body parts were taken to Dublin City Mortuary. The incident room was aware of Kieran Greene's confession and subsequent arrest. Given what he was saying, it seemed likely that the remains found in the mountains belonged to the missing woman Patricia O'Connor, but again nothing was being taken for granted.

A sample of hair was taken from the head for DNA analysis, and Dr Mary Clarke, a specialist oral surgeon, was also asked to attend the mortuary. There were seven teeth present in the lower jaw found by the Murphy family following their picnic at the Old Boley three days before. Dr Clarke examined them and took some notes.

The following morning, Patricia's orthodontist, Dr Edward Cotter, was asked to hand over her dental records. She had been a patient of his for years. Patricia became quite self-conscious about her teeth in her later years, and spent a lot of money on perfecting her smile. She took great pride in her appearance as she got older, and started to treat herself after a lifetime of hard work.

Patricia's dear friend Breda remembered her coming into work at Beaumont hospital one day without a tooth in her head. She had just begun her treatment. Breda got a shock when she saw her and remembered telling her she looked a mess, but Patricia didn't care.

'I'll have a mouthful of lovely teeth next week,' she said through a gummy grin.

Dr Cotter first met her in July 2007. She had no upper teeth at the time and wore a denture. She was looking for an alternative. Implants were the way to go, but she didn't have enough jawbone, so she needed a graft to transfer bone from her hip in order to build up her upper jaw.

It was a long and expensive road, but Patricia was determined. It was something she had always wanted to do. Dr Cotter made a cast of her implants and lower teeth just over a year later, and she was thrilled with the results. The dentures made her feel old beyond her years, and for a woman who liked to smile, she was so pleased she'd taken steps to correct the damage done through years of neglect. Little did she know that this big, happy smile she'd worked so hard for would be used a decade later in an investigation into her brutal murder.

Once Dr Clarke received Patricia's records, she was able to compare them with the dental structures observed on the decomposed remains she had examined in the mortuary the night before. The position of the teeth on the lower jaw matched. There was also evidence of a root canal treatment, and the presence of implants on the upper jaw. As far as she was concerned, there were 'no incompatible inconsistencies'. A positive dental identification was established. It was Patricia.

Like the rest of the country, Patricia's sister Rita was horrified by the discovery of body parts up the Wicklow Mountains. Many bodies had been found up there over the years, but the fact that some young lad had been dismembered and just discarded like that was particularly disturbing. Gangland murders had become almost daily occurrences. Life is cheap in the underground world of organised crime, and many people suspected that this was just another casualty of a bloody feud between rival gangs. 'Live by the sword, die by the sword' was the general consensus at the time.

Rita first heard her older sister Patricia was missing through another sister, Colette. Their sister Valerie had been in touch. She lived in Dublin, not far from Patricia's home in Rathfarnham. She bumped into Gus while out walking her dog one day, and he told her Patricia was missing. She thought it strange that he hadn't rung her to ask if she'd heard from her.

Colette remembered reading about the body parts found up the mountains. She couldn't stop thinking about the poor family who would soon get the most dreadful news about their loved one. Imagine getting that knock on the door, she thought to herself. Nobody deserves that. Sadly, it wouldn't be long before she knew exactly how that felt.

Shortly after Patricia's remains were identified through her dental records, Valerie called Colette to say the guards had been round to confirm that it was their missing sister. Colette didn't believe her. She was floored and just started cursing down the phone. It couldn't be. How could it be her? How could someone do that to her? It felt like a dream. A bad dream. A total nightmare. She was so small. She wouldn't have stood a chance.

Bad news travels fast, and as soon as Patricia's family were told it was her, her name appeared across all media platforms. The BBC even carried the story. The girls at Beaumont Hospital couldn't believe it. They knew their Trisha was missing because Louise had texted one of them a few days earlier wondering if she'd seen or heard from her mother. She thought it was odd at the time. It wasn't like Patricia to go missing like that, but she knew things weren't great at home. Still, the last thing she expected was for her body to be found strewn across the mountains like that.

Breda got the shock of her life when one of the girls rang her to let her know. She couldn't believe it. She had followed the story on the news and remembered that it was first thought they were male body parts, and then they were confirmed as female. How could this be her dear friend Trisha? It took a while to register. She just hung up the phone in disbelief.

Later that day, Dr Leo Varadkar was appointed Taoiseach.

8.

THE LONG TEN YEARS

Following his arrest, Kieran Greene was taken to Bray Garda Station. At this point, it was just over 24 hours since he'd walked into Rathfarnham Garda Station with his astonishing confession. Now that he was in garda custody, the option of walking out the door had gone out the window.

He was told he was under arrest on suspicion of murdering Patricia O'Connor, and that he was entitled to consult a solicitor if he so wished. He also had the right to contact another person to let them know he was in custody.

It had been a long day, and it was late by the time he was processed back at the station, so it was decided to let him rest for the night before conducting any formal interviews. This also gave the team some precious time to prepare.

Kieran could be detained for a maximum of 72 hours. The first 24-hour period had been approved by Detective Connolly as the arresting garda. A chief superintendent must approve a second 24-hour period of detention if it's required, and a suspect can only be kept for a final 24-hour period if a judge can be convinced it's absolutely necessary.

The clock starts ticking as soon as a person is arrested, and while it can be stopped at various points, such as rest periods or if the arrestee requires medical attention, the pressure to extract as much detail as possible from the interview process is immense. In the absence of any direct evidence, such as forensics or witnesses, it can be the difference between justice being served and someone getting away with murder. Preparation is key. Experienced interviewers will carefully plot out how they plan to tackle each interview in order to ensure that every aspect of the case is covered, and also to avoid wasting time by going over old ground.

Four gardaí are allowed to sit in on an interview, but no more than two can actually question a suspect. More often than not, the other members will watch the interviews from an adjoining room and will offer feedback to their colleagues in between interviews. If the need arises, the other detectives may be asked to take over at some point. This can prove useful if a suspect takes a dislike to an interrogator, or if the team feels a fresh perspective may reap rewards. The workload may even be divvied up, depending on the complexities of the case.

Kieran was examined by a doctor the following morning. He had complained of chest pains during the voluntary statements he gave after he handed himself in, and the team wanted to ensure he was fit for interview. Aside from that, they wanted to see if the injuries he complained of were consistent with being beaten with a hurley.

The doctor, Anthony Hooper, began by asking him some questions about his medical history and general health. Kieran told him he was attacked by someone with a hurley a few weeks beforehand. He told him he was hit 'three times, maybe more'. Dr Hooper wanted to know where he'd been hit, so Kieran put out his right wrist and also pointed to his temple, the side of his body and his stomach.

'The last one winded me and I got sick', he said.

Dr Hooper nodded as he scanned the body locations being presented to him. He took note of a number of marks. The right side of Kieran's temple looked tender, and there was a scrape on his right forearm. He also noticed an area of tenderness on his lower ribcage, but there was no visible bruising.

In Dr Hooper's opinion, the injuries could have been the result of direct or indirect trauma. In other words, they could have been caused by getting a bang, or banging against something. It was impossible to tell which. The injuries were consistent with what Kieran was telling him, and he couldn't rule out the possibility that the marks he examined were defensive wounds.

Fingerprints and a DNA sample were also taken from Kieran and sent to the forensics lab at Garda Headquarters in the Phoenix Park, where they would later be tested against various items seized as part of the investigation. This is common practice in all murder cases.

It was decided that Detective Connolly would lead the first interview that morning. Before they got started, he told Kieran that their conversation would be recorded. Kieran looked around the room. There was a camera pointed at him from behind the detectives and another directly overhead. Microphones were also mounted on the walls on either side of him. Three blank DVDs were unwrapped in front of him and inserted into an electronic recorder. The detective hit Record and the DVDs whirled into action. It was 10.03 a.m. on 14 June 2017.

Kieran was then cautioned and reminded that he didn't have to answer their questions, but whatever he did say would be taken down in writing and could be used as evidence down the line. It was also pointed out to him that the interview was being recorded. At the end of the interview, he would be given the opportunity to select one of the three DVDs, which would then be sealed and labelled as the master tape, to be passed on to the garda in charge.

'Kieran, let's go right back to something you said to us about living in the house with Patricia. You described it as a long ten years. What did you mean by that?'

'The ten years of hassle,' he replied.

'Yeah. What did you mean by that?'

'There wasn't one day she wasn't giving out. She used to assault the kids. It was constant. They used to hide under the table, and it was getting worse over the years. She fucked a shovel at one of their toys one day. Smashed it like. She used to throw out their Christmas presents too, which weren't cheap. She also spent all of Gus's savings.'

Kieran then went on to claim that Patricia was trying to kill Gus. He remembered Gus falling down the stairs of the house on two occasions, and he said he was 'nearly a hundred per cent sure' he heard Patricia's bedroom door close after he fell the second time.

'I felt she did something to push him down the stairs,' he said.

'Why would she do that?'

'She wanted him dead. She even told Louise that she'd sign the house over to her if she killed him. She manipulates things. Louise has Graves' disease, and she told her she could kill anyone and get away with it. She actually told her she [Louise] could get away with murder. She said there was a symptom of her condition called Graves' rage, where you can kill anybody and get away with it.'

'And what did Louise say?'

'She automatically said no. She wouldn't do it. It was nothing new that she wanted him dead. She'd been saying it for years. I felt for everyone's safety in that house. Sure, she kicked my eldest one out, and said she should be left on the street. It was just a week or two before her debs last year. It was a nightmare for the kids. They couldn't have friends over.'

Kieran broke down as he described how life in the house was for his three children.

'She called my son a faggot,' he sobbed. 'And he just kept asking me why she called him that. I just wanted them to be happy.'

Kieran was in free-flow now, making wild allegation after wild allegation about the woman he was claiming to have killed in self-defence. He was getting more and more upset as he outlined what life under the same roof as her was like, and Detective Connolly was reminded of something he said during one of his voluntary statements. He interjected.

'Kieran, you told us before that you felt free after burying Patricia. What did you mean by that?'

'That my kids would be safe. No one would have to fear her,' he answered. 'It would have been completely different if she wasn't there. The kids wouldn't be assaulted or abused. She used to call my little girl stupid all the time.'

Gus wasn't the only one Patricia wanted rid of, according to Kieran. He thought she was trying to kill all of them.

'Louise is allergic to penicillin,' he explained. 'She took a sip of Coke one day, and within minutes her lips swelled up. I think she was trying to kill us, but I couldn't prove it. She had this glare y'know. She'd just stare at you.'

With time ticking away, Detective Connolly decided to move on and steer Kieran back to the day of Patricia's death. He asked him to go over it all again. Kieran's latest version of events didn't stray too far from what he'd told them previously, but every account offered them an opportunity to test what he'd said earlier, and to garner a little more detail about what he claimed to have happened. It was a worthwhile exercise.

Once again, he explained to them how she came at him with the hurley in the bathroom. He said she looked 'angry' before she attacked him, and was at the door mumbling something like, 'get out, get out'. That was new. Again, he told them she hit him on the right arm and on his side.

'She was aiming for my head, but I blocked it.'

He then went through the struggle with her again. He described grabbing the hurley off her and hitting her 'maybe twice'.

'Where were you at this point?' he was asked.

'We were both in the bathroom. I was facing the shower and she was facing me.'

The struggle continued, and he told them they both fell to the floor. When he came to, he said, he saw blood. Again, he told them he saw his dead uncle standing there, telling him everything was going to be okay.

'My dead friend was there too,' he said. That was new.

He also told them he was on top of her when he woke up on the floor of the bathroom. That was also new. In previous interviews, he repeatedly said he was lying next to her when he woke up.

'How long were you struggling with her?'

'It seemed like forever. Maybe fifteen to twenty minutes.'

'And you only hit her twice during that time?'

'I definitely hit her two times, but I could have hit her a little more. She could have hit me more too.'

'Did she leave any marks?'

'Yes,' he replied as he pointed to the same areas he had shown Dr Hooper. 'She hit me on the right-hand side of the temple, and my right wrist.'

At this point in the interview, Kieran became somewhat agitated, and sensing they weren't placing too much weight on the injuries he claimed to have suffered at the hands of his partner's 61-year-old mother, he went on the defensive.

'This wasn't planned. I defended myself. I couldn't overpower her. If I wanted to kill her, why would I wait ten years?'

'Why didn't you shout for help?'

'I was still in shock. I was dazed. She had hit me on the head. We were all over the shop.'

'Kieran, there were seven others in the house. They would have come to help you. Why didn't you shout for help?'

'It wasn't really a noisy row. She was saying, "I want youse out," and she was saying she wanted us all dead. She kept saying it. She wanted Gus dead. She wanted everyone dead, all the way down to the kids. I'm not a bad person. She hit me hard and winded me. She slipped and hit her head.'

Kieran was riled up now, and his interviewers sensed it. It's very common for a suspect to get wound up under questioning. In fact, more often than not, it's expected and almost welcomed. The funny thing is that it can be looked at in two ways. On the one hand, he could be losing his cool because he's telling the truth and feels frustrated because nobody believes him. On the other, he could be lying and simply cracking under the pressure of trying to make his muck stick. Either way, this was a crucial juncture in the interview process.

Detective Connolly is the epitome of calmness and professionalism. Over the course of the previous two days, he had built up somewhat of a rapport with the man sitting across the desk from him. Experienced detectives know that if you push too hard too soon, you can quickly find yourself on the sidelines if a suspect chooses to clam up and avail of their right to say nothing. Cool heads always prevail, and so Detective Connolly proceeded with caution.

Kieran told them he was facing the shower during the struggle, and, given the layout of the bathroom he had inspected two days earlier, Detective Connolly knew this meant he had a clear exit behind him during this supposed struggle.

'Why didn't you just leave?' he asked softly.

'I didn't run because she kept hitting me. If I turned my back, she would have conked me.'

'But you had the hurl?'

'No. She still had the other end.'

Detective Connolly raised an eyebrow. Kieran had told them previously that he had grabbed the hurley from her before he struck her. He decided to press him on that.

'But you said you had it and hit her twice with it?'

Kieran was adamant he couldn't turn his back on her to leave the bathroom. He insisted he'd been left with no choice but to stand his ground and defend himself. If he was acting in self-defence and didn't want to or mean to kill her, the next logical question was why didn't he try to help her?

'I did courses on CPR, but I didn't do it on her. She was still warm when I checked her in the bathroom. I brought her upstairs and checked on her once or maybe twice. I was up and down. I was panicking, and didn't know what to do.'

'Why didn't you call an ambulance?'

'I didn't want anyone to see her.'

Kieran's demeanour had cooled somewhat, so Detective Connolly pushed a little harder now.

'You had the chance to save her, but you decided to leave her to die,' he said bluntly.

'She would have told them I hit her. She'd be believed,' he said as he blinked away tears.

'It wasn't planned. It was to keep my kids safe. I let her die so my kids would be safe.'

It had been decided beforehand that Detective Garda Owen Martin would focus on Kieran's second trip to the shallow grave in Wexford.

'Did you have your phone with you, Kieran?' he asked.

'When?'

'When you returned to Wexford.'

'No. It was at home charging. I didn't bring it with me. I didn't tell anyone where I was going either.'

'When exactly did you return to the grave?'

Kieran hesitated. He couldn't put an exact date on his return.

'Maybe five to seven days later,' was his best attempt.

He then described cutting up the body, opting to glaze over all the gory detail.

'After I dug her up, I scraped off all the muck and tried to lift the body. I couldn't lift it. I nearly gave up and told the farmer. I don't know how long it took, maybe hours. I got sick several times while doing it. I was seeing things as well. I cut it up where it lay.'

Detective Martin asked him to draw a sketch of the grave, which he did. He then asked him about dumping the remains afterwards.

'I can't remember exactly where I first stopped,' he said. 'But I do remember there was some foliage. I took out a bag with a body part in it. I couldn't tell you which part it was. It was a black plastic bag, and I just ripped it open and dumped the body part in the foliage. Afterwards, I put the bag back in the car, and kept driving. I was throwing parts away every few yards, or else I'd drive for fifteen to twenty minutes before dumping a piece. I put all the bags in the boot afterwards.'

'What side of the car were you dumping the parts from?'

'The left-hand side.'

'And what did you do with the bags?'

'I'd rip them open with my hands and then just threw them out randomly along the route before I turned for home.'

'Was there anyone with you, Kieran?'

'No. I was on my own all the way. I didn't stop off anywhere, and as I said my phone was at home charging. I told the family last Monday. I picked Keith up. He's the father of Louise's two eldest girls. I picked him up and brought him to the house, and then I told them all there at the same time. Afterwards, I drove straight here.'

'Why did you want Keith to be there?'

'He's family. I get on great with him. He had a right to know.'

'And how did he react?'

'He was shocked, but he didn't live with us. He didn't know the full extent of her anger. She attacked me. I've never been in trouble before.'

Detective Martin then turned his attention to the hacksaw Kieran claimed to have used to dismember his victim. He wanted to know more about it.

'It was in the shed for years,' he explained.

'Can you describe it to us, Kieran?'

'It was about a foot long. As I said, it had been there for years. My brother-in-law probably bought it.'

'Did you go anywhere on Friday, June ninth?'

Kieran paused. He looked confused, and it took a moment for his gears to start turning again. He wasn't great with dates, but this was the first time he'd been asked specifically about 9 June. He figured they were trying to pin down an exact date for his return to the shallow grave in Wexford.

Of course they wanted a more precise timeline of events, but 9 June was a date of huge significance because gardaí suspected that Kieran went shopping for tools to dismember his victim's buried remains on that date, and they also had reason to believe he wasn't alone.

9.

A VIOLENT DEATH

On 11 June 2017, Detective Garda Janette O'Neill, a highly experienced scenes-of-crime investigator, was asked to attend a crime scene near the Sally Gap up in the Wicklow Mountains. Her expertise is wide-ranging, and while most of her time is spent examining guns, ammunition and homemade bombs at the Garda Ballistics Section, she's also qualified in many other areas, including the collection of trace evidence or blood. Detective O'Neill is trained to collect almost any piece of forensic evidence except fingerprints.

As she drove up to the now cordoned-off crime scene, she was aware that a body part had been discovered the day before by a member of the public. The sight of human remains out in the open like that would sicken anyone, but Detective O'Neill had developed a strong stomach over the years and was unfazed by such grisly discoveries. She had to be. In order to extract as much evidence as possible, she needed to remain focused on the task at hand. Time is of the essence when a body is exposed to the elements. Mother

Nature can claim valuable evidence forever if it's not preserved swiftly, so there was no time to be queasy.

On arriving at the scene, she was directed to a ditch near Glencree Forest where, she was told, a family out picnicking the day before had stumbled upon the remains. It was part of a torso. In her report she described it as 'fresh' and noted 'very little insect activity'. It was clear it hadn't been there for very long.

The piece itself ran from just below the jaw as far as the ribs, and included the neck and upper torso. There were seven teeth present in the lower jaw, and she hoped they would identify this John Doe. Or perhaps it was a Jane Doe. It was hard to tell. After she finished her work on site, she oversaw the removal of the body part to Dublin City Mortuary, where an autopsy would hopefully unlock more clues about what had happened to this poor soul.

Detective O'Neill was kept busy over the next three days as more and more body parts were recovered. In total, fifteen parts were found in nine different locations across an area with a radius of 30km. Given the locations of the various pieces, she was of the view that the victim didn't die at any of the scenes she visited. In her opinion, the mountains appeared to have been used as a dumping ground by whoever had killed this unknown person.

As is common practice, the Office of the State Pathologist was also one of the first ports of call. The office's main activity is performing post-mortem examinations in cases of sudden, unexplained death where a criminal or suspicious element is present. This case certainly satisfied the criteria. The pathologists deal with homicides, as well as a wide range of natural and unnatural deaths, such as road traffic accidents, other accidents and drug-related deaths. Most of its workload involves state forensic cases.

In June 2017, Dr Michael Curtis was the Deputy State Pathologist. He received a call after the first body part was found. His diary was soon cleared for the next few days as each of the fifteen recovered pieces eventually ended up on his slab at the Dublin City Mortuary.

Appropriately enough, the mortuary, located on beautiful tree-lined Griffith Avenue in Whitehall, was once home to the local garda station. Whitehall Garda Station served its community for the best part of eight decades before it was shut down in 2012 due to cutbacks during the recession. It proved to be an ideal home for the mortuary, which had been making do with a temporary site in Dublin City Fire Brigade's training ground in Marino. The facility had moved there in 1999 following the demolition of the old Victorian City Morgue at Store Street. Autopsies weren't carried out at this site, and the move was supposed to be temporary, with work beginning on a new state-of-the-art facility at the O'Brien Institute in Marino in 2010. That project was soon mothballed, though, again due to the recession. Its partially completed structure was later torn down. The vacant Whitehall Garda Station was then refurbished to accommodate both the Office of the State Pathologist and the Dublin City Mortuary. Post-mortem facilities were also provided as part of the multi-million euro retrofit. The building is a protected structure, and many locals objected to it being used in such a way. Some wanted it to be turned into a community hall, while many were just creeped out at the thought of its proposed purpose.

Less than one year later, on 11 June 2017, Dr Curtis walked the gauntlet of knobbly London plane trees that line the street where his office is. Griffith Avenue was drenched in sunlight, but the footpath leading to his office was gobbled up by the long shadows cast from the tall trees above, offering a cool reprieve from the warm day. It was a sign of things to come. He wouldn't feel much sunlight where he was going.

Dr Curtis got to work. Over the course of the next few days, he was provided with all fifteen of the dismembered body parts, which equated to the entire body of an adult woman, who would soon be identified as Patricia O'Connor.

He made incisions with his scalpel down the front of certain body parts in order to extract and examine the organs within, and examined them carefully with the naked eye before dissecting them to look for any internal abnormalities.

With the exception of the wrists and hands, a common feature he noticed among the parts was that they all had sharply cut bone edges. This led him to believe that the act of dismemberment was carried out with a power tool, most likely a power saw. The edges of the wrists and hands were more irregular and ragged. He figured they were probably removed with a handheld saw.

Unsurprisingly, his examination of the skull found in the plastic bag unearthed the most clues. Dr Curtis noticed five lacerations to the scalp. Three of them were full-thickness splits to the front right-hand side. They were deep and went all the way to the bone. There was also a deep cut at the back of the scalp, and he also spotted another cut above the left ear.

From the fifteen autopsies carried out, he concluded that the woman had died from blunt force trauma to the head. She was hit at least three times. The sheer force of one of the blows transferred through the bones, causing multiple fractures.

The injuries also suggested death would have come quickly. Interestingly, when later asked if the large fracture to the skull could have been caused by falling on a step, Dr Curtis said he couldn't absolutely exclude it as a possibility.

Forensic anthropologist Lauren Buckley also attended the post-mortems. Her expertise in the examination of bones has helped to put some of Ireland's most notorious killers behind bars, including Gary McCrea. In 2004, he murdered his estranged wife Dolores in County Donegal, and burned her remains. With the fire still smouldering, the then State Pathologist, Professor Marie Cassidy, and members of the Garda Technical Bureau carefully sifted through the ashes, collecting the mother-of-four's charred bones.

Ms Buckley was then called in to piece them together for examination. She identified small fragments of teeth in the trays of items collected from the fire, which helped to identify Dolores through her dental records; crucially, she was also able to establish that the victim had been *placed* in the fire, and hadn't fallen into it accidentally. McCrea was convicted of murder the following year.

Ms Buckley made a number of important observations while examining Patricia O'Connor's remains. First, she noted that 'striations from a saw' were visible in cuts to the bones. She also noticed that the cut edges were relatively sharp and clean, so much so that the surfaces of some dismembered parts fitted together perfectly. Her examination of the hands led her to believe they had been sawn through at the wrist, and the cuts looked 'hacked and shredded'. She was also able to tell that the body appeared to have been buried before being exhumed and cut up, and that the first part seemed to have been dumped not long before it was found.

Dr Curtis also examined the remains for defensive wounds, especially on the hands and forearms. These types of wound can appear anywhere on a victim's body, but they're usually found on the back of the hands, the inside of the palms, and the inner side of the forearms. The different positioning and angles of the wounds can give a forensic examiner a better idea of the nature of the attack. In most cases, a victim will instinctively hold up their hands and forearms in front of the body in order to protect the face and chest from injury. Defensive injuries can also give you an idea of what type of weapon was used. Sharp weapons such as knives will leave cuts and scrapes, while a blunt object causes bruising.

In any event, the woman Dr Curtis now knew as Patricia O'Connor did not show any signs of defence-type injuries. She hadn't put up a fight.

As Dr Curtis progressed through his examinations, his findings were being relayed back to the incident room at Bray Garda Station. Superintendent Ward wanted to be kept right up to date. Kieran Greene was being held in the station for questioning, and the Deputy State Pathologist's observations and conclusions would soon be put to the suspect. The investigation was beginning to gather momentum. By now, Detective Inspector Brian O'Keeffe had been assigned the role of Senior Investigating Officer (SIO). Going forward, it would be his responsibility to lead the multifaceted investigation.

As Detective Connolly prepared to begin his second interview with Kieran Greene on the day after his arrest, 14 June 2017, he now knew Patricia O'Connor had died from blunt force trauma to the head. According to Dr Curtis, she was hit at least three times on the head.

Kieran was summoned back to the interview room just after 9 p.m.

Detective Connolly began by asking him to pick up where he left off earlier. He wanted to know more about the disposal of the body parts.

'What did you do with Patricia's clothes, Kieran?'

'What do you mean?'

'Her clothes, Kieran. What did you do with them?'

'I scattered them all over the mountains too. Pieces just came off while I was cutting her up. I put them in a bag, and then I just scattered them around the place.'

Another thing that didn't sit well with Detective Connolly was Dr Curtis's opinion that a power tool had been used to dismember all but Patricia's hands and wrists. Kieran had never mentioned a power tool of any description in his previous interviews, insisting at all times that he had used a single hacksaw he found in the shed at Mountain View Park. He claimed to have discarded that up the mountains too, but it hadn't been found. Power tools obviously need power, so Detective Connolly figured that Kieran was lying about where the body was dismembered. He put it to him that it appeared that the body hadn't been cut up in the cornfield in Wexford. Kieran had claimed previously that he had cut her up where she lay in the shallow grave because he couldn't lift her out of it.

'I'm telling you, it was,' he replied. 'Hand on heart.'

'Kieran, the evidence we now have is that a power tool was used to dismember her. Can you explain that?'

'No.'

The investigation of serious crime is like a living organism. The more you feed it, the more it grows. The more you get to know it, the more it tells you. As more jobs were being ticked off the list in Bray, more evidence was finding its way onto Detective Connolly's desk. Unbeknownst to Kieran, he was also in possession of the results of a technical examination carried out on Patricia's car. This was the silver Toyota Corolla Kieran claimed to have used to drive to the shallow grave in Wexford with his partner's dead mother in the boot. Kieran had given the keys to Sergeant Myles when he handed himself in two days beforehand. He had also given her permission to examine it.

A receipt for Mr. Price in Tallaght, dated 9 June 2017, was found inside. When Kieran was asked if he was in Mr. Price the week before, he said he was probably in there getting a few 'bits and pieces', but couldn't remember exactly what. His memory was refreshed for him. The purchase items included a jerrycan, tow rope, vinyl tape and some utility knives.

'Why did you buy a petrol can, Kieran. Was it to burn the body?'

'No, it was in case I ran out. The body wasn't burned. Nothing was.'

'And the blades?'

'I used them to clean grouting in the bathroom.'

The boot was searched for blood. Not a single drop was found. That in itself wasn't too surprising, considering the boot liner was missing, and the body had supposedly been placed on some blankets. That said, Detective Connolly did expect some blood to be found in the front of the car.

'You told us you didn't get changed after you killed her. You told us you were wearing the same clothes when you drove to Wexford?'

'That's right.'

'So, can you explain to us how there was no blood found in the car?'

He couldn't.

'Kieran, you claim you threw the clothes and tools out of the car?'

'Yeah.'

'We have hundreds of people searching up the mountains. They have found all of Patricia O'Connor's remains, and yet there has been no sign of any clothes or tools. Can you explain that?'

He couldn't.

'Were her clothes covered in blood afterwards?'

'I don't know. I couldn't see. I expected to see blood shooting up all over the place, but there was none of that.'

Detective Connolly revealed another card.

'Kieran, we now know Patricia's head has evidence of injuries that are not consistent with what you've told us. There were three injury locations. Three blows with a solid implement. One of the blows resulted in serious damage to the head.'

'That could have been when she fell.'

'No. Serious damage was caused to the right-hand side of her head. It doesn't tally with her fall. You said she was lying on her back. She was hit three times in the head.'

Silence.

Kieran stuck to his story. He denied researching online how to dispose of a body, and insisted that he had acted alone at all times. As far as he was concerned, he was left with no choice but to defend himself from attack. He didn't mean to kill Patricia, and his unspeakable acts afterwards were explained away through sheer panic and shame. He said his decision to dismember her and scatter her remains across the Wicklow Mountains was borne of a fear of getting caught. He wasn't thinking straight, apparently. Obviously not. To dig her out of the shallow grave he had put her in and display her remains for all to see across one of the most used beauty spots in the country made no sense. To go to all that effort to avoid detection, only to hand yourself in days later also defied logic.

'I told you everything from the beginning,' he said finally. 'I'm being honest. I did it for my kids.'

Sure, there were some holes in Kieran Greene's confession. Some minor details changed during the interview process, but the major ones didn't, and for the most part, his story seemed to hold water. There was still a lot of work to do, but the investigation team felt they had enough to charge him with murder. That decision lies at the door of the Director of Public Prosecutions, and it's a decision that isn't made lightly, especially when it comes to the most serious criminal offence a person can be charged with.

A decision not to prosecute can cause great stress and upset to a victim's family. On the other hand, if someone is prosecuted and later found not guilty, it can damage their reputation and they can suffer a lot of harm. As well as recognising the public interest in bringing a prosecution, the DPP must also consider the strength of the evidence, and the likelihood of getting a safe conviction across the line.

The investigation team, now led by Detective Inspector Brian O'Keeffe, had to convince Claire Loftus and her team at the Office of the Director of Public Prosecutions that the evidence was admissible, reliable, and enough to show that Kieran Greene had murdered Patricia O'Connor. They had a detailed confession, sprung from his own mouth, and signed with his own hand; they had the post-mortem results, which, for the most part, backed up what he was saying, but crucially laid the grounds for a challenge to his contention that he was acting in self-defence during a struggle. She had *no* defensive wounds.

It was a slam dunk, surely? The DPP seemed confident. After hearing the investigation team's pitch for a prosecution, it was decided that even if Kieran contested the murder charge, there was a good chance of convincing a jury that he did it. Shortly after the DPP green-lighted a prosecution, Kieran Greene was charged with the murder of Patricia O'Connor.

10.

IT WAS SELF-DEFENCE

Kieran Greene was charged with Patricia O'Connor's murder at 11.28 a.m. on 15 June 2017. He was taken to Tallaght District Court soon afterwards.

Unlike the Criminal Courts of Justice beside the Phoenix Park on Parkgate Street in Dublin 8, the facility in Tallaght isn't very accommodating to accused persons hoping to make a discreet entrance.

The Garda Press Office informed the media that a 32-year-old man had been charged with Patricia O'Connor's murder, and details of his pending court appearance were also attached in a press release. Unsurprisingly, a large media presence awaited Kieran's arrival outside the courthouse. This was the first time they'd lay eyes on the man suspected of carrying out this gruesome act. It had been front-page news for days. Rumour had it that it was Patricia O'Connor's son-in-law, and that he had killed her in a dispute over the house they shared.

The snappers arrived early in the hope of catching him before the hearing. They surged towards the unmarked garda car when it arrived, blindly firing off shots through the rear windows as it whizzed past them. Kieran was seated in the back, flanked by two detectives. He pulled up the hood of his grey top and pinched it tight to his face to try to hide from the world. He kept it up as he was escorted into the building.

The journalists piled into the courtroom just before his case was called, much to the bewilderment of those hanging around in the public gallery for their own cases to be heard. The photographers waited outside, flicking through their images to see if they had got their shot.

Detective Connolly gave Judge Patricia McNamara evidence of arrest, charge and caution.

'It was self-defence,' was all Kieran said after the charge was put to him, an early indication that this was going to trial.

There was no application for bail. Given the nature of the charge, that would have to be heard by a High Court judge, so Kieran was remanded in custody. Judge McNamara directed that he receive any medical attention required while in custody, and due to the fact that he didn't have a job at the time, she also assigned him free legal aid.

Kieran's knees wobbled a little as he took to his feet when his name was called. He had to take his hood down while in the dock, but he didn't address the court at any stage. He kept his head bowed and avoided the burning eyes of the media on the front bench just a few feet from where he stood. It was the first time they had seen his face. The hearing only lasted a few minutes, and before he knew it, he was once again running the gauntlet of photographers and TV camera crews outside. He made sure his hood was back up before he left.

Patricia's brothers and sisters were still trying to get their heads round what had happened to Trisha. Their world had been turned upside down. You never expect this to happen to your family. This is the stuff of nightmares. It was like a horror movie, and it didn't seem real. Being told their sister was dead was truly shocking. Words couldn't begin to describe how that felt. Learning how she died, and what happened to her afterwards, floored them. And to think the person responsible for all this was the father of three of her grandchildren, her daughter's boyfriend of ten years, someone who lived under the same roof as her. That was just too much to take in. They were uncomprehending when they heard Kieran had been charged with her murder. He was such a quiet guy. How could he do such a thing? Why would he do such a thing?

Patricia's body was released to her family a week or so later. She was cremated at Mount Jerome Crematorium in Harold's Cross after a small humanist ceremony. It was a very private affair, with only immediate family in attendance. Colette later regretted not doing more for her sister's final farewell, but Louise wanted to keep it low-key. The case was still attracting considerable media attention and she said she wanted to grieve in private, away from the glare of the public. Still, Patricia had a lot of friends who wanted to be there to say goodbye and to pay their respects – it didn't seem right. Louise went straight home afterwards.

Back at Bray Garda Station, the investigation into Patricia's murder continued. The team's work was far from over. Door-to-door enquiries at Mountain View Park hadn't thrown up much.

Nobody had heard or seen anything unusual coming from the O'Connor house on the night in question. The O'Connors' next-door neighbour, Sam Lin, had noticed that the children weren't out playing on the street in the weeks that followed. He thought that was odd, but assumed it was because of the bad weather. He didn't see anything out of the ordinary on the night of 29 May 2017. Gardaí noticed a CCTV camera mounted on the front of his house, and from the way it was positioned, it looked as though it captured a large part of the O'Connor property. Mr Lin said that he had another camera out the back, and that too appeared to be angled favourably from the investigation team's point of view. He was happy for them to take the system's hard drive, and he hoped it would be of some use to them.

The house at 66 Mountain View Park had been designated a crime scene and needed to be thoroughly searched and forensically swept for clues. Detective Connolly didn't notice anything out of the ordinary when he briefly inspected the downstairs bathroom on the evening Kieran handed himself in. There was certainly nothing to suggest a brutal murder had taken place there. During his interviews, Kieran told them he had mopped up all the blood with bleach, but it was hoped he'd left something behind for the crime scene investigators.

Ballistics expert Detective Janette O'Neill went to the house on the same day Kieran was charged with murder. She didn't see any signs of a struggle, but the walls in the hallway and bathroom looked like they'd been freshly painted. Cream and magnolia was her best guess. As she scanned the sloppy brush strokes, she tried to decide whether it was just a bad paint job or one that had been done in a hurry. Interestingly, she also noticed that the bathroom had been recently tiled.

John Hoade, a forensic scientist, also visited the house. He works for Forensic Science Ireland, which was set up in the 1970s to analyse samples taken from crime scenes and provide expert evidence in criminal trials. He was already involved in the case, having played a crucial role in identifying the remains through DNA analysis. He did so by comparing tissue samples taken during the post-mortem examinations with a DNA sample taken from Louise. He concluded that the profile from the remains was 'two million times more likely to be from Louise's biological mother than from somebody unrelated'.

Mr Hoade took some photographs of the bathroom when he arrived at the house. Just like Detective Connolly before him, he couldn't see any blood, so he snapped on some surgical gloves and reached for his forensic toolbox.

Bluestar is a crime scene investigator's best friend when it comes to finding old blood stains, or stains that may have been washed out or wiped off. It comes in tablet form, and when mixed with a special chemical, it can be sprayed onto surfaces directly. It's extremely sensitive and allows the naked eye to pick up the most minute traces or droplets that have been washed off, with or without detergent. Crucially, it doesn't destroy or alter the DNA of any detected traces.

Mr Hoade switched off the light and moved around the bathroom, carefully squeezing the plastic trigger of his Bluestar spray bottle over the tiles and other surfaces. Bluestar gives off a blue glow when it comes into contact with blood. That's why he needed the room to be dark. A small area on the floor, adjacent to the bath panel, lit up. The glow rose from the grout where the tile met the panel. Bluestar is just a detection tool, and it can produce false negatives if it comes into contact with certain chemicals found in paint and varnish, so Mr Hoade took a swab for further analysis. Back at the lab, he was able to establish that the blood came from a male source. He couldn't develop a DNA profile from the swab sample, but he was able to rule out Patricia O'Connor as the source.

Mr Hoade also examined a number of items seized from the house, including a child's hurley, which was found up against a fireguard in the kitchen. He didn't find any traces of blood on it. Likewise, no blood was found on the other items he tested, including some carpet taken from an upstairs bedroom, a piece of red and gold fabric, a tablecloth, tiling tools, hammers, saws and a grinder.

He was also asked to analyse a knotted area of a black plastic bag. This was the bag Patricia's head and hands were found in. The investigation team hoped that whoever tied the knot had left some valuable DNA evidence behind. Unfortunately, there wasn't enough on it to generate a profile. The bag was then sent back to the Garda Technical Bureau to be dusted for prints. Some marks were found on it, but again none of them had enough detail to develop any identifying features.

Mr Hoade tested the inside and outside of the Toyota Corolla. He noticed the boot mat was missing. Again, no joy.

The hair and piece of fabric found in the shallow grave also ended up on his desk. The hair was about 12cm in length and light blonde/brown in colour. Again, there wasn't enough DNA in the roots for him to generate a profile. The investigation team needed to know if it was Patricia's hair, so a decision was made to send two locks to a specialist lab in the UK for further analysis. A hair taken from Patricia's severed head was also sent as a reference sample, as well as a DNA sample from Louise. The UK lab found moderate support that it belonged to Patricia.

The piece of fabric was covered in earth, so John carefully rinsed it with water. He didn't measure it, but figured it was maybe six inches long, and noticed it had a floral pattern on it. He didn't examine it any further before handing it back to gardaí.

Sergeant Pat Carroll, the man behind the mammoth search recovery operation in the Wicklow Mountains, was also involved in the search of the house in Rathfarnham. His team moved in after the forensic experts were finished with it, and just like the approach taken with the search of the mountains, a lot of planning went into the sweep of the suspected murder scene. Officers were assigned specific rooms to search, and anything of interest was seized.

A black suitcase found in an upstairs bedroom was taken away in an evidence bag. It would later prove to be a crucial piece of the puzzle. A roll of black bags found in the shed at the back of the house was also seized. Gardaí wondered if bags taken from this roll had been used to dispose of the body parts.

Unsurprisingly, the bins are usually the first things to be examined during a house search, and a receipt from DIY retailer Homebase was found in the one in the living room. At first glance, it seemed innocuous enough, but its significance wasn't lost on its finder, given the circumstances of the case. According to the crumpled-up piece of till roll, somebody bought a five-metre cover mat and some grout from the Homebase unit in Nutgrove Retail Park at 12.33 p.m. on 30 May 2017. This was the day after Patricia went missing.

Another receipt was found in the top drawer of a plastic storage unit in the front bedroom. This receipt was dated 9 June 2017, 4.32 p.m. It was from another hardware store, B&Q in Tallaght. It was for two pairs of gloves, three saws and a cover sheet. That last item was of particular interest. No blood was found at the shallow grave where Kieran claimed to have cut Patricia's body up – perhaps the cover sheet had been put under her. Kieran denied using one when he dismembered her, and the searches to date hadn't turned up any, but this felt important.

Several other receipts of interest were found in the house, including another from Homebase. Four days before the cover sheet was bought in Tallaght, somebody bought coffee-cream coloured paint and PVA. Detective O'Neill figured the walls in the hallway had been recently painted when she searched the house a few days before.

A fourth receipt, from Woodie's DIY in Tallaght, had a 5.13 p.m. timestamp, again on 9 June 2017. It was for two axes and a pack of ten blades.

Just twenty minutes before that purchase, two pairs of green wellington boots were bought in Shoe Zone in Tallaght, according to another receipt found in a plastic storage unit.

Baby wipes and a pack of household gloves were on the items registered on a receipt dated 7.40 p.m., 9 June 2017, from EuroGiant at the Nutgrove Shopping Centre.

The significance of the items bought in the various hardware stores on the day before the first body part was discovered wasn't lost on the investigation team. It was decided to go to each of these locations to make controlled purchases of the listed items. Harvesting CCTV footage from the various shops was also added to the job list back at the incident room in Bray.

Detective Garda James Doolin was sent to B&Q in Tallaght to do just that. When he arrived, he spoke with the manager, who was happy to let him take a look at the store's CCTV footage from the date in question. The footage clearly showed Kieran Greene and Keith Johnston buying certain items. Detective Doolin then asked the manager to collect the exact items on the receipt that had been seized from the house. He returned with thirty extra-strong black sacks, two pairs of gloves, a ten-inch saw, two adjustable hacksaws and a light-duty protection sheet.

One of the black sacks bought was sent to Garda Headquarters to be tested at the Forensic Science Laboratory. It was a long shot, but gardaí wanted to know if was the same as the type of bag Patricia's head and hands were found in. They were also in possession of a roll of black bags seized from the shed at Mountain View Park, and that too formed a part of Nora Lee's analysis. Ms Lee, a forensic scientist with over thirty-five years' experience, found 'very strong support' for the proposition that the bag containing the body parts came from the same roll as the bag taken from the shed. However, she found it didn't match the bag from B&Q that she examined. That said, she couldn't rule out the possibility that the bag used to dump the body parts was bought in B&Q.

Keith Johnston wasn't a suspect at this time. He had assisted gardaí by giving them a witness statement, and while he mentioned buying some drill bits and grout to carry out some repair works in the bathroom at Mountain View Park after Patricia went missing, he conveniently forgot to mention that he and Kieran had gone shopping for hacksaws just a few days beforehand.

On the same day, Garda Garret Collins was asked to go to Woodie's DIY in Tallaght. Again, he asked to speak to a manager. As hoped, the CCTV footage harvested from Woodie's showed Kieran Greene and Keith Johnston wandering through the aisles of the hardware store. Kieran could be seen at the till paying for axes and a pack of knife blades. Garda Collins downloaded the footage and thanked the manager for his help.

11.

A FAMILY AFFAIR

Kieran Greene didn't fit the profile of a mastermind criminal, and gardaí found it hard to believe that he alone killed Patricia O'Connor and disposed of her remains in the gruesome way he had described to them. For starters, it seemed incredible to think that nobody in the house heard the struggle downstairs on the night in question. Kieran claimed that Patricia was shouting. He said the struggle with her lasted up to twenty minutes. The house was full. How could nobody have heard the commotion?

Kieran didn't know where he found the strength to drag her body upstairs afterwards. According to him, it was a 'miracle'. He suggested that his dead uncle – who was apparently watching over him that night – may have helped him. The ghost of his dead friend was there too, according to Kieran. Perhaps he gave him a hand too.

Kieran Greene has a very slight frame. Patricia O'Connor was much shorter than him, but she was stocky and would have been difficult for him to move on his own. Gardaí were convinced that others were involved, and they were not interested in investigating miracles or the supernatural, especially with good reason to look a little closer to home.

Over 300 hours of CCTV footage were harvested from the hard drive belonging to Sam Lin, the O'Connors' next-door neighbour. He had recently upgraded his system, and the quality of the footage was good. More important, one of his cameras covered most of the front of his neighbour's property. It took everything in except the footpath that led to the alleyway down the side of the house. Apparently, the alleyway was rarely used anyway. The kids used to dump their bikes there. The camera mounted to the rear of Mr Lin's house also took in a large portion of the back garden at No. 66, and the patio doors leading into their kitchen. He told gardaí they knew the cameras were there. It wasn't like he was hiding them, and he certainly wasn't spying on them. He installed them for his own peace of mind, and if they had an issue with them, they never said.

Examining CCTV footage for the purposes of a criminal investigation is a painstaking job that requires a good eye and a hell of a lot of focus and patience. It can often feel like searching for a tiny needle in a very large haystack. Garda Alan Thompson was among those assigned the unenviable task of sifting through 343 hours of recordings from Mr Lin's system.

CCTV evidence features in most criminal investigations these days, and it has been instrumental in securing many convictions. Like it or not, most public spaces in urban areas are covered by a camera of some description. Dashcams have also become a useful tool for crime fighters. The video quality has improved dramatically over the years too, which makes the work of people like Garda Thompson much easier.

The investigation team had drawn up a list of significant dates, the most important being 29 May, the day Patricia was killed, so that's where Garda Thompson started. It didn't take long for him to develop a clearer picture of what had happened that day. His work was about to hand many more leads to the investigation team. It would take them in new directions, and reinforce their belief that Kieran Greene wasn't acting alone.

After Patricia supposedly stormed out of the house on 29 May 2017, Kieran told Detective Connolly that she returned just after midnight. He claimed to have killed her in the bathroom shortly afterwards. The footage Garda Thompson looked at was two minutes slower than real time, so he adjusted accordingly. It showed the various comings and goings of the day, and a number of moments in particular caught his eye.

At 6.35 p.m., Patricia O'Connor was seen pottering around the back of the house. She was wearing a summer dress. As far as he could make out, the dress had some sort of floral pattern on it.

Less than twenty minutes later, Kieran Greene could be seen closing the curtains at the back of the house. One minute later, Louise and Stephanie left through the front door with the kids. Gus left shortly afterwards.

The next thing of note took place at 8.44 p.m., when Kieran opened the curtains. It had been almost two hours since he closed them. Louise, Stephanie and the kids returned twenty minutes later.

Garda Thompson hit pause on his monitor again when the footage reached 9.34 p.m. This was to prove a pivotal moment in the wider investigation into Patricia's murder. At that exact moment, a figure could be seen leaving the house from the front, and from what he could make out, it was a woman wearing a dark green jacket with the hood up. She had a suitcase in her hand.

One minute later, Louise appears in the same shot. She walks down to the end of the driveway and looks left. This tallied with her account of going outside to check which direction her mother had gone when she stormed out of the house. Louise emerges from the front door once more at 10 p.m. Again, she walks to the end of the driveway and looks to her left before returning to the house. She appears to have a phone in her hand, but later denied being in contact with anyone.

Garda Thompson hit rewind again. He watched this passage over and over. He was trying to figure out if the person seen leaving the house at 9.34 p.m. was Patricia O'Connor. The person in this frame had a hood up, so he couldn't make out her hair or any distinguishing features. He switched to the camera at the rear of Mr Lin's house.

This second camera revealed that on two occasions shortly before the unidentified figure left the house, Kieran, Louise and Stephanie were in their back garden. Both times, they appeared to be having a chat before going back inside. Garda Thompson wondered what they were talking about. He kept watching the footage. There was no movement at the back of the house for a short time, but then at 10.05 p.m. a woman carrying a suitcase and with a coat draped over her arm entered the frame and went into the house through the back door. Where did she come from?

Gus returned to the house with Sammy the dog twenty minutes later. He could be seen talking to Louise at the back of the house just before 11 p.m. Garda Thompson noted that he was picked up inside the house by the camera at the rear of Mr Lin's house on a number of occasions between 11 p.m. and his last sighting at 12.45 a.m.

Just a few minutes before Gus's final appearance on camera, in the early hours of 30 May, Kieran Greene could be seen leaving the house from the side where the gate leading to the alleyway is located. He was carrying two long-handled objects, which looked like shovels, before disappearing off camera.

Shortly after this, Garda Thompson scribbled another observation into his notepad: *12.40 a.m.: Toyota Corolla car is driven out of the driveway and reversed back in.*

Ten minutes later, he noted that he saw a man put a shovel into the car. He then recorded the car driving away at 2.09 a.m. He sped up the footage. The stillness of the night raced by on the monitor. The sun rose just after 5 a.m., breathing light and life back onto the dark screen. The car returned to the house just before 6 a.m. Again, it reversed into the driveway and Kieran could be seen going into the garden shortly afterwards with a pair of shoes in his hand. He came back into the shot moments later with black bin bags, which he used to put some clothes in. When he was finished, he scrubbed the ground with some water from a watering can. He left the house just before 9 a.m. to drop his sons to school.

Two days later, on 1 June 2017, Kieran could be seen putting a black sack into the passenger side of the car. Keith Johnston called over at 1.39 p.m., and from Mr Lin's camera at the rear of his house, he could be seen using a power saw to cut a plank of wood. When asked about it later, Keith said he noticed a piece of timber in the bathroom had gone soft, so he was just replacing it. Kieran didn't use the power tool. He just stood there watching his buddy and then helped him to carry it into the house later that evening.

Garda Thompson took notes throughout his extensive viewing. He marked out times he felt were of significance, and condensed the relevant footage into a shorter compilation for the investigation team to look at.

The CCTV evidence raised some interesting questions. What time was Patricia actually killed? Kieran said it happened just after she came home about midnight, but that was clearly a lie. It was more likely to have happened sometime between her final appearance in the footage at the back of the house at 6.35 p.m. and 8.44 p.m., when Kieran opened the curtains just before Louise and the kids returned home. If that was the case, then who was the figure leaving the house with the suitcase at 9.34 p.m.? By the way it moved and carried itself, it didn't appear to be a 61-year-old woman. And what were Louise, Kieran and Stephanie talking about in the back garden just before that person left the house? It was time to get some answers.

On 2 September 2017, Sergeant Barry Turner knocked on the door of 66 Mountain View Park. Louise had moved back into the house with her kids after the guards had finished combing it for clues. Keith was also staying there a few nights a week. Louise looked surprised to see Sergeant Turner. She seemed even more surprised when he arrested her on suspicion of murdering her mother.

Back at the station, Sergeant Brian Hanley asked her if she understood why she had been arrested.

'Not really,' she said. 'You have someone for the murder. He put his hands up.'

'The purpose of your arrest is to establish the truth about the death of your mother,' Sergeant Hanley explained.

It was clear from her response that she had no problem speaking ill of the dead, even if it was her own mother.

'I told everyone about her and nobody would listen,' she said. 'She used to tell me and Stephanie every day that we should have been aborted. We were always walking on eggshells around her. She wouldn't let my dad get a medical card. We'd fight over silly things.'

'Like what?'

'Bricks and mortar, mostly. My ma tried to beat the head off me with a teapot the day she left. I ducked and left the room. She kicked the cat around the place.'

'Why?'

'I don't know. It could have been over a claim on the car or the kids. She used to say the kids were useless and retarded. I love my kids. Dad is heartbroken. He's talking about selling the place.'

In one of Kieran's interviews, he claimed Patricia was trying to kill them all, Gus in particular. Louise told them she had been diagnosed with Graves' disease four or five years before, and claimed her mother used to ask her to kill her father so they could sell the house and split the proceeds.

'I said no. I don't want to go to prison. Da never laid a finger on her. Kieran got it as well. I told him he had to go back to his ma's to give us a break.'

Sergeant Hanley guided her back to that day in the house, 29 May. 'Can you remember what the fight was about that day? What was she saying?' he asked.

'I can't remember exactly what she said. Everyone was fighting. That's when we decided to take the kids to the park.'

The CCTV from Mr Lin's house showed Louise and the kids leaving the house at 6.53 p.m. that day. Gardaí now had reason to believe that Patricia was killed around that time, and they suspected that was why Louise took the kids to the park for the evening.

'We came back from the park,' she continued. 'And then two weeks later, Kieran tells us he killed her.'

'Let's go back for a moment, Louise. Tell us what happened when you returned to the house,' Sergeant Hanley asked, knowing that it was just after 9 p.m. when they got back and that Kieran had opened the curtains at the back of the house about fifteen minutes beforehand. If the garda theory was correct, and Patricia was killed sometime in the two and a half hours before, it was safe to say that her body was still in the house while the children were getting ready for bed.

Louise stuck to the story she gave to gardaí in her voluntary statement back in June. She told them she was in the toilet when she heard some shouting and then the front door being slammed. When she was asked what the shouting was about, again she said she heard her mother say, 'I'll be back when that bastard pops his clogs,' and she figured she was referring to her father. She said she didn't know where she was going, and she couldn't tell them what time she left to check what direction she was going in. Gardaí now knew she walked down the driveway at 9.35 p.m. and looked to the left, towards Nutgrove. She told them she had no way of contacting her mother because Patricia didn't have a phone.

She was clearly growing tired of all the questions, becoming agitated and frustrated as the interview went on. She was showing signs of impatience and apparently couldn't understand what she was doing there and why she was answering these questions. Eventually she lost it.

'Kieran put his hands up, so why are you asking me about all this?' she barked. 'There are only two people who know what happened that day, my ma and Kieran. Me ma is dead and Kieran is locked up. He broke down and said what he done. He went to the guards. I didn't know what happened to her. Nobody had seen her. I contacted her family in Kilkenny. The neighbours saw her carry on.'

Louise had not contacted her extended family to see if they knew anything about her mother's disappearance. She promised Richard that she would after he became concerned when he didn't hear from her on his birthday, but she never did. Louise's aunt Valerie let everyone in Kilkenny know after bumping into Gus in Dublin. About a week later, Rita, Anne and Colette drove to Tallaght Garda Station to try to get some answers. They were tearing their hair out and just wanted to know what was going on.

They introduced themselves to the garda at the front desk as Patricia O'Connor's sisters, and told her they wanted to speak to someone about her disappearance. The garda went out the back for a few minutes and when she returned to her post, she apologised and told them they had no idea Patricia had brothers and sisters living down the country. Nobody had told them. Rita later said it felt like 'a kick in the stomach'. Alarm bells started ringing straight away for her at that point. It was the first time she suspected something bad had happened to her older sister. She just couldn't understand why Louise had never told the gardaí about them.

Louise repeatedly maintained her innocence. She told Sergeant Hanley she couldn't understand why Kieran didn't call an ambulance, and she said she was looking for answers too.

'I'll go to the grave knowing I never harmed a hair on her head,' she said.

Sergeant Hanley wanted to know what she was doing out in the back garden with Stephanie and Kieran on the night in question.

'I was having a smoke on the swing. I was worried she'd come back and throw us all out.'

She was asked about the suitcase Patricia supposedly left the house with. Louise's best attempt at describing it was to say it was a 'small one'. She said her mother had lots of similar suitcases, and she wondered if it was part of a set.

'Why didn't Kieran follow you to the park?' Sergeant Hanley asked.

'He went for a shower. There are nine people living in that house. Getting a shower is like a miracle. I tried calling him, but it went straight to voicemail. Then I get a text from him asking me to pick up something for the kids' lunches, which I did.'

CCTV footage taken from the local Tesco showed Louise and the kids entering the supermarket at 8.24 p.m. that evening. Stephanie was wearing a wine-coloured coat and a black top with very distinctive markings on the sleeve. They arrived back at the house just over half an hour later, not long before Louise claimed her mother stormed out.

She became even more frustrated when asked for more detail about her mother leaving. She felt these questions should be put to Kieran, not her. She insisted she didn't know anything about what happened to her mother until he broke down and told them two weeks later.

Louise was sticking to her original version of events, and ahead of her third recorded interview later that evening, it was decided to show her the CCTV evidence that had been collected. The footage harvested from the local Tesco backed up her claim that she picked up groceries on her way home from the park.

She was also shown the various clips compiled by Garda Thompson from her neighbour's house. Without too much hesitation, she identified the figure leaving the house at 9.34 p.m. as her mother. She struggled to identify the person seen looking down the road a minute later, but figured it was her.

She was also shown a clip from the same camera taken much earlier in the day. The timestamp was 1.31 p.m., 29 May, and she was asked to describe what she saw:

'That's me ma. It's me ma's dress anyway. I think that might be her walking up the steps, probably taking in the bin.'

For the first time during the interview, Louise became visibly upset while watching the footage of her mother. She was handed some tissues.

'Despite everything, I really loved my mother, y'know. And it's really tough,' she said, wiping away tears and blowing her nose.

She was given a moment to compose herself before they pressed on. They still had a lot of questions to ask, and she was about to be shown something she certainly wasn't expecting.

'Louise, the footage we've just shown you was taken from the camera at the front of your neighbour's house. Did you know there was a camera there?'

'Yeah, we get on fine with all our neighbours. I knew it was there.'

'Okay. We're just going to show you another clip now, and we want you to tell us what you see.'

Interviewing a suspect in real life isn't quite like it's depicted by Hollywood. Nobody beats down on desks or throws furniture around the interrogation room, and nobody is going to drag a confession out of someone by throwing them up against the wall. If they did, it's fair to say it wouldn't stand up in a court of law. The process is far more subtle and nuanced. It requires great skill, and it's a joy to watch an experienced interrogator in action. Sergeant Turner had a plan, and he was executing it with surgical precision. He had a lot of evidence, albeit circumstantial, that painted a very different picture from the one Louise and the others had hung up in their previous exhibitions. That said, there's no point laying all your cards out on the table in one go. The best approach is to give them the opportunity to come clean. To tell the truth. Any deviation can then be rebutted with a piece of evidence, so it's far more effective to present the evidence in a piecemeal fashion.

Sergeant Turner hit Play on the next clip, then sat back in his chair and waited for the reaction.

Louise's eyes narrowed and focused on the monitor in front of her. She looked very uncomfortable as the screen warmed up with an image of her mother at the back of the house at 6.35 p.m. on 29 May – the last confirmed sighting of her on CCTV. Louise knew her next-door neighbour had a camera at the front of his house, and she seemed perfectly fine with the fact that it captured the comings and goings from her own home. However, she was taken aback when she realised the camera mounted to the rear of his house also took in a large slice of their back garden. Her initial response was telling.

'My neighbour's videoing into my house. Nice. Is that not against the law?' she asked. 'Like, invasion of privacy. That's fucking disgraceful.'

She clearly had no idea that Mr Lin's system covered this much space at the back of her mother's house. She was disarmed momentarily; it seemed that her mind was racing.

'What do you see in that clip?' she was asked.

'It's me ma at the door. Looks like she's opening and closing the door. At least, I think that's her. The dress. Yes, that's her. Everyone was in the house.'

She became upset for a second time. 'I'm sorry, it's just it's hard seeing me ma going around like that.'

They kept going. She was asked what she and Stephanie were talking about on the swing just after 9 p.m.

'Are you for real?' she asked. 'I haven't a notion what we were talking about.'

'Where was your mother at this stage?'

'I have no idea. Probably upstairs.'

'Louise, you're seen talking to Stephanie again out the back a short time later. It goes on for six to seven minutes. What was that about?'

'I don't know. It could have been nothing. We could have been sitting there in silence. Stephanie has a lovely heart on her.'

She was asked about the person seen entering the house from the back just after 10 p.m. Again, Louise couldn't believe her neighbour's camera was so intrusive. She claimed she couldn't make out who it was. She said it just looked like a 'white blur' to her. Sergeant Turner suggested the person was avoiding the camera out the front by using the side alleyway to come in through the back, obviously also unaware of the scope of Mr Lin's security cameras.

'Who is it, Louise?'

'I don't know. Houdini, maybe?' she cheekily replied. 'It just looks like a big splodge to me.'

Gardaí were confident that the 'big splodge' Louise spoke of was her daughter Stephanie, who had also been arrested on suspicion of being involved in her grandmother's murder. They suspected that she was the figure seen leaving the house on the evening of 29 May in the green coat with the hood up and carrying a suitcase. They believed she did this for the benefit of the camera at the front of her neighbour's house, which she knew about, and that she did it as part of a ruse to make it appear her grandmother was still alive. Why would she do such a thing if she wasn't complicit? Admittedly, it was hard to make out the face of the 'big splodge' in the clip, but the figure was wearing a dark top with the same distinctive markings running down its sleeves, the same as on the top Stephanie was wearing in the supermarket earlier that evening.

At the time of her arrest, Stephanie's hair was dyed blonde with pink at the front. Her hair colour was constantly changing. In her own words, she was 'naturally light brown or very dark blonde'. Like her grandmother, she took great pride in her hair. She used to dye it all the time, but it was fair to say her colour choices were far more adventurous than Nana's.

Detective Sergeant Eamonn O'Neill opened the first interview with Stephanie by asking about her family life, and she began by describing her grandfather Gus as 'the definition of an amazing person'. She said he was one of the most generous people you could ever meet. He and Patricia got on 'okay', according to Stephanie. They slept in separate rooms, and Nana spent most of her time watching TV in her bedroom.

After watching the CCTV compilation taken off Mr Lin's security system, gardaí had a number of areas they wanted to cover with Stephanie before they delved deeper into the content of the footage itself.

First, they wanted to know if the alley at the side of the house was used much. It may not have seemed like it to her without seeing the footage, but this was really important. The alley was a blind spot – it wasn't covered by Mr Lin's cameras, as confirmed by Garda Rowley Burke, who was also tasked with viewing the extensive CCTV footage. As well as being the figure seen leaving the house at 9.34 p.m. in the guise of Patricia O'Connor, gardaí also suspected Stephanie was the person seen returning to the house less than half an hour later with the suitcase. They believed she used that side alleyway to avoid being detected by the camera at the front. Clearly, she, like her mother, was unaware of the scope of the camera at the back.

She told them the alley wasn't used much. It was blocked off by bikes. She said she didn't have a key to the back door because they never used it to enter the house. They would always come in through the front door.

Now that gardaí had a much clearer picture about movements at the house on 29 May, Stephanie was asked about her recollection of the comings and goings that day.

'You won't find me very helpful,' she said.

'Why not?'

'I don't remember it all.'

'Tell us what you do remember.'

Stephanie began by going over some of the territory she had covered in the voluntary statement she gave to gardaí back in June. She described a fight over the cat, going to the park and Nana being in a very bad mood when they returned. She said she went to bed, and when she got up the next morning, her grandmother wasn't there.

'Whose decision was it to go to the park?'

'I'm not sure. Probably Mam. We all just needed to calm down. When we came back, Nana was banging around upstairs. I was watching TV with the kids, and then next thing I heard her clunking down the stairs before saying she'd be back when "that bastard" pops his clogs. She said she'd be back to get what's hers.'

'Were you surprised when she didn't come back the next day?'

'Erm, no. Not really. I mean if she wants to go, she'll go. She left before when I was a kid, so I thought it'd be okay. It didn't seem real, that night.'

'Did you get on with her?'

'Yeah.'

'Tell us what happened next.'

'Well, the truth came out two weeks later when Kieran broke down and told us what he did. That's when I found out. Kieran was telling my mam.'

'And how did you feel when he told ye?'

'Confused. Shocked. Angry. It was surreal. I didn't look at the newspapers. I just knew what Kieran had told Mam, that Nana attacked him with the hurley and that he took it off her and hit her in self-defence. It was in the bathroom. I heard what he said he did afterwards too, that he panicked and brought her to Wexford, and then the mountains.'

She paused for a moment.

'I don't know exactly what happened next,' she continued. 'I don't want to know, but I know she wasn't in one piece. Everyone was very emotional when he told us.'

Stephanie said it wasn't unusual for her grandmother to have two arguments in one day. She said she was in a particularly bad mood that day, and while she did get angry very easily, she described her as 'amazing' too.

Aside from suggesting that the back door was never used to gain entry to the house, Stephanie's first two interviews following her arrest didn't offer much more than she'd already said in her voluntary statement. She was smart and very composed for someone so young, especially considering the seriousness of the crime she was being questioned about. She came across as pleasant, intelligent and articulate. Her replies were robust, delivered slowly and in a very soft voice. She showed very little emotion and didn't seem fazed by the situation at all, despite being held on suspicion of murder.

It was time to show her the CCTV footage.

Stephanie identified her grandmother in a clip from 12.14 p.m. on 29 May. When asked to comment on the clip, she said she was taking the bin in to let someone out of the driveway. She described her grandmother as having her hair tied back, and wearing white shoes and a dress with 'peacock features'.

'Nana had lots of crazy dresses,' she said. 'It was her signature style.'

She was shown the footage of her in the back garden with her mother just after 9 p.m. She said they were just having a chat.

Crucially, she was shown the clip taken from the back of the house later that night. The one with what Louise had described as the 'big splodge'.

'Tell us what you see, Stephanie.'

'Someone going inside,' she said.

'Any idea who it is?'

'Me, I guess.'

When asked what she was doing out the back of the house at 10.05 p.m. that night, she became somewhat evasive. Her replies were delayed and short.

'What are you doing in that clip, Stephanie?'

'Going inside.'

'Where were you coming from?'

'I'm coming from around the shed.'

Conveniently for her, she couldn't quite remember how she got out to the shed. She was asked what she was bringing in.

'A bag,' was her delayed response.

Sergeant O'Neill had been very patient up to this point but it was clear that she was holding back, and it was time to take the kid gloves off.

'Time to tell the truth, Stephanie,' he said.

'There's nothing to tell. I'm bringing a bag in from the shed. I'm bringing in stuff from the shed.'

She pointed at the bag on the screen and told them her mother had asked her to bring it in.

'I just do what I'm told,' she said.

Louise claimed she didn't know what she and Stephanie were talking about in the back garden that night. As far as she knew, they could have been in complete silence out there. Stephanie remembered it as 'just a chat' and couldn't recall what they were talking about either.

Gardaí had an altogether different take on what was on the agenda at that late-night meeting. They believed that was when the two women hatched a plan for Stephanie to leave through the front door disguised as her grandmother. What's more, they believed Patricia O'Connor was dead at that stage, and that her body was still inside.

Stephanie has very distinctive hair. That's why the figure seen leaving the house with the suitcase had their hood up. Why else would it be up? It wasn't raining. They knew about the camera to the front of Mr Lin's house. They knew it would pick her up. They knew it would pick up Louise playing the role of a concerned daughter running out after 'her mother' shortly afterwards. They hoped it would throw gardaí off the scent. They were wrong.

'Is that all your mum asked you to do, Stephanie? To bring a bag in from the shed?'

She couldn't remember.

'Come on, Stephanie. Why did she want a bag brought in from the shed at ten o'clock at night?'

'She just asked me to bring in stuff from the shed. She'd seen Nana leaving with a bag and wanted to see if it was the bag from the shed.'

'What stuff?'

Again, she couldn't remember. She was asked more about the bag.

'It was a suitcase-type bag. I just brought it in and went to bed.'

'What was in it?'

'I don't know. I didn't look inside.'

'What colour was it?'

'I can't remember.'

'Was it heavy?'

'I can't remember.'

'Who owned it?'

'I don't know.'

For someone who had been very articulate up to this point, Stephanie didn't have much to say during this particular line of questioning. It was decided to call it a night.

Louise wasn't very forthcoming either as her interviews progressed, especially when asked about the figure caught on that pesky camera at the back of the house at 10.05 p.m.

'What do you see in that footage, Louise?'

'Someone walking into the house.'

'Come on now, Louise. What else do you see?'

'It's dark. It's hard to see. I see someone. They obviously came in the side door.'

'That person appears to be carrying something. Do you have any idea what it is?'

'I don't. I can't see.'

The footage was shown to her again. This time frame by frame.

'How about now?'

'It looks like the person is carrying something like a beach bag,' she eventually said. 'That could have been me or one of us in the house. I can't remember.'

'What would you have been getting from the shed at that hour?'

'I don't know. Blankets, a blow-up mattress ... it looks like a beach bag.'

Stephanie had told gardaí her mother asked her to fetch a suitcase from the shed. One of them was definitely lying, but it seemed more likely they both were.

'What colour is the bag?'

'I have no idea.'

She was politely asked to take another look.

'Why? I think you're expecting me to be a miracle worker here and see things I can't see. The person doesn't have a beard, so maybe it's me or Stephanie. It could be Kieran too if he shaved.'

And on that note, the interview was brought to an end.

Stephanie was interviewed again the following morning. She was shown the piece of fabric found in the shallow grave in Wexford. It had a green leaf pattern on it and looked just like the pattern on the dress Patricia O'Connor was seen wearing in the footage outside her house on 29 May. Stephanie was convinced the patterns on the dress her grandmother was wearing that day were peacocks.

'It doesn't match,' she said after inspecting the six-inch piece of fabric.

She was told where they found it, and it was put to her that it wasn't going to look the same after being buried.

She insisted it wasn't the same.

'Stephanie, did you kill your nana, Patricia O'Connor?' she was asked bluntly. This was the first time it was put to her.

'No,' she replied.

'Did you assist anybody in killing her?'

'No,' she said again.

Stephanie reluctantly accepted that the person seen on CCTV at the back of the house at 10.05 p.m. was her. She said she was bringing something in from the shed for her mother. The details about what she was bringing in were sketchy, but she was a hundred per cent certain of one thing: the person seen leaving the front of the house half an hour earlier was not her. Gardaí put it to her that it was. They put it to her that she agreed to leave the house disguised as her grandmother following a chat with her mother in the back garden. She denied that was the case.

Her mother was in denial mode too during the fourth of her five garda interviews. Detective David Connolly said straight out that he believed that what she had told gardaí about the night her mother went missing was a 'web of lies'. She insisted it wasn't.

'There was no big plot,' Louise said.

The black suitcase found in Gus's room at Mountain View Park was brought into the interview room and shown to her. She agreed it looked identical to the one captured on the CCTV footage, but she suggested maybe it was one of a set.

She described the suggestion that Stephanie was the one seen leaving the house with the suitcase as 'ridiculous'. While she had showed a little hesitation in earlier interviews, she was now absolutely convinced it was her mother.

'Your mother was seen wearing a dress earlier in the day. The person leaving the house in that recording isn't.'

'So? She obviously got changed.'

'The hood is up, but it wasn't raining. Why is that?'

'I don't know. What do you want me to say?' she asked rhetorically. 'Maybe they have sore ears, or maybe they're self-conscious.'

She was also shown the piece of fabric found at the site of the shallow grave. Again, she responded by saying she had never harmed a hair on her mother's head. She was asked if the fabric was the same as her mother's dress. She couldn't tell for sure but, unlike her daughter, she accepted that it looked like the same print Patricia was wearing that day.

The footage showing Kieran closing the curtains at the back of the house seconds before they left for the park was shown to her.

'Is that Kieran?' she was asked.

'Yeah. It's a bloke. Who else would it be?'

'Why would he close the curtains at that hour?'

'I don't know. Maybe he put on the TV. Maybe he was just blocking the light out, or maybe he was dancing around naked after his shower.'

'We think something happened in the house around that time. Just before 7 p.m. Around the time you left for the park with the kids.'

'Can we not go to the park? Is it against the law?' she again asked, without really expecting an answer.

'Was your mother dead when you returned from the park?' she was asked, and she was most certainly expected to answer this one.

'If she was dead, I would have called the guards and punched Kieran's lights out. You believe what you want to believe. You think I would hurt my mother. I didn't know what happened to her until Kieran had his meltdown two weeks later.'

She was shown the footage from the early hours of 30 May, and told that it appeared to show Kieran getting some shovels from the back of the house at 12.38 a.m. Another clip recorded five minutes later was shown to her. It showed someone at the back of the house closing a door. She accepted it looked like her dad. Kieran was then captured at the front of the house with a shovel.

'I know my dad. He's not involved. He wouldn't hurt a fly. I wouldn't believe it even if I saw him with a hatchet in his hand,' was her response to her father's cameo.

She was shown the footage of Kieran returning to the house just before 6 a.m. She was disgusted at being shown that clip.

'That's obviously when he took my ma and came back. That's a nice thing to see, isn't it? It's fucking horrible.'

'Did he manage to do this in secret?'

'What, kill my ma? Yeah. He's a fucking nut. He's destroyed our family.'

At 6.18 a.m. on 29 May, Kieran could be seen from the camera at the back of his neighbour's house talking to someone in the kitchen area of the house. This wasn't long after he returned from wherever he had been for the previous four hours or so. She was asked if she knew who he was talking to. She accepted they could have been up at that hour, but she couldn't remember anyone talking to him specifically.

'Jesus, I don't know what he would have been talking about after coming back from burying her. Why don't you ask him? He's a fucking nut. He's probably gone doolally.'

Louise was aware that her father had also been arrested. She was perplexed. She told gardaí he 'wouldn't hurt a fly'. Gus was living with Richard and his family in County Meath at the time. He was in the same garda station, also being questioned on suspicion of murder. He was interviewed four times.

In his first interview, he told Detective Garda David Jennings that everyone in the house got on well.

'There was rarely an argument. Patricia and I would argue from time to time, but only occasionally. It was a happy home,' he said.

When asked about their relationship ending, he just said, 'Whatever happened, happened.' He said he really loved her.

He told them it wasn't like her to go missing. He claimed they checked with her family 'down the country' and waited a few days. He thought she had maybe gone to England, but he knew she had no money so he thought she would come home.

On the night she supposedly went missing, he said he took the dog for a walk, and when he got home, he made a cup of tea. Before he retired for the night, he told gardaí that Louise told him Patricia had stormed out of the house earlier that evening. He said he was tired so he just went to bed and didn't get up again until nine o'clock the next morning. He said he had no reason to. He had gone to the toilet before he went to bed and slept through the night.

He wasn't to know it, but gardaí already knew he was lying to them. CCTV footage from the camera at the back of Mr Lin's house showed that he was up well past midnight. Not a good start.

He denied covering up for anybody. He said he did his own thing that day and insisted he wasn't hiding anything. He apologised for not being able to shed any more light on what had happened to Patricia. He also expressed regret at not being there to help his wife in her hour of need.

'I had nothing to do with it. Honestly. We didn't row before I left the house that evening. I was livid I wasn't there to stop whatever happened. I was also livid when I had to move out.'

The next day, he was shown a number of clips, including the one of the figure leaving the house with the suitcase. He said he couldn't make out who it was.

Detective Jennings looked at the clock. It was against him – Gus could only be kept for another twenty minutes or so. With time quickly running out, Gus made a remarkable admission. He told them he had lied about seeing Patricia on the day she went missing, and within the next few precious minutes of his final interview he made some startling revelations. That wasn't the only lie he had told them.

'I'm as bad as the rest of them,' he said. 'I'm as bad as them, but I didn't lay a hand on her.'

He went on to tell the detectives that despite what he said in his first interview, 66 Mountain View Park was not a happy house. He said he lied about all that to protect his daughter and grandchildren. He denied murdering his wife but told them she was dead when he came in from his walk that night. With his period of detention all but over, Detective Jennings needed more time to flesh all this out with him. He was out of time, but he hoped Gus would agree to give a voluntary statement. He did.

'When I arrived home after my walk, everything was normal,' Gus said. 'I did go into the kitchen to make myself a cup of tea before going to bed. Stephanie woke me up during the night. She asked me to come downstairs. The lights were on, but they'd been dimmed. I saw something big wrapped up on the floor in blankets. Louise said it was Patricia and that she was dead. I was told she attacked Kieran.'

Detective Jennings interrupted him to ask who was downstairs at that point. He told them Louise, Kieran and Stephanie were there. He said he just 'washed his hands of it' and went back upstairs to bed after telling them to call the gardaí.

'Not much was said about it the next day. I just left them to it. I knew the body had been moved and disposed of and I knew Kieran had left in the car, but I didn't know the body was in it.'

'Was the body cut up in the house before he left?' he was asked.

'As far as I know, it was whole when Kieran left the house with it,' he replied.

After telling them his piece, he repeatedly told them he was sorry. His statement was read back to him and he was asked if he wanted to add anything to it or make any changes.

All that was left for him to say was how sorry he was. He told them he deserved whatever came his way now. Despite everything, he insisted he still loved her.

'I didn't loathe her. I really loved my wife,' he said. 'She's probably with the angels now, my parents and hers.'

In her fifth and final interview, Louise was once again accused of telling a pack of lies and, once again, she insisted she was telling the truth.

'Tell us why you went to the park that evening, Louise. Come on now. Tell us the truth.'

'We went there to get peace from my mam.'

'Permanent peace?'

'No. She was freaking out about the cat that night. She was alive when we walked out. My ma walked out that door.'

It was put to her that her mother was dead when they returned from the park, and that she knew that the person who walked out the door a few hours later was Stephanie. Again, Louise denied that and insisted her daughter was in the living room when her mother stormed out with her suitcase.

'I know my ma was alive when I came back,' she said again.

'You know, it's not fair to put the burden on others.'

'I'm not putting the burden on anyone,' she quipped back. 'Kieran killed my mother. It's sick what he done.'

She denied talking about killing her mother with the other adults in the house, and again said that the first she knew of what actually happened was two weeks later when Kieran confessed to it.

Yet again, she was accused of lying.

'I know what I seen and heard,' she said with a sting in her tone. 'Kieran put his hands up for what he done and I know she walked out that door. Stephanie did not dress up as my ma. You are thinking it's some sort of stupid plot. It's not.'

She was angry now. Her interviewers asked her what she was most angry about.

'The whole lot of it,' she answered. 'It's like a bad dream.'

'Why would he kill her?'

'He was obviously under so much pressure. I can't understand a murderer's mind. If I knew something, I would have done some-thing. I would have rang an ambulance or got the guards.'

It was put to her that she left the house at 9.35 p.m. and looked down the road to add weight to the ruse involving Stephanie. It was suggested she only did it to give the impression her mother was still alive and that she was looking for her. Again, she flatly denied that was the case.

Finally, she was asked if she saw her mother's body downstairs that night wrapped in blankets.

Louise must have wondered where this question came from. That was the first time it had been mentioned to her.

'Absolutely not,' she said.

12.

I KNOW IT LOOKS BAD

Gardaí didn't think Keith Johnston had anything to do with the murder of his ex-girlfriend's mother, and he wasn't arrested on suspicion of murder like the others were. However, investigators were convinced that the self-confessed 'handyman' did more and knew far more than he was letting on. They didn't suspect him of having any involvement in the actual killing of Patricia O'Connor but had every reason to believe he was involved in the attempted cover-up afterwards.

For a start, he failed to mention the shopping spree he went on with Kieran Greene in the voluntary statement he gave to gardaí after his friend handed himself in. That looked bad. Surely that was important, especially in light of what Kieran had told them about how he dismembered and disposed of the body. If he had nothing to hide, why didn't he mention that?

Gardaí now had crystal-clear CCTV footage of him in Kieran's company while be bought specialised tools in places like Woodie's DIY and B&Q on 9 June. Granted, he didn't actually buy any of the items, but he could be seen carrying them around the stores and standing beside Kieran at the tills while he paid for the goods, so he couldn't argue that he didn't know what Kieran was buying. Gardaí believed these tools were used to dismember Patricia's remains later that day. It made sense. The first body part was found the very next day.

After examining the CCTV footage harvested from Sam Lin's home security system, the team was also aware that Keith had been in and out of the house at Mountain View Park in the days after Patricia went missing. He was seen going into the house with a bucket of paint on 5 June. He was seen with a paintbrush in his hand later that same day.

He told gardaí that he fixed a step and some broken tiles in the bathroom a few days earlier. He claimed it was to appease Patricia, whom he feared would throw them all out of the house when she returned, but gardaí suspected a far more sinister motive. They believed he carried out the refurbishment works in the bathroom to destroy evidence and help cover up what happened to her.

Another thing that wasn't fully explained during his voluntary statement in June was this 'nagging thought' he said he had while he was carrying out the repairs. He said he couldn't help thinking he was cleaning up a crime scene. Why would he think that? He had done work there before. Also, nobody had asked him to fix the step and replace the broken tiles. He did it off his own bat, apparently. Furthermore, this wasn't the first time Patricia had left the house, so he had no reason to think something bad had happened to her. Gardaí felt there were enough red circles peppered across the pages of his original statement to justify bringing him in.

In September 2017, Keith was back living in the house at Mountain View Park. He was arrested there on 26 September and taken to Bray Garda Station for questioning. Unlike the others, who had been picked up three weeks beforehand, he was told he wasn't being arrested on suspicion of murdering Patricia. Gardaí just wanted to find out the truth about what happened, and he was told that was the purpose of his arrest.

Sergeant Eamonn O'Neill began by asking him what his connection to the others was, and he told them he used to be in a relationship with Louise O'Connor. Stephanie was his daughter. Louise had another daughter from a previous relationship, whom he also cared for. 'Her father left when she was very young,' he explained.

He was asked about his relationship with Kieran, and while he admitted he didn't want him around when he first came on the scene, he said he grew to like him over time and they eventually became friends.

'Did you spend much time in the house?' he was asked.

'Ah yeah. I'd be there at least twice a week anyway.'

'And you're back living there now by the looks of it?'

'Not really. I mean, not full time. I only stay at the house two times a week.'

They wondered if he was back with his old flame, but he assured them he wasn't.

'That's all in the past,' he said. 'There's nothing romantic going on. I stay in Patricia's old room.'

Sleeping in the room where Patricia's battered and bloodied body lay just three months before was a chilling thought, and he later told them there was a 'dark cloud hanging over the house'.

He was asked how he would have described Kieran's relationship with Patricia.

'She would constantly give him stick,' he said. 'She had a special kind of giving out for Kieran. He had no life outside those four walls. He just got abuse.'

Keith had mentioned doing various odd jobs around the house when he gave his voluntary statement, and he was asked to give a bit more detail about that. He was the one who fitted the bathroom.

'When was that, Keith?'

'Erm, let me think. Maybe ten years ago. I've done a bit of work in the house since. Nothing major.'

Again, he was asked how he found out that Patricia was missing. He said that Stephanie's sister called him on 31 May, the day before Gus and Kieran reported her as a missing person. He called over to the house the next day. Kieran picked him up. On the drive over, he was pretty sure Kieran mentioned Patricia, and he figured he would have asked him what was going on, but he couldn't remember the exact detail of their conversation in the car.

While he was at the house, he said, he noticed that a piece of wood on a step beside the shower had gone soft. He told them he decided to fix it to avoid the others being served an 'eviction notice' when Patricia came back.

'I had to buy some tiles for the job,' he added. 'We regrouted the floor tiles but didn't get to finish it. All in, it took about three days, and I was in and out of the house during that time.'

That tallied with the CCTV evidence from Mr Lin's house.

He was asked more about Patricia's disappearance at the time. He seemed very relaxed about her going missing like that.

'Were you not concerned about her? I mean, she had gone missing without a trace and gardaí were investigating. Surely that was a cause for concern?'

'No, not really,' he replied. 'I was fully convinced she'd be back within 48 hours. I really wasn't worried at the time.'

He said his main concern was getting the bathroom in order. Nobody asked him to do it, but he knew it would please Patricia. He said he genuinely feared she would throw everyone out if she came home and saw the bathroom like that.

One of the more pressing questions was then put to him.

'Keith, you mentioned in your voluntary statement that you thought at one stage that you could potentially be cleaning up a crime scene. What did you mean by that? Why did you think that?'

'I was joking,' he replied.

'Joking?'

'Yeah. I said it in my mind and then I just forgot about it and put it out of my head. I'm sorry I mentioned it at all.'

Keith was probably understating how he felt about saying that – more likely he was absolutely kicking himself for it. Its significance was obvious. If he felt he was cleaning up a crime scene that day, how could he not suspect something was up when he went shopping for axes and saws with Kieran a week later?

'And what about this sneaky look around the house you said you took after becoming suspicious?' he was asked.

'Well, I was in most rooms in the house while doing the work.'

'Okay, and you say nobody asked you to fix the bathroom?'

'No.'

'You're sure about that?'

'Positive.'

Keith couldn't remember when he last saw Patricia alive. He was then pressed a bit more on why he carried out the repairs in the bathroom. The timing of it all was highly suspicious. The bathroom had been fitted over ten years ago and hadn't been touched since. Surely he could appreciate how it looked. Nothing touched for over a decade, and then all of a sudden, he's fixing steps and replacing tiles just three days after someone is beaten to death in there. The whole thing stank.

'Keith, we don't think you fixed that step and regrouted those tiles out of some act of kindness. We believe Patricia's blood was there, and you were helping to hide it.'

'But it wasn't regrouted,' he interjected.

'You told us it was.'

'No, I just started it and there were a few scratch marks. I didn't take the bathroom apart. I know it looks bad, but that's just the way it is. I was trying to do a good thing for the family.'

He wasn't overly convincing, but he was sticking to his story.

'Hand on heart, that was me just trying to help the family out. So they wouldn't get chucked out.'

At this point, he tried to shift the focus away from himself by saying he was struggling with the concept that Kieran did what he did and then managed to hold it together for two weeks.

'He's a good buddy,' Sergeant O'Neill said.

'He *was* a good buddy,' Keith replied.

He then went on to describe all the other work he did in the house, again in an attempt to explain away the suspicious repairs carried out in early June.

'You can't just say I did one thing to make it look like I was up to something because that's not the case. I also fixed the roof, presses and doors.'

He broke down and put his head in his hands when he was asked what he thought of what Kieran did.

'It was horrible and sickening,' he sobbed, but he insisted Kieran never approached him for help. He accepted he went to the shops with him to get a 'few bits', like plywood and tiles, and he told them the work was done in two or three blocks. He repeatedly denied regrouting any of the floor tiles. According to him, he just replaced three broken tiles. That was it. Blood from an unidentifiable male source had been found in one spot on the floor during the forensic sweep of the house. It was found on the grout where the tile meets the panel, but he was adamant the original grout was still on the floor.

'Where did you get the hacksaw used for the repairs?' he was asked.

'From my own home,' he replied.

'And you were there on the first of June, as well as the following two days?'

'I think so.'

He was asked specifically about 9 June. This date didn't ring a bell. Not a loud one anyway. He accepted Kieran brought him to a few places to get 'bits and pieces' over the week or two after

Patricia went missing. He remembered going to Woodie's, B&Q and Homebase, but nothing stood out about 9 June. Gardaí found that hard to believe. It was a standout day, and he appeared to be acting aloof about it.

'What about the next day, Keith? June the tenth?'

That was the day the picnicker found part of Patricia's torso near the Sally Gap. Again, nothing unusual about that day for Keith. He remembered how he heard that remains had been found up the mountains. He was watching Dublin playing on TV that day, and the news at half-time mentioned something about it.

When asked about Kieran's confession after he picked him up and drove him to the house in Rathfarnham two days later, Keith said Kieran just started 'babbling'. He described him as 'gasping' as he told Louise that he had killed her mother.

'He just said, "That is me," and when we asked him what he was on about, he said he left the body up the mountains. I told him he'd have to hand himself in. I mean, what else was he going to do? He couldn't go on the run.'

'And how did he take that?'

'That's the strange thing. He just logged it.'

'Did he say why he killed her?'

'No. He just said he did it. I didn't hear a motive anyway, I don't think.'

Keith wasn't a hundred per cent sure about a lot of things. He said he didn't like thinking about it, and he felt 'lost' when he did. Despite his sketchy recollection of events, he was absolutely certain of one thing: he told gardaí that there was no way Louise had known what happened to her mother on 29 May. He had no doubt in the world that she was completely in the dark, until Kieran confessed to everyone before he handed himself in on 12 June.

Sergeant O'Neill was giving Keith every opportunity to come clean. He just knew he was hiding something. He became uncomfortable and somewhat evasive whenever he was asked specifics about the story he was spinning. Despite failing to mention his shopping spree with Kieran when he gave his witness statement in June, he had now referenced visits to various hardware stores. That was a start, but he had failed to tell them that the purchases included a wide selection of what could be described as body-dismembering paraphernalia.

He also wouldn't commit to that all-important date, 9 June. But he'd soon have to. Before they laid their cards out, he was given once last chance to tell the truth. The next question would be crucial. The whole interview process had been building up to it.

'Keith, do you have any idea where Kieran got the tools used to dismember Patricia O'Connor?'

'The shed would be my best guess,' he answered without hesitation. 'There was all sorts in there. Loads of tools, including hammers, chisels, a tile cutter and pickaxes.'

'Who owned the tools?'

'Half of them were mine, and the rest belonged to Louise's brother, Richard.'

'Did Kieran use them?'

The very notion of Kieran using the tools amused Keith. He described him as 'useless' when it came to that kind of stuff. It just wasn't his thing. Not many things were.

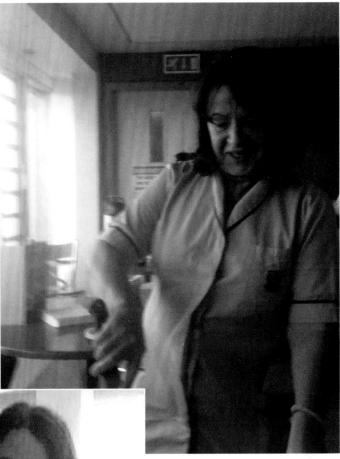

Patricia O'Connor working at Beaumont Hospital. She spent over 30 years in the hospital's catering department. (*Courtesy of Breda Wosser*)

Gardaí preparing to search a field on the Kilmuckridge Road, just outside the village of Blackwater in Co. Wexford, where Kieran Greene initially buried Patricia O'Connor in a shallow grave. (© *Mary Browne/Browne Photography*)

Superintendent Pat Ward of Bray District, speaking with members of the search operation near the Sally Gap, Co. Wicklow. (© *Collins Photo Agency*)

A forensic expert entering 66 Mountain View Park, where Patricia O'Connor was beaten to death on 29 May 2017. (© *Collins Photo Agency*)

Crime scene investigators combing 66 Mountain View Park for clues. They didn't find any forensic evidence inside. The bathroom where Kieran Greene beat Patricia to death was thoroughly cleaned and refurbished after he killed her. (© *Collins Photo Agency*)

Gardaí searching ditches off the Military Road in the Wicklow Mountains following the discovery of human remains there in June 2017. (© *Collins Photo Agency*)

Members of the Irish Defence Forces taking part in a massive search operation that resulted in fifteen body parts being found within a 30km radius in the Wicklow Mountains. The remains made up the body of Patricia O'Connor. (© *Collins Photo Agency*)

Kieran Greene, the father of three of Patricia O'Connor's grandchildren, claimed he was acting in self-defence when he killed Patricia in the home they shared in Mountain View Park, Rathfarnham.

Kieran Greene arriving at Tallaght District Court in Dublin on 15 June 2017, shortly after being charged with Patricia O'Connor's murder. (© *Collins Photo Agency*)

Patricia O'Connor's husband Augustine 'Gus' O'Connor leaving the Criminal Courts of Justice in Dublin. (© *Collins Photo Agency*)

Patricia O'Connor's daughter, Louise, preparing to cover her face with her scarf on her way to the Criminal Courts of Justice in Dublin. (© *Collins Photo Agency*)

Patricia O'Connor's granddaughter Stephanie walking towards Dublin city centre after a day in court. (© *Collins Photo Agency*)

The 'trusted handyman' Keith Johnston leaving court after a day of evidence. (© *Collins Photo Agency*)

Louise, Keith and Stephanie doing some shopping in Dublin city after a day in court. A rare glimpse of the trio without their faces covered. (© *Collins Photo Agency*)

Louise walks past some of her mother's former colleagues and friends following her sentence hearing before the Central Criminal Court. (© *Collins Photo Agency*)

Christine Murphy leaving court after giving evidence. She found the first body part while picnicking near the Sally Gap in the Wicklow Mountains in June 2017. (© *Collins Photo Agency*)

Patricia O'Connor's next-door neighbour, Sam Lin, leaving court after giving evidence during the trial. Footage taken from his home CCTV system proved crucial to the case. (© *Collins Photo Agency*)

Members of the investigation team pictured after the jury returned its guilty verdicts. From left to right: Garda David Hamblyn (Bray Garda Station), Detective Garda David Connolly (Rathfarnham Garda Station), Garda Garret Collins (Bray Garda Station), Detective Sergeant Eamonn O'Neill (Bray Garda Station), Detective Garda Tom Bissett (Bray Garda Station), Sergeant Kieron O'Neill (Rathfarnham Garda Station), Detective Inspector Brian O'Keeffe (Senior Investigating Officer). (© *Barry Cummins/ RTÉ*)

One of the key members of the investigation team, Detective Garda David Connolly, arriving at the Criminal Courts of Justice complex in Dublin. (© *Collins Photo Agency*)

The trial judge Mr Justice Paul McDermott leaving court. (© *Collins Photo Agency*)

Detective Sergeant Lucy Myles leaving court. She was the first to take a statement from Kieran Greene after he handed himself in. (© *Collins Photo Agency*)

Former Deputy State Pathologist, Dr Michael Curtis, leaving the CCJ after giving distressing evidence about the post-mortems he carried out on the remains of Patricia O'Connor. (© *Collins Photo Agency*)

Richard O'Connor and his wife, Martina, arriving at the courthouse ahead of the sentence hearing. Richard delivered a powerful victim-impact statement. (© *Collins Photo Agency*)

Patricia O'Connor's sisters Rita (left), Valerie (centre) and Anne (right) leaving court after Kieran, Louise, Stephanie and Keith were convicted. (© *Collins Photo Agency*)

Patricia O'Connor's son, Richard (centre left), and his wife Martina (centre right), posing for a photo with his mother's former colleagues from Beaumont Hospital. From left to right: Breda Wosser, Kim Bermingham, Sandra Flynn and Josie Dunne. They presented Richard with a memorial photo montage after the sentence hearing at the Central Criminal Court. (© *Collins Photo Agency*)

Patricia O'Connor's sister Colette holds a framed photo of 'Trisha' after the final sentences were handed down. (© *Collins Photo Agency*)

'Kieran didn't use tools and never bought them. He just bought cheap stuff in the pound shop.'

Sergeant O'Neill rattled off two key quick-fire questions to nicely cue up his great reveal.

'When do you think he chopped up the body, Keith?'

'The day before the Dublin match, I presume.'

'Okay. And do you have any knowledge of where he got the tools to chop up her body?'

'No, everything was in the shed.'

Keith didn't know that gardaí had ironclad evidence that he went shopping with Kieran for axes, hacksaws and blades the day before the Dublin match. He just told them this was the same day he believed Kieran dug his girlfriend's mother up and dismembered her. They had clear CCTV evidence showing him floating around the aisles of various hardware stores for items that he didn't think it relevant to mention and, what's more, he was saying he figured Kieran used tools from the shed to carry out this grisly deed. He was pressed a little further.

'What about the saw you used to cut the piece of timber for the step in the bathroom. Was that in the shed too?'

'No. Some fella gave it to Kieran.'

'Can you describe it to us?'

'It was an electric saw with a small blade, kind of like a hedge trimmer. I'd never seen anything like it, so I was curious and he showed me how to use it.'

'Kieran showed you?'

'Yeah, and then I used it to cut the new board for the step.'

'Did you ever go shopping for tools with Kieran?'

'Yeah, plenty of times. We'd get stuff for the house, and sometimes not even his house. He'd often give me a lift if I needed stuff.'

'And you're certain you have no knowledge of him buying things to cut up the body?'

'No, never.'

At this point, the full deck of receipts seized from the car and house were laid out on the table in front of him. The receipts proved that certain items were bought at certain locations at certain times, but they alone couldn't prove who made the purchases. The CCTV footage did, though.

Keith could argue that he didn't buy any of the tools, but there was no hiding the fact that he was with Kieran in the relevant stores on this pivotal date, to which he struggled to attach any significance. Moreover, he couldn't deny that he knew what was being put in the shopping baskets. He could be seen holding some of the items. He had a lot of explaining to do.

He was first shown the receipt from Mr. Price in Tallaght, and asked why Kieran bought a tow rope, knives, tape and a petrol can. He said he didn't remember.

He told them that he presumed this was the day Kieran cut Patricia's body up. It seemed incredible that he didn't wonder what Kieran was doing buying these items, and it was even more incredible to think he didn't feel it important enough to mention it after Kieran handed himself in.

'Keith, this was the day before the body was found. Did you not associate this with what happened up the mountains?'

'No. I didn't put two and two together,' he replied.

He was asked his shoe size.

'Nine,' he answered with a look of puzzlement. 'Why?'

The receipt from Shoe Zone in Tallaght was produced.

'Can you tell us why Kieran bought two pairs of size nine wellington boots from this shop? Size nine. Your size, Keith.'

He claimed they were for fishing and he said they left them in the car.

'Where else did you and Kieran go that day?'

He couldn't remember.

The receipt for Woodie's DIY was produced in an attempt to refresh his memory. He was asked why Kieran needed two axes and a packet of blades.

'The axes were for chopping firewood,' he said. 'They were going cheap so we picked them up.'

'Did you buy a saw?'

'Yeah. I wrecked my own doing the work in the bathroom.'

'Did you need two?'

'What?'

'Two saws were purchased. What did you need two for?'

'Kieran bought one for himself. A lot of it was just to replace stuff I got in the house. I buy tools all the time.'

'Yes, but you said Kieran *never* buys tools, so what's he at then? Did you not think that was strange?'

'They're not tools. They're *items*,' he said smugly.

At this point, it was decided to show him the video footage harvested from the various stores visited by gardaí when they made controlled purchases of the items listed on the receipts. The first clip showed him and Kieran in Mr. Price, and he could be seen holding the jerry can that Kieran later purchased.

'Did you not wonder what he needed a petrol can for? Were you not curious enough to ask him what it was for?'

'No. It didn't bother me. I wasn't curious.'

'Come on now, Keith. Tell us what the shopping spree was actually for.'

'I've told you,' he said. A hint of frustration was starting to set in. 'It was to replace lost and damaged tools and for fishing. Kieran bought me a hacksaw because he damaged mine.'

He was asked where the tools were now. He didn't know. He was shown the controlled purchases made by gardaí in yet another attempt to jog his fractured memory. No joy. Although he did accept that some of the items looked familiar.

When asked why he hadn't mentioned this shopping spree before, he insisted he had. A memo of his previous interview was read out to him, and there was no mention of visiting those hardware stores on 9 June.

Keith exploded.

'I know for a fact I said B&Q and Woodie's. Fuck off, youse lying swines.'

His outburst let his interrogators know they were on the right track and pressing the right buttons. It was so obvious to them that he knew what those tools were to be used for. If you were to believe that he genuinely didn't, then surely he would have realised after Kieran handed himself in three days later. Keith Johnston was drowning. He was now in survival mode. He knew it didn't look good. His story didn't hold water.

Sergeant O'Neill pushed another button.

'You got sucked into this,' he said.

'I wasn't sucked into it.'

'We believe the body part found on the tenth of June had been left there late on Friday, June the ninth, or in the early hours of the following day. Where were you on the evening of Friday June the ninth?'

'I was at home.'

'You're sure?'

'Yes.'

'What time did you leave Kieran that day after your little shopping trip?'

'I can't remember.'

'When did you see him next?'

'I can't remember.'

'Did you stay up late that night?'

'I don't think so.'

'Did you have any visitors?'

'No, I don't think so.'

One of the black bags found in the shed at Mountain View Park was spread out on the table in front of him, and he was asked if he had anything to say about it.

'It's a black bag,' he deduced with tongue very much in cheek. 'I don't know,' he continued. 'They're found in every house.'

'Indeed. The thing is, this bag was examined by a scientist and there's strong support that it was made by the same machine that made the bag Patricia's head was found in. What do you have to say about that?'

'You mean they don't know? What they do with their bags is their business,' he replied unhelpfully. He was right, though. They couldn't tell for sure if the bags came from the same roll.

Gardaí again appealed to his sense of self-preservation by putting it to him that he'd been 'sucked in'.

'Stop saying that. I didn't do anything. Go back and live in your fantasy world,' was his response.

'But you said you had a feeling you might be cleaning up a crime scene when you were working in the house. You must have known.'

'Stop twisting my words,' he said.

'Tell us again about the saw.'

Keith sighed before again telling them that Kieran bought it. 'Ask him yourselves,' he suggested.

They moved on. They couldn't prove it, but they suspected that Keith went to the shallow grave with Kieran to dismember Patricia's body. If anyone was there with Kieran, it was Keith, but he strongly denied that was the case. Throughout the interviews, he painted Kieran as someone who wasn't used to getting his hands dirty.

'Was he any use with a shovel?' Keith was asked.

'No, he was useless. Worse than useless.'

This portrayal of his friend was backed up by the others during their interviews and didn't do much to support a scenario whereby Kieran acted alone at all times. He seemed incapable of doing so.

'Keith, did you have to go down to Wexford to help him?'

'What? Dig her up? Are you kidding? No, I've told you everything I know. The answer is the answer. It's not going to change. I told you twenty times already.'

His interviewers decided to take a different approach. They wheeled out the DVD monitor and showed him some footage from the back of the house at Mountain View Park on the evening of 29

May. The timestamp was 10.06 p.m. Gardaí believed Patricia was already dead at this point. They believed her body was still in the house, and they suspected the figure seen leaving from the front door roughly half an hour earlier was Keith's daughter Stephanie, disguised as her grandmother.

At 10.06 p.m., somebody could be seen inside the house closing the back door. This was one minute after a female figure, who gardaí again believed to be Stephanie, entered from the rear. Stephanie had already identified herself in the shot. Her uncle Richard had too, but Keith followed in Louise's footsteps, telling them he couldn't say for sure who it was.

He was asked how he felt about what Kieran had done. 'Horrendous,' he replied. He was asked how he felt about his daughter and her mother being arrested. He said he was angry.

It was put to him that Kieran had involved Louise and Stephanie in this dreadful crime.

'No way,' he said. 'There's no way they'd get involved in a murder.'

'You became involved too, Keith. You came involved with them because of the clean-up operation.'

'No, I did not,' he replied.

The investigation team didn't believe Kieran had acted alone. Was he protecting the others? And if so, why? Why would he take the fall? Did he think he would get off? Did he think they would believe he was acting in self-defence?

Whatever about that, the investigators just knew the others had played pivotal roles in the attempted cover-up. During his interviews Keith repeatedly insisted that wasn't the case; time after time, he denied the allegations being put to him. But it just made so much sense that he was involved. He had to be, and he wasn't doing much to lift the cloud of suspicion from his door.

Just before they wrapped up his third interview, he was asked if there was some sort of agreement that Kieran would admit to all this.

'No. I don't know,' he replied.

The most fundamental elements that needed to be proved in the case against Keith Johnston were that he knew Patricia had been killed when he carried out the repairs in the bathroom, and that he knew what the axes, saws and other tools were to be used for when he went shopping with Kieran just over a week later. Getting to the bottom of those burning issues was the main focus of his fourth interview.

With that in mind, one of the first questions asked after the Record button was hit was when he really found out that Patricia was dead. He maintained his line that the first he learned of it was when Kieran confessed to the whole family in the house at Mountain View Park just before he handed himself in at Rathfarnham Garda Station.

Again, he denied going to Wexford to dig up Patricia's body from the shallow grave, and he was really starting to get fed up with that accusation.

'You have your facts wrong. Stop asking me about things I know nothing about,' he said.

'Ah, come on now, Keith. Are you really trying to tell us Kieran did this all on his own? He didn't know one end of a saw from another. You said it yourself.'

'Come on. He's not a two-year-old,' Keith said.

'What is all this?' he was asked.

'A big steaming pile of shite.'

'And where do you see it ending?'

'Off a cliff.'

A DNA sample had been taken from Keith when he was first brought in for questioning. Standard procedure. He was asked if he thought his DNA would turn up in Wexford.

'No. Not a hope in hell,' he said with confidence.

In his fifth interview, it was put to him that Patricia was killed sometime between 7 p.m. and 9 p.m. on 29 May, and that Louise, Stephanie and Gus all knew she was dead on that night. Keith said that wasn't the case. For a start, it was his understanding that she was killed much later. Kieran had told gardaí that he killed her shortly after midnight when she returned to the house after storming out in a rage a few hours earlier. The CCTV evidence didn't support that claim, and suggested she was murdered much earlier than that.

With time running out before a decision on whether to charge or release Keith had to be made, Sergeant O'Neill again put it to him that he helped clean up the murder scene. It was clear as day as far as the gardaí were concerned, and at the very least the optics didn't look good for the handyman.

'No, I didn't,' he said. 'Put whatever you want in your notebook, it doesn't make it true. Youse are a joke. I'm not involved in any murder. I didn't help Kieran in any way. I had nothing to do with it.'

After Kieran's confession on 12 June, Keith accepted that he should have twigged what he was buying the tools for, but he didn't.

Before they wrapped up his final interview, he was asked what he thought might happen to the others.

'Worst-case scenario, everyone goes to jail,' he said.

He was asked if he thought he might go to prison too. He supposed he might but hoped he wouldn't. He wouldn't today anyway. His confidence that his DNA would not be found in the field in Blackwater, County Wexford was well placed. Not a single cell was found. He was free to go.

13.

A SEA CHANGE

F ollowing his first court appearance after being charged, Kieran Greene was taken to Cloverhill Prison on the outskirts of Dublin city. It is a short drive from the city centre, maybe 10 kilometres to the south-west. The prison is a closed, medium-security facility, which holds mainly remand prisoners from the Leinster area. It has 431 beds, and most of them are full all year round. On the back of damning reports from various advising committees down through the years, management at Cloverhill have worked hard to try to address overcrowding issues, but with more and more people being sent to jail, it has proved to be quite a Rubik's Cube.

It's a busy prison and a tough place to work. In 2008, staff threatened to walk off the job over concerns for their safety. Thankfully, those issues have been resolved over the years, but prison officers are not immune to being verbally and physically abused at work. For the most part, though, there's a good rapport between prisoners and officers.

In 2017, one of the biggest issues for the inmates related to the tuck shop. Some prisoners were upset with an increase in the price of cigarettes and the method of accessing tobacco, but that resolved itself over time. A lack of toilet privacy was also a concern at the time. So too was the number of prisoners being held in three-bed cells.

A bloody gangland feud was still raging in Dublin at the time. In fact, most people initially thought that the discovery of the remains found in the Wicklow Mountains was another casualty of the feud. Unsurprisingly, gang culture within the walls of Cloverhill prison was a serious problem in 2017. The number of prisoners seeking protection was high, with up to a quarter of its population availing of the special status throughout the year. Protected prisoners are immediately separated from the general population or from specific prisoners identified as presenting a threat, which can cause a strain on already stretched resources.

Drug use in the prison was also of major concern. The prison authorities were doing their best to keep them out. Screens were put in place to prevent visitors passing drugs to their loved ones, and sniffer dogs were brought in on Sundays for unscreened family visits. But where there's a will, there's a way. One spot outside the prison walls proved popular for mules with good arms: with a well-aimed pitch they could lob drugs straight over the netting above the yard.

Cloverhill District Court is located on the prison grounds, which makes life a little easier for the prison officers who have to produce inmates for their court appearances every morning. If it's just a regular update of where their case is at, a prisoner can agree to appear via video link at the discretion of the court. Kieran did just that a week after he appeared before Judge Patricia McNamara in Tallaght. He addressed Judge Victor Blake only to confirm his name and that he could see and hear the court. Detective Garda David Connolly got back into the witness box. He told the court he was still awaiting formal directions from the Director of Public Prosecutions. Kieran agreed to a four-week remand, before being taken back to his cell.

Kieran kept himself to himself in prison. He was very quiet and caused no issues for the prison officers. The prison governor was reasonably pleased with how he was settling into prison life, although several officers had described him as being restless. His mother also expressed concerns about her son's health when she visited him. She felt it had deteriorated while he had been in custody. He had lost a bit of weight, was very tired and withdrawn. He was paranoid and saying all sorts of things during her visits. As far as she knew, he was put on some medications.

Louise was one of the six people on Kieran's list of approved visitors. After he nominated her to be added to his list, he was asked what his relationship to her was.

'Girlfriend,' was his reply.

She first visited him on 17 June, five days after he confessed to killing her mother. She had to leave her phone and other personal items at the visitors' centre before entering the prison.

Keith Johnston was also on his list. He called to see him on his own on 2 September, the same day the others were arrested. Kieran had described him as a 'friend' to the prison authorities.

Louise and Keith visited him together the following month, and again on 16 November. The kids were brought in to see him too.

Anyone charged with murder is tried on indictment, which meant that Kieran was going to stand trial for murder before a judge and jury at the Central Criminal Court, which is located just up the road from the prison in the impressive Criminal Courts of Justice facility beside the Phoenix Park.

Prison staff noticed he was out of sorts around this time, particularly after Louise and Kieran's second visit. He wasn't sleeping and he seemed agitated. It would pass. Part and parcel of prison life, no doubt.

A few weeks later, Kieran's solicitor contacted the investigation team to say that their client wished to speak with them immediately.

On Saturday, 9 December 2017, Detective Sergeant Brian Hanley and Detective Garda Declan O'Brien drove to Cloverhill Prison to see him. They were taken to a visiting room on arrival. Detective O'Brien knew the prison didn't have any way of recording interviews, so he brought a camcorder with him.

Kieran looked like a man who hadn't slept in a while. He declined an offer to consult with his solicitor before the interview began. He seemed nervous, but eager to talk.

'Basically, I want to discuss the case,' he began.

His interviewers were all ears.

He began by returning to the night of 29 May, and the alleged assault he suffered at the hands of Patricia O'Connor. Again, he told them *she attacked him* in the bathroom with a hurley.

'She was hitting me a lot. I was trying to get it off her … to stop her. I kept asking her why she was attacking me, and she just kept saying, "It's my house. I can do what I want." She hit me in the arm, stomach and side.

'I was trying to grab it [the hurley], and we were struggling. I got it off her and hit her twice, but she grabbed it again. She was hitting me. The two of us were holding it. She winded me and I hit the ground.'

Kieran paused for a moment at this point as he gathered his thoughts. His interviewers hadn't said a word yet. For the moment, they were happy to just hear what he had to say.

'After I hit the ground, I heard someone come down the stairs,' he continued. 'It was Mr O'Connor.'

'Gus O'Connor?' he was asked.

'Yes. He came into the bathroom and was giving out to her. He said, "What the fuck are you doing?" She was giving out to him too.'

He then claimed Patricia swung the hurley at Gus, but missed.

'Gus had some sort of a black bar or crowbar in his hand,' he said. 'He hit her in the head. Twice. She hit the floor, and then he turned to me and said, "I'm defending you, so you can take the rap for this." We panicked and brought her upstairs.'

This was an incredible turn of events. And Kieran wasn't done yet. Detective Sergeant Hanley prompted him to tell them what happened next.

'Well, a few minutes later Louise came downstairs after hearing the noise. We told her what happened and she said, "You can't leave her here," so we brought the body back downstairs and put her into the boot of the car. I grabbed a shovel and got in.'

He was asked where Gus was.

'I don't know where he went. I didn't know where I was going. I just kept driving. I stopped for petrol at some point, and just headed down the M50, past Bray.'

In his previous statements, Kieran had said he was on his own when he drove to Wexford that night with the body in the boot. He said he was on his own when he dug the hole in the cornfield at Blackwater and buried her. He was asked over and over if there was anybody with him, and he repeatedly told gardaí he acted alone at all times.

'When I got back to the house, Louise was cleaning the bathroom. I told her that I'd buried the body,' he added.

In one fell swoop, Kieran implicated his girlfriend and her father in this gruesome crime. Both had been arrested and questioned for their suspected involvement, but neither had been charged. Kieran wasn't finished, though, and his 'friend' Keith Johnston soon found himself in his crosshairs.

'I told Keith a couple of days later, and asked for his help. I had never been in this predicament before, and I didn't know what to do. He told me to leave it with him and he came back to me with a plan a day or two later.'

'What was his plan?'

'Well, we went to a few shops. We bought a petrol can and some Stanley blades in Mr. Price.'

After that, he described going to B&Q, where they bought 'black bags, a tarp and a hacksaw'. He said they grabbed some spare Stanley blades and a 12" hatchet in Woodie's on the way home. It was still early, so they returned to the house afterwards, he said.

At about 9 or 9.30 p.m., Kieran said he and Keith drove to Wexford, only stopping for petrol along the way. When they got to the cornfield, he said he showed Keith where the shallow grave was.

'We dug her up and Keith started cutting her with the saw. He did that. He was putting all the parts into bags, and we'd tie knots on them and put them in the boot. Afterwards, we drove up the mountains and about five minutes past the viewpoint, he shouted "Stop!"

'He got out of the car, took a bag from the back and just emptied it. He kept doing this for a few miles until all the bags were gone. Then we just turned the car around.'

Kieran said they changed their clothes and put on some spare ones they'd brought with them. On the way home, he claimed Keith then turned to him and said, 'I know this is on you, brother, I have a background in drugs. I can't get into any more trouble.'

He said Keith told him they'd go easy on him because he didn't have a criminal record, so he agreed to take the blame.

In his original story, Kieran claimed to have used just one hacksaw to cut up Patricia's body. He said he couldn't lift her out of the pit he had put her in, so he butchered her where she lay. He claimed to have thrown the saw away up the mountains, but despite the best efforts of the search team, it wasn't found during the extensive four-day operation. Four months before this astonishing turn of events, metal detectors were used to sweep beneath the cornfield where the shallow grave was, but again nothing was found.

Detective Sergeant Hanley asked him what they did with their tools afterwards.

'We drove to the Dodder Valley Park in Tallaght and he took out the saw and all I mentioned earlier,' he said. 'He came back then with nothing in his hands.'

He said they drove to another location afterwards, where they burned the clothes.

'What happened then, Kieran? Did you two go your separate ways after that?'

'Yeah. Keith called over then maybe a day or so later and scraped the grout in the bathroom and shower and painted the walls as well.'

Kieran's revelations had just turned everything upside down. The investigation team would have to check out everything he'd just told them to see if it all stacked up. He still wasn't done, though. There was still room for one more person under the bus, and he soon threw Stephanie there too. He told them what they always suspected about her, that she had dressed up as her grandmother to make it look like she was still alive at a time when she knew she was dead.

'I was persuaded to take the blame for all this,' he said. 'So I said I would. I took the blame. I don't know why. I went and told the gardaí I killed her, even when I didn't.'

The red light on the camcorder was still blinking away as the two police officers sitting across from Kieran wondered why he was telling them all this now.

'We all agreed I would take the blame. The gardaí thought I was messing. I told them I wasn't. I feel I shouldn't be taking the blame for all this. I feel like I was set up because my missus and Keith are going back out. I reckon this was all planned. They are out there and I'm taking the rap for it.'

It all made sense now. The green-eyed monster had finally

raised its ugly head. Keith was back living in the house. Of course. He claimed nothing romantic was going on between him and his ex, but that could have changed in the three months since his arrest. Or perhaps they were together long before that? They had been visiting the prison together to see Kieran. Patricia was out of the way now too. Everything was coming up roses for them as far as Kieran was concerned, and here he was rotting away in a cell.

Jealousy is a dangerous emotion. It can make you say and do crazy things. This green-eyed monster was angry and had to be approached with caution.

It had been six months since he handed himself in. His timing was certainly interesting, but he claimed the only reason he didn't say anything sooner was because he was concerned for the kids. Following Louise's arrest, his mother agreed to take them in if necessary, so he was no longer worried about them. They would be taken care of if he and Louise both ended up in jail. That said, he had known for some time now that their futures were secure. His mother had signed a document agreeing to guardianship almost three months before this new confession.

Many question marks hung over Kieran's renewed version of events, so gardaí probed him for a bit more detail.

They began by asking him exactly where Gus had hit Patricia on the head. Kieran indicated that it was the left-hand side. That didn't tally with the evidence. In his post-mortem examination of Patricia's head, Dr Curtis found injuries to the right side, not the left.

Some of his timings in relation to what he accused Stephanie of doing didn't stack up either; he became flustered when that was pointed out to him, and he accepted they could have been wrong. He wasn't great with timings, apparently.

He was asked to remind them what Gus said to Patricia when he came into the bathroom.

'He said, "What the fuck are you doing? Why are you doing that to him?" He then hit her hard,' he said.

'Did you check her after bringing her upstairs?'

'I thought she was dead.'

He said he used a mop and bleach to clean the bathroom afterwards.

'I did the first one and Louise did it then after. She did it a couple of days later,' he said.

He insisted Louise was the one who told him to get rid of the body, and he claimed Keith suggested putting her deeper in the shallow grave.

'Did you help Keith cut her up, Kieran?'

'No, I was getting sick into a bag while he did it. I did help him put the parts into the car, though,' he said.

He was asked for more detail about Stephanie's supposed role in the ruse that evening.

'I don't fully understand it,' he said. 'I only heard about it after she had done it. Her and her ma said she was going to dress up like Patricia to show she had gone missing. I wasn't aware until I came back from Wexford that she did that.'

That didn't make sense either. Kieran was in the house when Stephanie left that night. He was spotted out the back at one point, chatting to Louise and Stephanie. It seemed incredible to think he didn't know what the plan was. That said, why would he lie about it now, given everything he had just told them?

He was asked who told Stephanie what happened to her grand-mother, and he told them Louise did.

Before they wrapped up the interview, he was asked if every-thing he had just told them was the truth. They had a long list of reasons to doubt him, but he assured them he was telling the truth.

'A hundred per cent, yes,' he replied. 'I wanted to get this off my chest. I was persuaded to do all this. I was concerned if I got arrested and Louise got arrested. I was concerned for the kids. Now I know they are going up to my ma,' he said.

'I honestly didn't do it,' he said. 'I'll swear on anyone's life, I didn't do it, you have to believe me.'

On the back of this revised version of events, a search team was sent to the Dodder Valley Linear Park in south Dublin. The park covers over a hundred hectares and stretches six kilometres from Old Bawn Bridge in Tallaght to Rathfarnham. It links the Dublin Mountains with Dublin's southern suburbs. This was where Kieran claimed Keith threw away the tools used to dismember his victim.

Garda Joseph Waldron was one of the officers assigned to search the suburban park on 2 January 2018. While combing through some brambles, he found a hacksaw with a black and white handle. Garda Seamus Murphy found an identical-looking saw in some undergrowth near the river. The only difference between the two was significant. On closer inspection, Garda Murphy noticed the one he found had some hair on the blade. The sample was sent to the same UK lab that had examined the piece of hair found at the shallow grave in Wexford. Again, it matched the reference sample provided and offered moderate support that it originated from the head of Patricia O'Connor or a close maternal relative. A small hatchet with an orange handle was also found at the river's edge. The next step was to compare the tools with the controlled purchases of hacksaws and axes made by gardaí following the discovery of the receipts in the house and car. Unsurprisingly, they were perfect matches. They were made by the same manufacturers, they were the same size, and their handles were the same colour.

Despite initially lying about what had happened to the tools after Patricia was dismembered, Kieran now seemed to be telling the truth. The question was, who put them there? Keith was rearrested, but nothing of note emerged from the interview that followed. He maintained his innocence. The allegations made against Louise and Stephanie were also put to them. They were invited to add to their statements if there was anything they wanted to say in response to what Kieran had told gardaí. They declined the opportunity. Gus, who Kieran now claimed to be the killer, was defiant in his response to this most serious allegation.

'I never laid a hand on my wife,' he insisted.

14.

THE TRIAL

Kieran Greene may have been telling the truth about the location of the tools used to dismember Patricia, but that didn't mean everything else he said was true. Aside from leading the investigation team to the park along the River Dodder where the hacksaws and hatchet were found, his statement from prison didn't assist gardaí in any other meaningful way. There was nothing to corroborate his wild accusations.

Sure, he told them about the ruse involving Stephanie dressing up as her grandmother, but they were satisfied a jury would figure out that much for themselves on the evidence they had already gathered. In their minds, she had sealed her own fate when she identified herself as the figure seen at the back of the house half an hour after the woman with the suitcase left from the front. She confirmed it was her when it was shown to her initially, but then rowed back on it when its significance dawned on her. Her uncle Richard had also identified her when the footage was shown to him. Even if he hadn't, the top this figure was wearing bore a striking resemblance to the distinctive top Stephanie had on in the footage recorded in Tesco a few hours beforehand.

None of the others was charged with murder, but in October 2018, a decision was made to charge all four with impeding the apprehension or prosecution of Kieran Greene. A jury would be required to decide whether or not they tried to help him get away with murder.

Keith Johnston was initially just charged in relation to the shopping trip he went on with Kieran the day before the first body part was found. Gardaí believed the tools his friend bought that day were the ones used to dispose of the body. Aside from Kieran's word, there was nothing to prove Keith had anything to do with the act of dismemberment itself. Two months later, Keith was re-arrested and charged with a second count of the same offence, this time in relation to the refurbishment of the bathroom in the days after Patricia was killed. The investigation team strongly believed he knew what happened to her and they were convinced his work in the bathroom was done with a view to protecting Kieran from getting caught. The DPP agreed there was enough circumstantial evidence to put it to a jury, and she was confident of getting a second conviction across the line.

Kieran didn't apply for bail before his trial. All the others did, and they were all successful. By now, the once-swollen house at Mountain View Park was empty. Keith Johnston was living with his mother in Tallaght. Gus moved in with him for a while, before Richard took him in. Louise and her children moved back into the house as soon as the strips of crime-scene tape were lifted from the front door, but Gus didn't approve of her return. He might have decided to leave the house, but in light of everything that had happened, he didn't want her there and he finally asked her to pack her bags. She refused. In the end, he sent her a solicitor's letter threatening legal action if she didn't go. She and the kids soon found themselves sharing a room in homeless accommodation. The council found them an apartment in Dundrum, but she was told she'd have to give it up if she was found guilty of the crime she was being accused of. A lot more than her freedom was now riding on the outcome of the trial.

A jury was due to be sworn in to hear Kieran's murder trial on 3 December 2018, but the date was pushed back when the prosecuting barrister assigned to the case, Mary Rose Gearty SC, asked the court for all five to be tried together. The defence teams opposed her application, but a joint trial was eventually approved. A last-ditch effort to get separate trials was unsuccessful, and the trial was pencilled into the Central Criminal Court's legal diary for 13 January 2020.

Back in Windgap, County Kilkenny, Rita was told a new trial date had been set. She'd be there no matter what. She still couldn't believe the others had somehow been involved. She knew they'd been charged, but she wasn't privy to the precise details of the investigation. In her mind, Kieran had owned up to it. She thought he did everything on his own. It was too much to take in. How could Gus and Trisha's own daughter be involved? And Stephanie? Her sister adored Stephanie. The thought of her being involved in some way turned Rita's stomach.

Her stomach was still doing somersaults when she boarded the train to Dublin for the opening day of the trial. She and her siblings had been shown around the courtroom beforehand. Attending court can be a daunting experience to the uninitiated, so they were offered a tour in the lead-up to the trial to put their minds somewhat at ease.

•••

The Central Criminal Court sits in the impressive ten-storey Criminal Courts of Justice (CCJ) complex on the junction of Parkgate Street and Infirmary Road in Dublin city. It's also home to the Dublin Metropolitan District Court, Dublin Circuit Court, the Special Criminal Court and the criminal division of the Court of Appeal.

The courthouse is a short stroll from Heuston Station, which made Rita's daily commute from Kilkenny much more tolerable. Before the €140m facility was built next to the Phoenix Park in 2010, the Central Criminal Court lived under the iconic green dome of the Four Courts a little further down the quays. Few of the courts were suitable for jury trials, though, and many were moved to ad hoc locations that weren't fit for hosting modern-day criminal trials.

The true might of the CCJ isn't immediately obvious from the outside. Its shiny shell is made up of enormous double-storey glass panelling to give the impression that it's only five storeys high. Its design was a clever and deliberate ploy by the architect to make the building blend into its surroundings. For those approaching from the park, it rises majestically from behind a wall of tall ash trees tucked in just off the road. A large insignia of Lady Justice marks the entrance.

Rita was blown away by the sheer size of the building when she was waved through by the friendly security team at the screening area just inside the front door. A huge amount of the building's interior is taken up by a great hall, four times larger than the Four Courts' Round Hall and as wide as the Pantheon in Rome.

Twenty-two courtrooms surround the hall. Sixteen of those have jury boxes. The designer's brief included a specific instruction to keep the appearance of the courtrooms low-key to create an atmosphere of dignity and calm. Acoustics and sight lines were considered top priorities too. Given the nature of the work conducted by the criminal courts, it's important for people to be able to hear and see everything, regardless of where they sit.

The complex has over 600 other rooms, including judges' chambers, jury rooms, consultation rooms, media rooms and holding cells for up to a hundred prisoners. There is a canteen on the second floor, where it's not unusual to see lawyers, gardaí, victims and accused persons milling about the dining area at lunchtime. Patricia's family members were shown the layout of the courtroom and told who sits where. The trial was expected to attract a lot of media attention, so they were shown where the journalists would be seated. The press bench is sandwiched between the public gallery and the rows of benches closest to the judge where the lawyers set up camp. Rita's eye was drawn to the empty dock. It was hard to imagine how she'd react when it was filled by so many familiar faces. On that front, they were told to remain impassive throughout the trial, and advised to leave if they felt they couldn't do so during difficult pieces of evidence. Easier said than done. Due to the nature of the evidence to be called and the close ties to those in the dock, gardaí knew it would be an emotionally charged atmosphere in the courtroom at times, but any outbursts could be seen as an attempt to influence the jurors. The last thing Rita wanted to do was to collapse a trial, so she promised to bite her tongue, for now.

Rita was glad of the walk-through, but nothing prepared her for the first day of the trial. She was very apprehensive. She would make the trip from Kilkenny almost every day for the next seven weeks with her sisters Anne and Colette and brother Michael. It didn't get any easier. Members of the family who were living in Dublin, including Valerie, Breda and Kathleen, also attended as often as they could. Not one day of the long trial passed without somebody being there in Trisha's memory.

Kieran Greene looked nervous on the opening day too. He was brought to court in custody which, luckily for him, meant he didn't have to try to dodge the snappers outside every day. The others were all out on bail, so they had to walk through the public entrance like everybody else. They did their utmost to hide their identities by wearing hats or putting their hoods up. They wrapped scarves around their faces and Stephanie wore sunglasses most days too. Every morning turned into a game of cat and mouse between the photographers, TV camera crews and the hooded trio of Louise, Stephanie and Keith. They successfully avoided the cameras for weeks, until one of the photographers enlisted the help of a friend, another photographer based in the Four Courts. Stephanie and her parents got the Luas into the city centre after court most days. One day, the CCJ-based photographer spotted them as they made their way to the nearest Luas stop. They'd often step off at the Jervis Shopping Centre. The other photographer, who they had never laid eyes on, positioned himself nearby with his camera locked and loaded. Sure enough, they got off the tram at the Jervis stop and went into a nearby Dealz store. They hadn't quite let their guard down at this point, but when they emerged from the shop a few minutes later, all three had pulled their hoods down and unwrapped the scarves from around their faces. Stephanie had taken her sunglasses off. In the distance, a camera with a long-focus lens clicked into life.

Gus didn't seem too bothered about having his picture splashed all over the newspapers and evening news. He wore a dark flat cap to court most days, but that seemed more like a conscious fashion choice than a shield from the public glare.

The trial date, 13 January 2020, was a Monday, the busiest day of the week for the High Court's criminal division. All cases listed for trial that day came before Mr Justice Michael White in Court 6 on the second floor of the CCJ. The room was abuzz with lawyers. Solicitors weighed down with files rushed to the front benches alongside barristers dressed in long black robes with bright white legal collars and bands.

The registrar's booming voice brought the room to a hush. There were six cases listed for trial. Journalists squeezed together on the end of one of the long wooden benches cocked their ears. The case they were there for was the last on the list. They drew their pens and snapped open their laptops when Kieran Greene was eventually brought up from his holding cell. The others, who were all on bail, joined him in the dock.

Nothing prepared Rita for the sight of her brother-in-law, niece and grandniece in that courtroom. She'd never met Keith

Johnston. He had been at Patricia's funeral, though, and now the very thought of that day made her feel queasy. Louise had wanted to keep everything hush-hush, which Rita thought odd at the time, but she had respected her wishes. Now she knew why. The low-key affair really upset the wider family because Patricia had made so many friends at Beaumont Hospital and they all wanted to be there. There were so many others back home in Windgap who would have made the trip too, but Louise wouldn't allow it. Kieran was in custody at the time of the funeral, but all the others in that dock were there, supposedly paying their respects. Rita remembered going over to Louise at one point to give her a hug. It wasn't a normal hug, though. Louise's body went limp and she didn't hug her aunt back. She just seemed to wither when Rita threw her arms around her. Stephanie was the same. It was so strange. Looking back now, Rita really regretted going over to them at all, but hindsight is twenty-twenty. She could never have predicted this reunion three years later.

Mr Justice White was told there had been a development in the case. Gus O'Connor wished to plead guilty. This posed a potential problem. Assuming he was now going to admit that he knew Patricia was dead when he reported her missing on 1 June 2017, the question arose as to whether that admission could potentially prejudice the cases against those who remained in the dock. It was an issue that would have to be thrashed out by the legal teams before the trial could begin. In the end, it was decided that a joint trial for the remaining four accused persons could still go ahead, provided there was no mention of Gus's plea or the evidence gathered specifically in relation to him.

Rita was gobsmacked by the development. She couldn't believe it. She was also angry that he had left it until the eleventh hour. Why now? she thought. Why not be a man and say it when you're being questioned? Get a bit of a backbone and say what you did instead of waiting until the last minute.

Gus had made up his mind after his application to be tried separately from the others was denied. Perhaps he felt he had a chance of getting off if he went before a jury on his own. An admission of guilt now would mean a lighter sentence down the line.

Before the jury selection process got under way the following day, the charges were put to the remaining four accused. Each of them stood in turn to be arraigned, and each of them replied 'not guilty' when the charges were read out to them.

Mr Justice White then told the jury panel waiting downstairs that it would be a long trial. If called upon, they were told, they would be required to commit to it for up to seven weeks. Anyone of a 'squeamish disposition' was advised not to sit on the jury. They were warned that the case involved evidence of 'the disinterment and dismemberment of body parts of the deceased'.

The first wave of potential jurors filed into the courtroom when their names were called. Some of them approached the bench and whispered into the judge's ear before being excused. Several others were challenged by the various defence teams. In the end, six men and six women were sworn in to hear the trial. The case was moved to Court 13 before Mr Justice Paul McDermott, the man who presided over the harrowing trial of two boys who murdered 14-year-old Kildare schoolgirl Ana Kriégel. The jurors were asked to elect a foreperson and to return to court the following day when the prosecuting barrister, Róisín Lacey SC, would address them for the first time. The case had landed on her desk just two months beforehand. Another senior barrister, Mary Rose Gearty, had been due to lead the prosecution – but the government had agreed to nominate her as one of five new judges to fill vacancies in the High Court.

Ms Lacey took to her feet at 2.20 p.m. on the opening day of the trial, 15 January 2020. It would take her the best part of an hour to deliver her opening remarks and outline the prosecution's case to the jurors. She warned them that her synopsis of the case was not to be taken as evidence. The only evidence they would be concerned with would come from the witness box or through various exhibits. She told them they would have to treat each case separately. Yes, the four accused were being tried together, but she warned against lumping them all together. Inevitably, one person's case had the potential to bleed into another's, but the jurors were told they couldn't use what one accused person said about another as evidence against that other defendant. It was a warning they would hear time and time again from all legal quarters throughout the trial.

Ms Lacey then introduced the quartet squeezed together in the packed dock. Stephanie sat in the middle, flanked by her mother Louise on the inside, and her father Keith on the outside. A glum-looking Kieran Greene sat detached from the others on a small bench next to the dock. Stephanie had kicked up a fuss before the trial got under way – she didn't want to sit anywhere near him – so he sat alone on his own perch with the others in his direct line of sight. He didn't know where to look most of the time, so he kept his head bowed and just stared at his feet with the neat parting in his hair facing the jury.

From her seat in the public gallery, Rita glanced over at the overcrowded dock. Seeing all those familiar faces felt surreal. It was hard to look at them. She never got used to it. A few minutes would go by, and she would start questioning if it was real. It was like something you'd see on TV, she thought to herself. It just wasn't normal and she couldn't believe it was actually happening. Those in the dock all glanced over at the public gallery from time to time. Louise used to stare them out of it, which Rita found very unsettling. They had done no wrong. It was a horrendous experience. Rita described Louise in particular as 'stone-faced' throughout. She wondered if she had been advised not to show emotion. Worryingly, Rita suspected she didn't have to be told.

Ms Lacey told the jury that for them to find Kieran Greene guilty of murder, she would have to prove to them 'beyond a reasonable doubt' that he *intended* to kill her or cause her serious harm. She also gave them a crash course in Section 7 (2) of the Criminal Law Act 1997. This was the offence faced by the others, twice in Keith Johnston's case. She told them there must be an *act* – they must have actually done something. There must also be *intent* to either impede Kieran Greene's apprehension or prosecution, and she said the act must be done 'without reasonable excuse'. Explaining the legal principles is the judge's job, so she didn't trespass on his territory for too long before giving the twelve men and women of the jury a roadmap of the case the prosecution was going to present to them over the next few weeks. For Rita and the other members of Patricia's family not sitting in the dock, this would be the first time they heard some of the gruesome details about what happened to their beloved Trisha.

'Patricia O'Connor was 61 years old,' began Ms Lacey. 'She lived in a modest four-bedroom house at Mountain View Park with her husband Gus, daughter Louise, Louise's partner Kieran Greene and Louise's five children, including one of the accused, Stephanie. The living conditions were quite cramped. It appears tensions in the house were high and stressful at times. There were also some interpersonal conflicts between individuals living there.

'On 1 June 2017, Gus O'Connor went to Rathfarnham Garda Station to report his wife as a missing person. She had been missing since 29 May 2017. A report was created and gardaí began investigating. They checked with relatives. They checked her bank account. They found nothing.

'Between 10 June and 14 June 2017, various body parts were found in the mountains, just off Military Road, in an area covering 30 kilometres. In total, fifteen body parts were located at nine different scenes. Members of the public found the first parts. The rest were discovered during a search involving gardaí and the army.

'The sum of these parts was found to be Patricia O'Connor. She had been dismembered. In the early stages of the recovery process, it was believed the parts related to a man in his twenties. That turned out to be an error. There was nothing to identify the remains initially, but DNA analysis led to a positive identification with the assistance of dental records. Patricia had a considerable amount of dental work done during her life and her dental surgeon will give evidence in due course. He provided her records to assist with the investigation.'

Ms Lacey then moved on briefly to the post-mortem evidence that would be presented during the trial. Patricia's siblings braced themselves on the hard public benches, mindful of the advice not to react to any of the evidence.

'The Deputy State Pathologist Dr Michael Curtis carried out a post-mortem on the dismembered head,' Ms Lacey continued.

'It was found in a plastic bag with right and left severed hands. He concluded that the head had been struck a minimum of three blows with a solid implement. He also found that the underlying skull showed a "circular depressed fracture" from which there was a "large hinge fracture" along the base of the skull. There was also another fracture a little further back on the head. In his opinion, cause of death was blunt force trauma to the head.'

Poor Trisha, thought Rita. She wanted to scream.

Ms Lacey went on to outline the voluntary statements made by Kieran Greene after he handed himself in on 12 June 2017. She said that body parts were still being discovered at this point, and it would take another two days before everything was recovered from the mountains. She summarised what Kieran had said during those interviews. The jury would hear a lot more detail about them at a later stage.

'Kieran Greene admitted killing Patricia in or around 29/30 May 2017. He told gardaí there had been a dispute in the bathroom, during which she hit him with a hurley. He said he grabbed it from her and hit her a few times with it. He said she fell.

'In his first interview, he said he took the body up the mountains in a Toyota Corolla. Patricia O'Connor owned a Toyota Corolla and he had access to it and was allowed to drive it. He said that was the car in which he put her in the boot. He said he acted alone at all times and that none of the family was aware she was even deceased. He gave gardaí the same story in his second interview that night.

'Gardaí still thought the body found in the mountains belonged to a male in his twenties, so there was some scepticism about what he was saying. He was not arrested. He left in quite an emotional state but told gardaí he was happy to return the next day, and he did so. He repeated his story to them and told them he first took her body down to a location in Wexford, where he buried her in a shallow grave. He said he returned to that location on 9 June, dug her up and dismembered her. Again, he said he did it all by himself. He said he put the parts into plastic bags and placed them in the boot of the car. He then drove up the mountains where they were thrown from the car.

'That afternoon, he agreed to take gardaí to an area near Blackwater, County Wexford to show them the shallow grave in the cornfield. Gardaí saw what appeared to be a shallow grave. They also saw what appeared to be hair and a piece of fabric with a floral pattern on it. Kieran Greene was then arrested for murder and taken to Bray Garda Station for further questioning. Gardaí were now aware that they were dealing with a female body.'

Twelve pairs of eyes stared down at Ms Lacey from the jury box. The twelve men and women hung on her every word. Her composed delivery was punctuated every now and again by the sound of wooden benches at the back of the packed courtroom creaking under the strain of curious members of the public moving forward to catch every word of this grisly story. The frantic pecking of keyboards behind her did little to distract from or drown out what she was saying.

She gave the jury an overview of what Kieran said during the interviews conducted with him following his arrest.

'He told them there had been a row over a cat. He said Patricia O'Connor stormed out and came back about midnight. He said everyone else was in bed. He claimed she came into the bathroom where he was and struck him several times with a hurley during a struggle that lasted between fifteen and twenty minutes. He told them he disarmed her and struck her a number of times in the head. He said they both fell and he blacked out. He said he couldn't remember much more about what happened, just that when he came around, he saw blood everywhere, so he brought her upstairs. During the night, he told them, he took her body to Wexford in the boot of his car. Again, he said no other family member was present. He said they were all ignorant of what had occurred because they were in bed at the time.

'He said he returned to the burial site on 9 June with a hacksaw and some gloves, dug up her body and dismembered her. He said he put the body parts into bags and discarded them along with the tools and clothes in the mountains. When the discovery of body parts became media news, he said, he decided to confess.'

Ms Lacey spoke about the voluntary statements taken from Louise and Stephanie, in which they both described Patricia as being 'in a rage' before she stormed out of the house on 29 May 2017. She said they both told gardaí they heard Patricia shout, 'I'll be back when that auld fella pops his clogs,' and she told the jurors they figured the 'auld fella' she was referring to was Gus. They claimed the first time they heard about what had actually happened was when Kieran Greene sat them down to make his confession before he handed himself in.

She walked them through some of the other evidence that would be presented to them as part of the prosecution's case, including the receipts found in the house and car. She said CCTV footage would also feature during the trial. In relation to footage harvested from a neighbour's house, Ms Lacey said the prosecution's case was this:

'On 19 May 2017, Patricia O'Connor can be seen going about her business in a floral dress in her front garden. The last sighting of her on camera was at 6.35 p.m. when she is seen going into the house from the back garden through the patio doors and into the kitchen area of her home.

'At 6.53 p.m., Kieran Greene closes the curtains at the back of that room. Louise, Stephanie and the kids leave the house shortly afterwards. The evidence will show that they went to a local park. They didn't return until about 9 p.m. Gus didn't return to the property until 10.30 p.m.'

The jury was told that it was the prosecution's case that Kieran Greene murdered Patricia O'Connor shortly after she came back into the house from the garden. She said they would be shown CCTV footage from later in the evening that showed Louise and Stephanie chatting in the back garden between 9 p.m. and 9.30 p.m.

'Four minutes later, someone is seen emerging from the front of the house, wearing trousers and a jacket with the hood up,' Ms Lacey said.

'This person has covered their face and hair and can be seen carrying a suitcase and leaving the property in the direction of Nutgrove. One minute later, Louise O'Connor emerges from the front of the house and looks to her left, in the direction of where this person has gone.

'At 10.05 p.m., a woman can then be seen entering the house from the rear. The only means of access to the back garden without entering the house is through an alleyway at the side of the house where there's a white gate leading the way. At the time this happened, that alleyway was like an obstacle course with kids' bikes strewn all over it. The figure seen at the back of the house is a woman, carrying a suitcase and a coat under her arm. It is the prosecution's case that this woman is in fact Stephanie O'Connor. Furthermore, we believe the person who left from the front of the house half an hour or so beforehand was also Stephanie O'Connor.'

Ms Lacey explained that a thorough examination of CCTV footage from that evening revealed that at no point after Stephanie O'Connor returned to the house at 9 p.m. could she be seen as Stephanie O'Connor leaving the property from any exit. Ms Lacey said it was her belief that the person who left with the suitcase is the same person who returned with the suitcase and entered through the back with a coat over her arm. Crucially, she said, she believed this was all planned:

'This, we say, was a ruse. A ruse engaged in by way of pretence, to have it recorded on CCTV that Patricia O'Connor had stormed out with her suitcase and that she was a missing person. We say she was dead in the house at the time, and that her body was later removed from the house and taken to Wexford, where it was later disinterred and dismembered.'

The case against Keith Johnston centred on his alleged actions in the days and weeks after Patricia was killed. Ms Lacey told the jurors she believed the so-called 'refurbishment works' he carried out on the bathroom floor, where Kieran Greene had confessed to beating Patricia O'Connor to death, were done with a view to hide or destroy evidence. She said he replaced tiles and oversaw the painting of a wall by Kieran Greene, all the while having a 'nagging thought' that he could potentially be cleaning up a crime scene. She briefly mentioned the shopping spree he was alleged to have gone on with his friend. In his initial statements to gardaí, he told them the only DIY items he remembered being bought for the house were 'tiles, drill bits, plywood and adhesive'. The receipts found during the course of the investigation showed axes, hacksaws and blades were also purchased. In addition, Ms Lacey told the jurors, she would present evidence that proved that Mr Johnston was with Kieran Greene when these items were bought in various hardware stores on 9 June 2017 – the day before the first body part was found.

She said, 'Patricia O'Connor was lying in a shallow grave at the time of this shopping spree. Her body was intact, having not yet been dismembered. We say Keith Johnston was aware of this, and we also say he was helping Mr Greene with the purchase of those items for the purpose of concealing her remains.'

Ms Lacey briefly touched on the forensic sweep of the house at Mountain View Park. She said that Louise and Stephanie moved back into the house afterwards. Interestingly, so too did Louise's ex, Keith Johnston. The jurors were told about their arrests in September 2017, and how they all denied any involvement in Patricia's gruesome murder and the attempted cover-up afterwards.

Jaws dropped even further when Ms Lacey moved on to Kieran Greene's renewed statement from prison in December 2017. She told them that he got in touch with the investigation team to tell them that he wanted to change his story. His updated version of events pointed the finger of blame at Patricia's husband, Gus, whom he now claimed had killed her and forced him to take the blame.

'Kieran told gardaí that Gus came into the bathroom with a crowbar of some sort after he had fallen to the ground during a struggle with Patricia. He claimed Gus hit her twice in the head, causing her to fall. Afterwards, Kieran said Gus turned to him and told him that he was defending him, so he would have to take the rap for it. Furthermore, Kieran claimed Louise was aware of what happened and that she helped them put her mother's body into the boot of the car. He also said she cleaned the bathroom up afterwards.'

Ms Lacey outlined what Kieran said about the alleged involvement of the other two. The jurors were told that he said that Louise contacted Keith to tell him what happened, and that he was the one who dismembered Patricia. He said it took between three and four hours. Afterwards, he said, Keith disposed of the tools in a park near the River Dodder and they burned their clothes. He also told them that Stephanie had dressed up as her grandmother on the night in question to pretend she was still alive. Ms Lacey told the court that Kieran claimed he had then been persuaded to take the blame and now felt he had been 'set up' by the others.

An eerie silence descended on Court 13 when Ms Lacey eventually resumed her seat. It was a lot to take in. The clickety-clack from the press bench came to an abrupt end as exhausted hands closed laptops and journalists raced downstairs to the media room on the ground floor to file their stories. The jurors were told to ignore the reportage. 'It is not relevant to your deliberations,' Mr Justice McDermott said. 'You must only concern yourselves with the evidence you hear from the witness box in this courtroom.' He also warned them not to discuss the case with anyone apart from each other. This motley crew had only laid eyes on one another for the first time the day before. They had entered each other's lives in the most random of ways, and over the next seven weeks or so, they would develop a close bond. A bond that would only be broken after they had made the most difficult decisions of their lives. Their work for the day was done.

As is common practice with all criminal trials, the next step was to show the jurors the maps and snaps. Garda photographers and mappers were called into the witness box the following morning to point out the various crime scenes, including the house, the car and the nine locations in the Wicklow Mountains where Patricia's scattered remains were found. They were also shown the location of the shallow grave in County Wexford, as well as the various shops and hardware stores relevant to the case.

The first civilian witness called to give evidence was Christine Murphy, the young woman who stumbled on the first body part while out picnicking with her family two days before Kieran handed himself in. Her brother and aunt were also called to give their accounts of what they saw. The various gardaí who attended the scene on 10 June 2017 also took the stand. So too did Noel Ruane, who found the second part of the torso at Glenmacnass Waterfall on the same day. Rita often thought about all those who came across her sister's remains. She felt sorry for them. Nothing could have prepared them for what they saw that day, but she was so grateful to them for coming forward and assisting with the prosecution. She even had the opportunity to thank them in person after they had given their evidence. Who knows what would have happened if they hadn't found her? She thanked them for calling the gardaí and for giving evidence at the trial. They told her there was no need to thank them – it was their duty – and they just hoped she and her family got justice for Patricia. Rita wanted that more than anything. Nothing was going to bring her sister back, but it would be of some comfort to know that those who were responsible didn't get away with it.

It took days to present the jury with all the evidence relating to the search of the Wicklow Mountains. The prosecution had to prove, beyond a reasonable doubt, who found what and where. Sprawling maps spun around in the jury box as the jurors tried to orientate themselves with the multiple crime scenes.

Among the exhibits shown to the jurors in the opening few days of the trial were the two hacksaws and the hatchet found during a search of the Dodder Valley Linear Park in Tallaght on 2 January

2018. They were told that some human hair was found on the rusty blade of one of the hacksaws, an image that didn't sit well with anyone in the courtroom, especially Patricia's brothers and sisters. Understandably, the evidence was particularly difficult for them to take in. Rita had to get up and leave a few times. Determined not to let Patricia down by getting upset in front of the jury, she'd run to the toilet and take a few minutes to compose herself before returning to the courtroom. The various defence barristers rose from time to time to cross-examine prosecution witnesses, but the evidence called in the early stages of the trial went largely unchallenged.

The receipts found in the car and house were produced for the jurors to look at. Garda Andrew Quinn gave evidence of Gus and Richard O'Connor reporting Patricia as a missing person on 1 June 2017.

At this point, the jury had no idea that on this date Gus already knew that Patricia was dead. A reporting restriction had been put in place after he entered his plea, so the gathered journalists were not allowed to mention it in their coverage. To do so would have been contempt of court. Gus had yet to be sentenced too because the court had adjourned his sentence hearing until the others were dealt with. There was no objection to him being granted bail while he awaited his fate, and he attended the court most days to hear the evidence. Whether intentionally or not, he used to base himself directly behind his in-laws. He came over to them at one point, but Rita didn't want anything to do with him. She was disgusted with him. Patricia had been nothing but kind to him. Sure, things hadn't worked out for them, but she still took care of him, and this was how he repaid her kindness. He wanted to explain himself, but Rita didn't want to listen to his excuses; she could barely stand being in the same room as him. She made her feelings known by not engaging with him in the slightest, and yet he continued to sit behind them every day. She found it uncomfortable and disrespectful.

Garda Patrick Foley took the stand on the fifth day of the trial. He was the first person to speak with Kieran Greene when he handed himself in on 12 June 2017. He described him as being of a 'nervous disposition' before he approached the hatch at the public desk. He told the jury about the 'altercation' Mr Greene claimed to have had with Patricia O'Connor. He also demonstrated the 'chopping motion' Kieran made with his arm as he described what he did to her. Under cross-examination by Kieran's barrister, Conor Devally SC, Garda Foley accepted that the use of words like 'altercation' and 'unresponsive' in his direct evidence was 'Garda speak', and he agreed that Kieran may have used other terminology during their three-minute conversation.

In keeping with the timeline of events, Detective Sergeant Lucy Myles was next up. She was the member in charge of Rathfarnham Garda Station on the day Kieran approached Garda Foley, but she has since taken up a role with Europol, the law enforcement agency for the European Union. She told the jurors about the voluntary statements she took from Kieran Greene that day. Mr Devally questioned her about her decision to interview him on her own. She had done nothing wrong and defended her decision to take his statement without a colleague in the room. She also pointed out that Kieran's statement was read back to him and that he signed it without raising any issues about how it was taken. He told her that everything in his statement was true and he didn't wish to add anything else or change it in any way at that point. Mr Devally then focused on his client's assertion that he acted alone at all times.

'Mr Greene accounted for having done all that on his own, both the murder and concealment. Is that so?' he asked.

'That's correct, Judge,' replied Detective Sergeant Myles.

'Anything involved in her death, removal, burial, exhumation, dismemberment and disposal was all his doing?'

'Yes.'

'And the subsequent concealment?'

'Yes.'

'There was nobody else around?'

'That's what he said.'

Later that afternoon, the jurors heard about the voluntary statements taken from Kieran Greene after his initial conversation with Sergeant Myles. They were read out in full for the benefit of the jury, with Detective Connolly confirming their contents from the witness box. Afterwards, he told them about the trip to Wexford where he saw what he believed to be a shallow grave, exactly where Kieran told them it would be.

The following morning, Patricia's son Richard assumed his seat on a hard bench outside Court 13. It was a seat he had taken up every day since the beginning of the trial. As a prosecution witness, he wasn't allowed to sit in the body of the court until he had given his own evidence. He cut a lonely figure sitting there day in, day out. His mind wandered. It was always racing. He hadn't enjoyed a decent night's sleep since his mother's death, wondering if he could have prevented all this. There were countless nights where sleep simply didn't come to him. Understandably, he was still trying to come to terms with what had happened. The most frustrating thing was that he still had no idea *exactly* what had happened to his mother. He had been told so many lies he didn't know what to believe anymore.

• • •

A few days before the first anniversary of Patricia's death, Richard convinced his father, who was living with him at this stage, to call Louise. Richard wanted to find out the truth once and for all, so he told his father to call her in the hope of extracting a confession from her. He put her on speaker so that he could secretly record the conversation. Gus pretended he was calling to have a family photo album returned to him. All Patricia's clothes and photos had been destroyed after she was killed, and any letters in her name were burned. Richard suspected this was done as part of the attempted cover-up, to make it look like she'd taken everything with her when she supposedly stormed out of the house a year ago.

Richard brought the charade to an end by cutting across his father during the phone call and demanding the truth from his sister.

'Ask Dad,' she replied. 'Ask him. Tell him to finally tell you the truth and to stop being such a fucking coward.'

'I *have* told him the truth,' was Gus's answer.

'The truth would shock the fucking life out of you,' Louise told her brother before the line went dead.

Richard could never forget finding out about how his mother died and the unspeakable way her body was then so cruelly mutilated. He felt anxious going back to his childhood home after what had happened. Cherished memories made there had been destroyed forever. He often thought about his mother's funeral. It upset him beyond belief. There were people there, quietly moving through the small crowd, saying horrible things about her. They shouldn't have been there. He got angry thinking about how they tried to blacken her name at her own funeral. He decided he would mark her death properly when all this was behind him.

• • •

For now, Richard was solely focused on the trial. He found it draining, both emotionally and physically. He put all his trust in the gardaí, the DPP and the jurors.

While he desperately wanted to be in the courtroom with his family, part of him must have been relieved to be spared the gory details of how his mother's remains were discovered in the mountains. Day six would have been extremely difficult for him to sit through too.

There was no plan to call Richard that day, but again he showed up and sat on the sidelines outside court. Unbeknownst to him, inside the court his mother's character was being torn to shreds and dragged through the mud. The jurors heard how Kieran blackened her name during his cautioned interviews with gardaí. He made outrageous claims about her insulting and beating his kids, her grandkids. He claimed they were all living in fear of her, and he went so far as to accuse her of wanting them all dead, especially her husband.

Richard may have been oblivious to what was being said beyond the two sets of double doors separating him from the courtroom, but his aunts and uncles listened intently to every word. They were horrified by what they were hearing. They couldn't believe this monstrous depiction of their Trisha. Not for the first time during the trial, Colette turned to Rita and just shook her head in disbelief. None of them knew their sister to be an angry person – she didn't have a bad bone in her body. Listening to all these horrible things being said about her really tested their patience. How could he say such things? Rita squeezed her husband's hand and forced herself to stay rooted to her seat, listening with gritted teeth. Her siblings all took the same dignified approach. They just sat there and listened, dumbfounded at what was being said.

Kieran told gardaí that the house was a 'nightmare' for the kids. The family knew better. They knew Trisha idolised her grandchildren. They meant the world to her. There was no way she would beat them and mock them in the way being described here. They really hoped the jurors would see through all these lies. Kieran's gaze never drifted from the floor as his horrible words were read into the record.

The Deputy State Pathologist, Dr Michael Curtis, took the stand that afternoon. Post-mortem evidence is always particularly difficult for loved ones to sit through, and before the jury was brought in to hear his testimony, Rita and the others were told what was in store. Mr Justice McDermott warned them that the evidence might be difficult to sit through and they were told they could wait outside if they so wished. They opted to stay.

The jury filed back in after lunch, and those huddled together in the public gallery braced themselves once more. They had sat through some extraordinary horrors so far, but Dr Curtis's evidence was especially harrowing.

He described the five cuts to Patricia's scalp in excruciating detail. He said 'they went right down to the bone'. To illustrate how deep they were, he said he could fit his fingers between her scalp and skull in one of them. It was a powerful image. Everyone squirmed in their seats at the thought of it. He went on to say the bone had been pushed right into the brain. He suspected she would have suffered brain damage as a result, but he wasn't in a position to say so conclusively because the brain was too far decomposed to examine it properly.

Rita found this part of the trial 'absolutely horrendous' to sit through. The clinical and emotionless delivery of such sensitive evidence is always unsettling for family members. It can come across as cold and dispassionate, but it is never personal. The facts and findings must be delivered clearly and coldly. Rita sat frozen in her seat with a lump in her throat, trying not to cry. She looked over at the dock at one point, and was taken aback by the lack of emotion on the faces looking back at her. Patricia's own daughter. Her granddaughter. It was incredibly hard to listen to, but they just sat there looking completely uninterested, bored even. Kieran never raised his head during the post-mortem evidence. Not once. It was as if he was just trying to tune it all out. Rita couldn't imagine how anyone could do such a thing. It was barbaric.

Kieran initially claimed that he had killed Patricia in self-defence with a hurley. In his revised version of events, he accused

Gus of beating her to death with some sort of iron bar. A child's hurley was taken from the house during the garda search, but there was no forensic evidence to suggest it was the murder weapon. No iron bar or crowbar was ever found either. To that end, Mr Devally asked Dr Curtis under cross-examination if it was possible that the large fracture found on Patricia's skull could have been caused by her falling on a shower step. Dr Curtis told the jury he couldn't absolutely exclude it as a possibility. Mr Devally also asked him if he thought death would have been instant. The pathologist said he believed the survival time would have been shorter rather than longer. A small mercy, Rita thought to herself.

• • •

The trial took its toll on those closest to Patricia. There was wall-to-wall coverage every day – there was just no getting away from it. The latest revelations from Court 13 were splashed across the front pages of the newspapers most days, and TV and radio reports were updated almost hourly, with every report preceded by content warnings. Viewers and listeners were warned that the reports contained distressing details of disinterment and dismemberment. They certainly weren't suitable for young ears or for the squeamish. Patricia's friends back at Beaumont Hospital followed the trial closely, and some attended on their days off. It was always the main topic of conversation in the tearoom. Like Rita and the others, they just couldn't believe what they were hearing and reading about in the news. This wasn't the Trisha they knew and loved. It just didn't tally, and they didn't believe a word of it. They knew better, and they prayed the jury would see through it too.

It wasn't the first time they had prayed for their friend. In September 2017, they held a remembrance mass for her at the hospital chapel. Over a hundred people from all departments attended to pay their respects. They would have loved to do the same at Patricia's funeral, but they didn't hear about it until it was too late. They figured the family wanted privacy, given the circumstances.

Breda was responsible for organising the collections for parting members of staff. She was also the one who organised remembrance masses for colleagues who had passed away. She never thought she'd end up doing both for her dear friend Trisha. Photos of Patricia were displayed outside the chapel, and a book of condolences was opened for people to sign. Breda provided a lovely photo of Patricia in her uniform for the mass leaflet. She looked happy.

• • •

Given the number of accused persons in the dock, and the number of statements taken during the garda investigation, it took weeks for the memos of interview to be read into the record, but it was a faster process than playing the video recordings in full.

From time to time, the Exhibits Officer was called on to fetch a piece of evidence for the jury. As well as the two hacksaws and the hatchet found in the park beside the River Dodder, all the controlled purchases made by gardaí using the receipts found in the car and house were also offered up as exhibits. Among those items was a roll of 'extra-strong black sacks'. Under cross-examination, Detective Garda James Doolin was asked to try to rip one of the bags with his bare hands. It was a struggle. The jurors were also invited to feel the bag for themselves.

All the relevant CCTV footage was also shown during the trial. Sam Lin, the neighbour who had provided gardaí with the hard drive from his security system, took the stand at the end of the second week of the trial.

The dock is located right next to the witness box. There are two routes for witnesses to choose from when they're called to give evidence. They can avoid the glare of those sitting in the hot seat by walking up a ramp at the back of the dock, or they can take the more direct route straight past the accused. Mr Lin opted for the latter. Louise, who had been mostly impassive throughout the opening stages, watched his every step with a scowl on her face.

Mr Lin had nothing but kind words to say about his former neighbours. He knew everyone in No. 66. The younger ones used to play on the street with his son. He described them as 'good neighbours' and 'very nice people'. If his alarm went off, he said, they'd get in touch to let him know. He took the security of his home very seriously, so he always appreciated the heads-up. Other neighbours also spoke kindly of the O'Connors. One of them used to leave her kids with Louise from time to time. She described her as a 'wonderful mother who lived for her children'.

Mr Lin said the first he knew about the case was when gardaí knocked on his door on 13 June 2017, the day after Kieran handed himself in. He told them about his cameras, and they took his details and returned the following day for the hard drive. Little did he know that it would play such a pivotal role in this high-profile trial. Under cross-examination, he confirmed that the O'Connors never spoke to him about his CCTV system. He walked straight past the dock again when he finished giving his evidence. Louise's scowl followed him out the door. The reason behind her dirty looks wasn't immediately obvious. However, a few days later, the jurors heard about her explosive reaction when she found out that one of his cameras could see into their back garden. No wonder she wasn't pleased to see her old neighbour.

Richard finally took the stand on 31 January 2020, over two weeks after the trial started. It was a long walk to the witness box. His sister was closest to him as he gave evidence. She was just over his right shoulder if he cared to look. He didn't.

When asked about his mother during his evidence-in-chief, he told Ms Lacey he had a good relationship with her. She left the house when he was maybe nine or ten, but he said they remained close, especially in later years. He described her as a 'straight shooter' who couldn't stand laziness.

'If you were in the wrong, she would tell you you were in the wrong, and if you needed a kick in the arse, she'd give you one,' he said.

Rita smiled. That was her sister alright.

He told the jurors he moved out of the house at Mountain View Park about twelve years ago, maybe longer. When asked what the situation was like in the house after he left, he said there was a 'fair bit of friction', which he put down to his sister not keeping up with the usual upkeep of the house. He spoke about how he became concerned about his mother when he didn't hear from her on 30 May 2017, his birthday.

He told them about Louise's reluctance to report their mother as a missing person after she had apparently left the house in a rage with her suitcase. He also noted that Kieran didn't open his mouth when he called over to the house to see what was going on. Louise did all the talking. Over a week later, he remembered walking to the local Tesco with Kieran. His mother had been missing for almost two weeks at this stage, and he was worried sick. He went through all the possibilities he could think of along the way, but he said 'there wasn't a budge out of Kieran'. All his queries fell on deaf ears. He found that very odd.

Mr Devally was first to his feet after Richard finished giving his direct evidence. He wanted to know what the situation in the house was like after his mother moved back in. Richard said the house was already 'packed', and he accepted that her return made it even more overcrowded. Mr Devally asked him if he thought Louise was 'sharper' than his client. In response, Richard described Kieran as someone who 'listened more than actually contributed', and he said his sister was 'cute enough', adding that he thought the dynamic between Louise and Kieran was 'very odd'.

When asked what his mother was like to live with, he described her as a 'doer'.

'She was a Kilkenny woman. She would always get stuck in. She hated laziness', he said. He said she was an active person, who was physically competent; she was strong, but very small.

When asked how his father was when they reported her as a missing person, Richard said he seemed 'normal enough'.

A few days later, the jurors heard about a laptop that was seized from the house on 21 June 2017. Stephanie's barrister, Garnet Orange SC, asked Detective Garda Gary Collins about it. Mr Orange said it belonged to his client, and he wanted to know what was found on it. Detective Garda Collins said he was given a copy of the computer's hard drive to analyse. He was mainly concerned with any activity on the laptop from the night Patricia was killed, 29 May 2017. Two email accounts were associated to it. One belonged to Stephanie, and the other was linked to another family member. That was easily explained – the laptop belonged to Stephanie, but everyone in the house had access to it. A scan of the device's browser history revealed it was mostly used to access websites associated with anime cartoons. YouTube was frequently visited too. Detective Collins agreed with Mr Orange that the laptop 'went quiet' at 6.07 p.m. on the evening of 29 May. He said it remained dormant for just over three and a half hours. The next time it was used was at 9.40 p.m. that night. It was 'revived' again half an hour later. Again, YouTube and anime cartoons were viewed. Mr Orange asked the detective about later searches, and he was told there was a search for job vacancies at Penneys in Dundrum at 11.05 p.m. Dropbox was signed into a few minutes later, and a CV was downloaded from a personal account linked to Stephanie on the cloud storage device. The CV was emailed to Penneys at 11.09 p.m.

The jury spent the next few days watching CCTV evidence of the various comings and goings at 66 Mountain View Park on the day of the alleged murder.

The first major legal hurdle arose in the fifth week of the trial. Kieran's defence team wished to focus on the renewed statement made by their client in December 2017. The jury had already been told that Kieran claimed it was Gus, not him, who killed Patricia. During some legal argument in the absence of the jurors, Mr Devally indicated his side's intention to rely on what Kieran said to gardaí while awaiting trial in Cloverhill prison, as opposed to the initial statements he made after handing himself in six months beforehand. Because of his guilty plea, Gus had essentially been whitewashed from the prosecution's case. The jury still wasn't aware of his plea. As far as they were concerned, the only significant reference to Patricia's husband was in relation to his role in reporting her as a missing person on 1 June 2017.

Mr Devally wanted to question the Senior Investigating Officer, Detective Inspector Brian O'Keeffe, about what he felt was the investigation team's 'failure to rigorously pursue' certain aspects of Kieran's later version of events, particularly his claim that Gus was the one who killed Patricia. He sought to criticise the follow-up investigation in front of the jury. The issue for the court to rule on was whether he should be allowed to put those questions to him in light of Gus's guilty plea. Mr Devally felt the jury should be told that Gus knew his wife was dead when he and Richard reported her as a missing person. Mr Devally believed the follow-up investigation was 'insufficient'. Kieran's accusation was put to Gus, and he denied it in the strongest terms, but Mr Devally didn't think that was good enough. He wanted to plant a seed of doubt in the jurors' minds about who should actually be in the dock for murder. Seeds of doubt can grow into acquittals.

Mr Justice McDermott agreed that the line of questioning was relevant and he accepted that Mr Devally did have a basis on which to explore the issues he raised, but he questioned whether the jury needed to know the full extent of Gus's admission. He wanted to ensure that everyone received a fair trial. In the end, he decided to allow the question to be put to Inspector O'Keeffe, but it was agreed that an edited version of Gus's plea would be put to the jury. They would simply be told that he had admitted a charge of impeding the apprehension or prosecution of Kieran Greene by reporting his wife as a missing person at a time when he knew she was already dead. No other details would be put to the jurors at this stage. Rita and the others would have to wait until Gus's sentence hearing to learn the finer details of what he did or, more important, what he *didn't* do.

When the jury returned to the courtroom, Inspector O'Keeffe confirmed to Mr Devally that Gus was arrested on suspicion of murder in September 2017. After being questioned, he told the jurors, he was released without charge. This was three months before Kieran accused him of bludgeoning his wife to death in the bathroom. Mr Devally then took him in a slightly different direction. He asked him if there was any basis to arrest the others on the back of what Kieran said in his initial statements in June 2017. Inspector O'Keeffe told him there wasn't. Mr Devally then asked him if it was fair to say that he wasn't allowed to re-arrest someone 'on a whim'.

'It has to be lawful,' he added. 'If nothing new comes to light, you can't make the decision to re-arrest someone unless you can convince a judge you have good reason to. Is that correct?'

'Yes, that's correct,' confirmed Inspector O'Keeffe.

Mr Devally was stacking his hand nicely.

'Would new evidence be justification for a re-arrest?' he asked.

'Yes,' replied the witness.

He then quizzed him about what action, if any, was taken in response to the allegations made by Kieran against the others. First, Inspector O'Keeffe told him that the park where Kieran claimed the tools used to dismember the body were dumped was searched. He accepted that they wouldn't have looked in that park if it weren't for this new information. The discovery of the hacksaws and hatchet also helped them to convince a district court judge to give them permission to re-arrest Keith Johnston. Nothing of significance came from the questioning that followed.

Inspector O'Keeffe said that, 'at some point afterwards, Mr Johnston, Louise and Stephanie were all charged with the offences they now stand trial for'. (They were all charged in October 2018.)

Crucially, the jury was now told that Gus was part of the trial until he pleaded guilty to the charge he faced some weeks ago. As per Mr Justice McDermott's ruling, all they were told was that he knew his wife was already dead when he reported her missing, and by doing so, he impeded the apprehension or prosecution of a perpetrator.

Mr Devally concluded his cross-examination by asking Inspector O'Keeffe if Gus had been invited to react on what Kieran said about him.

'He was, yeah,' was the reply. They couldn't take it any further than that, and they didn't.

The prosecution rested its case.

With no more witnesses to be called by the prosecution, the defence teams were then given the opportunity to call their own. As is the case with every criminal trial, they were under no obligation to do so. In fact, at no point during the trial were they required to put forward any type of defence. They didn't even have to cross-examine prosecution witnesses. It's entirely up to the prosecution to prove its case beyond a reasonable doubt. Defence barristers can sit on their hands throughout, if they so wish. Of course, they rarely do, but all accused persons are presumed innocent, and that shield protects them throughout all stages of the process until such time as a jury of their peers finds them guilty.

When the jurors returned to court a few days later, they were told that one of the charges against Keith Johnston had been dropped. In their absence, his barrister, James Dwyer SC, successfully applied to have it withdrawn. Mr Justice McDermott simply told them that, as a result of legal argument, they wouldn't be involved in the decision-making role in relation to the charge. The first charge accusing Keith of refurbishing the bathroom between 31 May and 9 June 2017 in order to conceal evidence was no longer a concern for them. That didn't mean he was free to go. The jury would still have to consider whether he helped his friend to buy various implements used to dismember Patricia, the day before the first body part was found.

With the jury updated, Mr Devally then seized the opportunity to go into evidence by calling his client's mother to the stand. Joan Greene began by telling the jurors that Kieran had a younger sister. She confirmed that he had been living in the family home at Millbrook Lawns in Tallaght, until he moved in with Louise. She said her now 35-year-old son had needed extra help in primary school because when he was about seven he was assessed to be behind his classmates.

Mr Devally then asked her about a guardianship agreement she had entered into with Kieran and Louise in relation to their children. She said she had agreed, if required, to take in her three grandchildren.

Louise's barrister, Michael Bowman SC, asked her to confirm the date she signed the agreement.

'15 September 2017,' she said.

By then, Kieran was in custody after being charged with murder, and Louise had been arrested on suspicion of murder two weeks earlier. They were clearly concerned about their own futures, and plans were afoot to make sure their kids were looked after if they both ended up behind bars.

Mr Dwyer also had a few questions for Kieran's mother on behalf of his client, Keith Johnston. He wanted to know what Kieran's mindset was like when she visited him in prison. She told him she was a bit concerned about his health.

'I noticed he'd lost a bit of weight when I saw him,' she said. 'He was tired and very withdrawn too.'

'Would you say he was paranoid at the time?' asked Mr Dwyer.

'Yeah, I think I would.'

Mr Dwyer was trying to ascertain whether the man who had accused his client of cutting up Patricia was maybe suffering from a mental disorder or having some sort of episode while in prison.

'Was he seeing things?' he asked.

'He wasn't seeing things,' she answered defiantly. 'He was *saying* things.'

After the lawyers were finished asking Mrs Greene questions, she was free to go. She rose from the witness box and made her way back to the public gallery. It was hard not to feel sorry for her as she passed her only son in the dock. She had done no wrong. Kieran's head hung lower than usual while she was giving her evidence just a few feet away.

As she shuffled across the long pew in the public gallery to resume her seat, Mr Devally rested his case. The barristers representing the three others said they wouldn't be calling any evidence, and just like that the trial entered its final stages. After weeks of harrowing evidence, the next step in the process would be closing speeches. All five barristers would be given a final opportunity to address the men and women of the jury before it was entirely out of their hands.

One last pitch.

15.

ALL RISE

In cases where the evidence against an accused person is purely circumstantial, a lot hinges on the closing speeches. Just like a prosecutor's opening address, jurors are always warned that closing speeches are not to be considered as evidence. That said, it's the only opportunity for lawyers to give their opinions on the evidence heard during a trial. The jurors are then free to accept or reject their interpretations of it.

There's a skill to the delivery of parting words to jurors that can't be taught in a lecture hall. To the layman or laywoman, legal proceedings can be overwhelming. The best criminal barristers in the country are the ones who can break down complex legal issues and present them in a way that's easily understood, without coming across as patronising.

Ms Lacey is a highly skilled and experienced legal practitioner. In 2017, just one year after becoming a senior barrister, she successfully defended one of the so-called 'Jobstown Six' before Dublin Circuit Criminal Court. Her client was one of six men accused of falsely imprisoning former Tánaiste Joan Burton TD during a water charges protest in Dublin three years before. But this was to be the biggest test of her career. What made her performance throughout this trial even more impressive was the fact that she took on the case only two months before it got under way, due to Mary Rose Gearty becoming a judge. It was a lot of hard work, but with her junior counsel, Geraldine Small BL, also in her corner, Ms Lacey was confident they could get up to speed quickly. They carved up the towering book of evidence and looked at the complex case from every conceivable angle. Sleep became a luxury during the trial itself. There was barely any time to take stock after a day in court. As soon as the jury was sent home for the evening, they'd have to turn their attention to what was in store for the next day. All their hard work boiled down to these final moments. They were crucial.

It had been a gruelling trial for all involved, and Ms Lacey had to be mindful of that when she sat down to prepare her final speech. She had to find a way to cover all aspects of her case, without overwhelming, and potentially losing, the jurors. Capturing and retaining their full attention was vital. Every word counted. What's more, she also had to predict what her opposite numbers were going to say in their closing speeches. The defence teams aren't given an opportunity to address the jury at the beginning of the trial, but they are given the last word after the prosecutor has spoken at the end. This puts them at a slight advantage. Each of the four defence barristers lined up to Ms Lacey's left would be able to mark her every word. They would then be given an opportunity to challenge everything she said. Once she resumed her seat, she wouldn't have a right of reply. Her only redress would be after the event if she felt something said was inaccurate or needed to be qualified for the jurors. She had to pre-empt their attacks in order to mount a proactive defence. No mean feat.

At 2.17 p.m. on 17 February 2020, Ms Lacey rose to her feet to address the jurors one last time. It had been 33 days, almost to the minute, since she first addressed them. It somehow felt longer.

It was standing room only in Court 13 when the jury returned. In the later stages of the trial, with the end in sight, more and more people started to attend. The press bench was even more crowded than usual. Latecomers squeezed onto the edges of public benches; others stood at the back with battered notebooks in hand. Rita and her siblings took their places. The little red light on the slim microphone in front of Ms Lacey blinked. Pens on the press bench clicked into life. Mr Justice McDermott welcomed the jurors back and invited the prosecutor to begin her address.

Careful not to trespass on the judge's territory, Ms Lacey touched only lightly on some of the legal principles in the case. Mr Justice McDermott would go into greater detail in his final charge to the now six men and five women of the jury. (The sixth woman sworn in to hear the trial had been excused from duty for personal reasons.)

Before diving into the deep pool of evidence heard during the previous six weeks, Ms Lacey reminded the jury of a warning that prefaced all the statements and memos of interview read out during the trial: 'What one accused says about another is not evidence against that other accused.' In other words, Kieran's allegations couldn't be used against the other defendants, and vice versa. Four people were in the dock, but the case was essentially being run as four separate trials. That said, Ms Lacey did later point out that it was the prosecution's case that there was a 'coherent narrative' here, made up of different actors performing different functions, but that they were essentially acting together for a common purpose. She described the whole thing like a 'jigsaw,' with one piece fitting into the other through admissible evidence.

They weren't entitled to speculate, but Ms Lacey told them they could draw inferences from the evidence heard. This would be particularly important when considering whether Louise, Stephanie and Keith knew or believed that Kieran had killed Patricia. Without the ability to read their minds, the jurors would have to try and figure out their mindset through their actions, and the actions of others. A daunting task, no doubt. But Ms Lacey hoped that by the time she had laid out all the pieces of evidence, and attached what she believed to be of significance to them, they would be left with no doubt about each person's knowledge at the time.

Cruelly for Rita and the others, who had once again made the trip to the court, Ms Lacey had to revisit the post-mortem evidence heard during the trial. As Deputy State Pathologist, Dr Michael Curtis was considered an 'expert witness', a status which basically means he's free to give opinions on his evidence; more important, his opinions matter. She focused on his examination of Patricia's head. Dr Curtis described the fractures to her skull as 'full-thickness splits'. This was important, according to Ms Lacey, because it demonstrated the ferocity with which the blows were delivered. They all cut through her skin and went right down to the bone. The presence of crushed blood vessels led Dr Curtis to believe that she was still alive when she was struck. One aspect of his evidence that Ms Lacey really wanted to drill home to the jurors was that Patricia O'Connor had not fought back.

'I want to emphasise this,' she said. 'Despite Dr Curtis's thorough examination, he was in a position to tell you there were no defensive wounds. No evidence of a single defensive wound.'

She paused and let that statement hang in the air for a moment before she moved on. It was a powerful image.

One of the main hurdles for the prosecution to get over was the lack of forensic evidence in the case. Given the deep wounds on Patricia's skull, you'd expect a lot of blood to have been spilled on the bathroom floor. If there had been, there was no evidence of it. John Hoade, the forensic scientist who had searched every inch of the bathroom for traces of blood, found just one small drop between the tiles. They couldn't establish who it belonged to, but it wasn't Patricia's. No blood was found in her bedroom or in the boot of her car either.

To that end, Ms Lacey pointed the jurors to what Kieran said to gardaí the day after he handed himself in. He told them he used hot water and bleach to mop the blood off the bathroom floor. He used tissues too, which he flushed down the toilet when he was finished. He said he also used bleach to clean the floorboards of her bedroom where he lay her body after moving her upstairs. He even scraped between the boards with a plastic blade to remove all the blood. The lack of forensic evidence found in the car was also easily explained by the fact that the boot liner had been removed.

The lack of gore at the site of the shallow grave where Kieran claimed he cut up his girlfriend's mother was another curious feature of the case. Again, not a drop of blood was found. Ms Lacey told the jurors that a cover sheet bought in a DIY store had never been recovered. Perhaps that was placed under the body to avoid leaving any evidence behind. Kieran denied it, and there was no way of proving it, but the jurors were again reminded that they were allowed to draw inferences from the evidence. The purchase of a 'light-duty protection sheet' that was now nowhere to be found was certainly suspicious.

Two crucial pieces of evidence were found in that field, though. Ms Lacey said it was the prosecution's case that the pattern on a piece of fabric found at the grave bore a 'remarkable resemblance in terms of design and pattern' to the one Patricia was seen wearing on 29 May 2017. She was still wearing this 'flowery frock' when she was last seen entering the house from the back at 6.34 p.m. The evidence also supported the prosecution's belief that the strands of hair found at the grave belonged to her too.

Ms Lacey then turned exclusively to the only one of the four facing a murder charge.

'Our case is that Kieran Greene murdered Patricia O'Connor on 29 May 2017,' she declared.

Kieran had put forward two versions of events. His initial account, in which he said he alone beat Patricia to death, was the one pursued by the prosecution. Ms Lacey had to prove beyond a reasonable doubt that Kieran *intended* to kill Patricia, or at least cause her serious harm, when he attacked her with the hurley. In his original statements, he claimed he was acting in self-defence. In Ms Lacey's mind, the evidence just didn't support his contention that he was the victim of an unprovoked attack, but she had to consider that scenario for the jurors in case they believed him. If raised successfully, the claim of self-defence can reduce murder to the lesser charge of manslaughter. It can even result in a full acquittal if the force used is considered to be appropriate to the nature of the attack.

'If you accept she was the aggressor, then you have to consider what actions he took in his defence,' Ms Lacey said. 'There was nobody else in the bathroom, according to him. On his own account, he says he disarmed her, and then repeatedly hit her with the hurley. Multiple blows.'

Kieran was left with a 'little red mark' on his wrist. Patricia was left with three catastrophic injuries. Every inch of her was examined for defensive wounds, and not one was found. If the jurors did somehow believe that Kieran had acted in self-defence, surely they couldn't accept his response was appropriate. Surely he couldn't walk free for what he did? In legal terms, it was the equivalent of bashing a fly with a sledgehammer. Ms Lacey also reminded the jurors that a claim of self-defence couldn't be made in a situation where you disarm someone and then turn the weapon on them in such a way.

Dr Curtis couldn't entirely exclude the possibility that Patricia died after falling over and hitting her head off the shower step. 'But if Kieran was closest to the door,' argued Ms Lacey, 'there was an obligation on him to retreat, and he could have. There were plenty of areas for him to retreat to.'

According to Kieran, there were several others in the house at the time. Ms Lacey wondered why he didn't call for help. She, like many others in the courtroom, found it impossible to accept the suggestion that the only way he could defend himself against a 61-year-old retired grandmother was to beat her to death.

'His defence doesn't hold water. He adopted a highly aggressive stance in a sustained attack that lasted between fifteen and twenty minutes. Why would it take that long if he had disarmed her? He bore her an ill will. He had a bad feeling against her, and we say he wanted to remedy what he described as an intolerable domestic situation.'

Ms Lacey hoped Kieran's self-documented ill will towards Patricia would lead the jurors to conclude that he had had the intent to murder her.

Before the trial got under way the next morning, Mr Devally asked if his client could sit facing the jury. From where Kieran was seated, the jurors could only see his side profile, and he felt he was at a disadvantage at this crucial stage of the process. A chair was brought into the dock and placed next to Keith. Stephanie shuffled a few inches closer to her mother. Everyone in the dock looked even more uncomfortable than usual.

When the jurors were ushered back in, Ms Lacey turned her attention to the prosecution's case against Stephanie. It made sense to deal with her before her mother because the allegations against both of them were inextricably linked. If the jury didn't believe that the figure seen leaving 66 Mountain View Park at 9.34 p.m. on 29 May 2017 was Stephanie disguised as her grandmother, then the case against Louise fell too because she was accused of agreeing to her daughter adopting the disguise.

Stephanie returned to the house with her mother and younger siblings at 9 p.m. As far as the prosecution was concerned, she didn't leave as Stephanie again that night. Throughout the trial, several of the defence barristers put it to various gardaí that a person could actually leave and enter the house from the front without being captured by Mr Lin's camera because part of the driveway is in a blind spot. To do so would involve scuttling along by the front window. Ms Lacey felt they were seeking to inject doubt into this aspect of the case through speculation and hypothesis. She anticipated that this theory would feature in Mr Orange's final address, so she wanted to put it to the sword while she had the chance.

'We say it is simply a suggestion of counsel that she left in that manner. It is an invitation to you to speculate that she left in that way, but their theory implodes when you look at the reality of the case,' she said.

If Stephanie did leave the house like that, she never mentioned it to gardaí in her interviews, and Ms Lacey made sure to remind the jurors of that.

She also reminded them of what Stephanie told gardaí about the alleyway at the side of the house that led to the back garden. In fact, she read from her memo of interview verbatim. When asked if the family used it to access the house from the rear, Stephanie said, 'No, we just don't find the need for it. We use the front door.' Ms Lacey suggested there was 'nothing ambiguous' about her answers. They simply didn't use the alleyway. But, Ms Lacey believed, she used it that night because she knew she would be invisible to her neighbour's front camera.

In due course, the jurors would be provided with the DVD compilation of the CCTV footage from Mr Lin's home security system.

Ms Lacey suggested they compare the footage of Patricia O'Connor from earlier in the day to the clip at 9.34 p.m.

'We say that if you look closely at the manner in which the figure comes down the steps at that time, you'll notice it does so in a sprightly fashion. It's a matter for you to decide, but we say the manner in which this person moves is very different to the deportment of Patricia O'Connor.'

Supposing for a moment that the figure seen leaving the house was Patricia, Ms Lacey wondered aloud about Stephanie's where-abouts at the time she claimed her grandmother 'stormed out' of the house with her suitcase.

After returning from Tesco at 9 p.m., Stephanie told gardaí she heard shouting for maybe ten to twenty minutes. She told them she was watching TV with the kids at the time.

'If that's true,' Ms Lacey said, 'then she's placing herself in the living room for up to twenty minutes after 9 p.m. But that's simply not so.'

On at least two occasions during that 20-minute window, Stephanie was caught on camera in the back garden with Kieran and her mother. She was outside for four minutes the first time, and almost seven minutes the second time.

'This is all lies,' Ms Lacey said. 'She's lying about what she was doing. Her presence in the garden, we say, is evidence tending to show something was being discussed. There's no audio, but you're entitled to infer that much. We say that's where the plan was hatched for Stephanie to leave as Patricia, a plan that was executed to create an illusion that she's still alive when the opposite is the case.'

Ms Lacey urged the jurors to find Stephanie guilty. If, and only if, they did, they would then have to consider if her mother was in on the act. Louise had emerged from the house a minute after the figure with the suitcase left. When asked about it, she claimed she was checking to see which way her mother went. She left the house again less than half an hour later, supposedly to see if her mother was coming back. Taken in isolation, Ms Lacey said her movements might give one 'pause for thought', but she asked the jurors to look at the whole picture. She was so convinced, she claimed, that the figure seen leaving the house at 9.34 p.m. was her mother that she declined an offer to view the footage a second time during her garda interviews. She barely looked at it. She identified herself leaving the house moments later, and again confirmed it was her mother she saw walking up the street, suitcase in hand. Like her daughter before her, Ms Lacey suggested, she was lying:

'She is positive in her assertions, identification and recognition of this person as her mother. There is no margin for error. If you believe that the figure is in fact Stephanie O'Connor, then Louise is lying.'

Once the charade was complete, Ms Lacey said, Stephanie was free to come back in, through the rear door. She finished by saying that Louise's actions were intended to 'prop up the ruse'. With that, Louise bit her lip hard and whispered something angrily from the corner of her mouth.

They were all getting a little restless in the dock. Keith turned to Stephanie for a chat after Ms Lacey started walking the jurors through the many facets of her case against him, a man she described as a 'trusted and integral part of the family'. Something

Keith said to gardaí long before his arrest came back to haunt him once more. He must have been kicking himself for telling them that he had a 'nagging thought' that he could be cleaning up a crime scene when he was carrying out repairs in the bathroom in the days after Patricia went missing. He tried to pass it off as a joke when he was eventually questioned under caution, but he wasn't believed. It certainly wasn't a laughing matter. He even tried to retract his voluntary statement afterwards, claiming he was 'off his bin' on Valium. Keith Johnston might have avoided being prosecuted altogether if he hadn't said that. He probably felt that he was deflecting attention away from him and towards his supposed friend, but in reality, he was doing quite the opposite. Ms Lacey laid out the significance of this 'nagging thought' for the jurors in the simplest of ways: she said the timing of it was important because it *preceded* the shopping spree.

Whatever Keith Johnston said in his interviews, even more significant was what he *didn't* say. In Ms Lacey's words, he was 'remarkably silent' about his shopping spree with Kieran. In his initial voluntary statement, he told gardaí he just went to Homebase to pick up drill bits, screws and tiles to fix the bathroom. When pushed, he told them he 'might have gone to some shops in Nutgrove and Churchtown'. Ms Lacey reminded the jurors that he failed to mention any of the other hardware stores he went to. 'Why the secrecy?' she wondered aloud. Kieran had already handed himself in by the time he spoke to gardaí. If he had nothing to hide, why didn't he tell them at that point? Ms Lacey urged the jurors to really consider the purpose behind this lack of memory.

When gardaí 'refreshed his memory', Keith was left with no choice but to accept he was also in those stores with Kieran. After all, the camera never lies. But while he went so far as to admit he was there helping him out, he insisted he didn't know what the 'items' were to be used for. Ms Lacey suggested that this too was a lie. The type of tools was significant. What did he think they were going to be used for? Kieran Greene was not very handy around the house, and Keith knew it. Ms Lacey reminded the jury how he described his friend as 'useless' when it came to DIY work. He used to buy everything in pound shops, and Keith said himself he wouldn't get Kieran to help him with any odd jobs he did around the house. He told gardaí Kieran 'wasn't a normal bloke'. According to him, he didn't like fishing, football, tools and power tools, and Ms Lacey said he should know. They were friends, after all. Keith went even further with his scathing criticism of Kieran's prowess when it came to manual labour. He said he simply wasn't able for it and 'never worked hard enough to take his top off'.

'So what did Keith think was going on when he purchased all these tools?' asked Ms Lacey. 'Did he not wonder why he was buying all these tools?'

The timing of the shopping spree was also of interest. By 9 June 2017, the repair works in the house had already been carried out. Even if they hadn't, the two men's shopping list on that date didn't tally with the work that was carried out in the bathroom.

Another curious feature of their lengthy shopping list was that they bought two sets of certain items. Two hacksaws, two axes, two pairs of wellies. Ms Lacey described it as 'DIY's version of Noah's Ark'. Why did they need two of everything? Kieran wasn't flush with cash, and yet here he was buying duplicates of expensive tools that he had no legitimate use for.

Ms Lacey found it incredible that Keith 'didn't put two and two together', as he said himself. She said it was 'disingenuous' of him to say he didn't know what Kieran used to dismember Patricia. He knew that she had been missing for eleven days when they went shopping together. He knew Richard and Gus had reported her missing over a week beforehand. If he didn't know exactly what happened to her, he must have had his suspicions. In fact, he did, according to himself. That unfortunate 'nagging thought' he had while carrying out the repair works suggested he had reason to believe she was dead. That belief would be enough.

Ms Lacey also said it beggared belief to think he didn't at least ask his friend what he was up to. When asked why he didn't, Keith simply said he didn't care. To wrap up her case against Stephanie's father, Ms Lacey attacked his credibility:

'His stance is unbelievable to the core,' she said. 'It's just unbelievable that he would accompany him on a shopping trip without asking him what he was doing. It's simply not a credible position. When you look at the evidence, I think you'll have no difficulty in reaching the conclusion that he knew, or believed, that tools were being purchased for the purpose of dismembering Patricia O'Connor.'

Ms Lacey finished her final address to the jurors by accusing all those sitting in the dock of being liars. People lie for lots of reasons, but she felt the lies she accused them of telling could be relied on by the jury. She said she believed the lies showed a 'lack of credibility' that directly related to their guilt. In other words, they told lies to cover for themselves or others.

By now, Ms Lacey had been on her feet for quite some time. Before resuming her seat, she swivelled round to see if her junior counsel Ms Small wanted to add anything. She didn't. The senior counsel had summed everything up clearly. All bases had been covered and she had painted a very clear picture of the prosecution's case against each of the four accused. It was now time for her opposite numbers to make their final pitches to the attentive jurors. Aside from offering the odd peek during the cross-examination of prosecution witnesses, this would be the first time the defence teams revealed their hands.

Mr Devally was first up. He began his speech by describing this case as 'more bloody, more gruesome and more horrifying' than most that came before the court. As if on cue, a howling wind could then be heard swirling around in the ventilation system high above the courtroom. It was so loud, it forced Mr Devally to pause for a moment.

'A ghost in the machine,' he joked.

Mr Devally's instructions were clear. His client had given two accounts of what happened in the house that night, one in June 2017 and the other, six months later, in December 2017. Kieran insisted that his earlier version wasn't true. He claimed that he had agreed to take the fall, but changed his mind. As far as Kieran was concerned, the wrong man was in the dock. He blamed Gus, and he also implicated all the others in the attempted cover-up.

Mr Devally had his work cut out for him. He had to convince the jurors to set aside what Kieran originally said to gardaí, and instead focus on his later account. By criticising the garda investigation and subsequent prosecution, while also portraying his client as someone who couldn't possibly pull off such a brutal crime without some assistance, it was hoped enough question marks would be raised to leave some doubt in the minds of the jurors. Doubt is a defence barrister's best friend. It was a hard sell, though.

The experienced barrister accepted that there were holes in both of Kieran's stories. Ms Lacey was relying solely on the June 2017 version, which laid all the blame for Patricia's murder at Kieran's door, by his own admission. However, Mr Devally accused his opposite number of 'cherry-picking' the pieces of that statement that suited her narrative and ignoring the rest. Lies were exposed in the earlier version. For starters, Kieran told gardaí that he killed Patricia sometime around midnight after she returned to the house. The evidence didn't support that timeline. The prosecution believed she was killed several hours earlier. He also insisted that he had acted alone at all times, and that nobody knew what he did until he confessed. Looking over at the crowded dock, Mr Devally now wondered how that could possibly be true.

'You are being asked to consider as false anything inconsistent with a guilty verdict,' he told the jurors. 'There's an awful lot in the June account that must be false if the prosecution is right, yet you are being asked to treat it as a full confession of murder. You're being asked to rely on it, where it suits, and to reject anything contradictory as lies.'

The June account was riddled with lies. Kieran told gardaí that everyone else was asleep when Patricia returned, but that was 'nonsense', according to Mr Devally. He was also wrong when he said the body parts were scattered across the mountains in six bags and that he ripped them from the bottom. Mr Devally urged the jurors to try and do that with one of the roll of bags that was bought as a controlled purchase. He lied about the disposal of the tools of dismemberment. He didn't dump them up the mountains, as claimed.

Mr Devally then asked the jury whether his client came across as the type of person who could pull off something like this on his own. He reminded them of how Richard had described him as 'nothing but a moron' and a 'fool' in his evidence.

'Remember how Richard and Keith treated him in the back garden in the video clip of them talking?' Mr Devally asked. 'Nobody addresses him. He is detached. He's just part of the furniture. He's a moron, he's useless. Maybe they treat him with some disrespect, maybe he's a bit of a donkey, a beast of burden for the house.'

Mr Devally proposed that nobody else was interested in protecting Mr Greene, and that his state of mind in June 2017 was to ensure that the others didn't get into trouble. He suggested Kieran didn't have the imagination to come up with a story like the one pitched to gardaí when he handed himself in.

'How does he come up with this story?' he asked. 'Do you think it was his idea to get somebody to dress up? We say he was well primed by others.'

Mr Devally contended that the December version was the 'proper story' of what happened that night. Sure, there were some inconsistencies in it; for example, Kieran maintained the fiction that Patricia was killed around midnight. His lies were a bit confusing at times, but Mr Devally suggested that was because he wasn't very good at telling them. He suggested Kieran changed his story because there was no point lying anymore. The reason he lied in the first instance, according to Mr Devally, was so that his children would have a mother and grandfather to take care of them in their home. By December 2017, they'd all been arrested too, so his 'martyrdom' no longer had a purpose, or so he claimed.

'My client was wrongly prosecuted,' he declared.

When looking at both versions, Mr Devally accepted there were lies in both; but he argued that there were more truths in the later version. One of Kieran's claims had even led gardaí to discover the hacksaws and hatchet supposedly used to dismember Patricia's disinterred body.

'December is still messed up,' he said, 'but there's an awful lot of truth in it.'

He criticised the detectives for what he claimed was their failure to thoroughly investigate the allegations made by his client from prison. He suggested they had a man with a confession and just 'nailed it down' that he was the murderer. Case closed. By doing so, Mr Devally told the jurors, it was difficult for them to get justice for Patricia O'Connor.

Turning his attention to Gus, Mr Devally wondered if there was a reason he didn't go to the park with the others on the evening in question. He was caught coming back later in the night with Sammy the dog.

'Maybe Gus had to take the crowbar with him. Someone had to dispose of that.'

Despite telling gardaí that he went to bed soon after returning to the house, Mr Devally said the CCTV was 'peppered with sightings' of Gus later that night. The light in his bedroom didn't go off until 1.05 a.m. At this time, Mr Devally said Kieran was supposed to be 'acting solo' in the disposal of the body. Nobody else knew, apparently. Mr Devally said he didn't believe that was the case. He said he believed Gus was 'intimately involved'.

Not surprisingly, given that he had specifically asked the pathologist the question earlier in the trial, Mr Devally also asked the jurors to consider the possibility that the blow to the back of Mrs O'Connor's head was consistent with her falling onto a step. Dr Curtis couldn't rule that out.

Before concluding his address, Mr Devally again asked the jurors to look at his client. With Kieran looking doe-eyed over his shoulder, he asked them to remind themselves of the evidence his mother gave on his behalf.

'He's not very bright,' Mr Devally said. The court would break for the day when he was finished, so he wanted his final words to really hit home.

He continued: 'When the gardaí were interviewing him, they treated him as if he was slow and not the full shilling. He's the donkey. The others will sit on their backsides and let him take the kids to school because that's what Kieran does.

'He then reaches a point where he knows all the sacrifice he made isn't working and he knows he's no longer able to protect his children from their mother being prosecuted. Even if you prefer the June account, you can't discount as possible that when he comes forward in December, it's because he wants to tell the truth. His whole reason for hiding what happened is gone. It's a very distinct possibility that he was persuaded to act the way he did. And in doing so, he is being condemned for that which he did not do.

'There are two accounts, ladies and gentlemen. One is full of truths, the first one is not. None of what he says in his earlier version has been corroborated.

'He's such a sap. He's described as a moron, and yet here he is, Machiavelli himself. A mastermind. It doesn't add up and I suggest it should compel you to acquit him of murder.'

Louise grunted and shook her head when she heard Mr Devally's closing remarks, but she had resumed her composure by the time he resumed his seat. Her daughter's barrister would make his final pitch in the morning.

For his opener to the jury the next day, Mr Orange borrowed the opening line from a famous nineteenth-century novel.

'All happy families are alike; each unhappy family is unhappy in its own way,' he said.

The line, taken from Leo Tolstoy's 1878 masterpiece *Anna Karenina,* was brilliantly appropriate. At over 800 pages, the novel is a long read with multiple complex characters. It deals with themes of betrayal, family and marriage.

It's an attention-grabber of an opening line, and Mr Orange certainly had his audience's undivided attention.

Stephanie giggled when her lawyer described her as 'the girl with the odd-coloured hair'. Ice blue was the colour of choice on this bitterly cold February morning.

Mr Orange continued his address by pointing out the obvious to the jurors: 'none of us were present in the house that night, and yet you're being asked to come to very firm and clear conclusions as to what happened there. You have to rely on evidence and words from people outside the house.'

He spelled out to them in no uncertain terms how serious their job was, by telling them their decision 'would affect the fate of a complete stranger'.

He then focused his attention on the complete stranger he was representing. He said that much of the prosecution's case against Stephanie was based on a circular logic: *post hoc ergo propter hoc*. Those five little words drew puzzled looks from the jurors. The literal translation of the informal Latin fallacy is 'after this, therefore because of this'. It arises when a person reasons that because one event happened after another, the first event caused the second.

One famous example involves Brazilian football legend Pelé, who believed a rare dip in form was the result of him giving his match shirt to a fan. Pelé became so convinced that the events were linked that he sent his friend out to find the shirt. After it was returned to him, his form quickly recovered, cementing his belief that it had been the cause of his poor performances. What his friend failed to tell him was that he couldn't actually find the original match shirt – the one he returned to Pelé was a replica.

Mr Orange used an example closer to home to enlighten the jurors. He reminded them of the 'soft landing' our politicians promised us in 2007, just before the Irish economy entered severe recession.

'We thought we were well set up. Most of us bought into that,' he said. 'We believed our politicians, and they believed the experts. Why? Because it suited.'

With that in mind, he asked them to be careful when assessing the prosecution's case against Stephanie.

As anticipated by Ms Lacey, he also reminded the jurors that the CCTV footage from Mr Lin's property only covered 'a third, maybe a quarter' of the garden, and they couldn't therefore exclude the possibility that other people had come and gone during the night. For example, Patricia was seen earlier in the day dragging a wheelie bin up the side of the house, but she wasn't captured going into the house.

'Great care must be taken in relation to the CCTV,' he urged.

He told the court that the defence only became aware after the trial started that the investigation team had sought a height analysis report in relation to the figure seen leaving the house with the suitcase. If such a report was compiled, its findings were not called as evidence by the prosecution.

'Why?' he wondered. 'Perhaps it was because it didn't suit them, so they chose not to use it or disclose it.'

He said it was 'simply impossible' to identify who leaves the house at 9.34 p.m. on the night in question.

'Ms Lacey told you the fabric found at the grave *matched* the clothing worn by Patricia O'Connor. That's all well and good, except for the fact that another garda noted that Stephanie quibbled that it wasn't the same.'

This, according to Mr Orange, was 'confirmation bias'. He warned the jury against blindly accepting it was a match, and to instead look at all the evidence before making their minds up one way or the other. *Post hoc ergo propter hoc.*

In relation to the computer evidence presented late in the trial, Mr Orange accused the prosecution of ignoring the fact that it actually supports Stephanie's case in relation to her state of mind on the night. There were no Google searches for alibis or how to dispose of a body. She was looking at anime cartoons at 10.10 p.m. An hour later, she was applying for a job. He suggested her online activity was not in line with someone who knew there was a dead body, and a murderer, in the house.

If the jury were to believe that a plan had been hatched to disguise his client as her grandmother, Mr Orange said, 'it requires the assumption that everyone involved in the so-called plot actually had the same understanding as to what was happening, or what had happened.' This was the fallacy at the heart of the case against Stephanie.

Did she really know what happened? Kieran Greene claimed she did, but the jurors couldn't use his words against her. That said, it's hard to ignore something when it's said. Mr Orange was conscious of that threat and suggested that Kieran became obsessed that his girlfriend was back with her ex, Keith Johnston, and just lashed out in every direction, bringing everybody's house tumbling down. His view was that Kieran didn't care about the collateral damage of his actions.

'I suggest to you, these are lies and should play no part in your deliberations. Six months had lapsed. We don't know what was going on in his mind while he was in prison. Even if he wanted to tell the truth, he still managed to get the details wildly wrong.'

Mr Orange asked the jurors to consider a number of key questions in relation to his client.

First, he asked them to consider *when* Patricia died. He said that the only thing they could be absolutely certain about was that she died sometime between her last sighting on the CCTV footage at 6.35 p.m. on 29 May 2017 and the afternoon of 10 June 2017, when the first body part was found.

If the jury believed that Stephanie was the one seen leaving the house 'in disguise' at 9.34 p.m., they would have to be convinced beyond a reasonable doubt that her grandmother was dead at that stage and, crucially, that Stephanie knew she was dead.

In Mr Orange's opinion, there were three possibilities in relation to a potential time of death. Patricia could have been killed between the time she was last seen going into the house at 6.35 p.m. and the time the others left for the park at 6.53 p.m., but that would involve the act being carried out in a crowded house with young children around. Also, it was inconceivable that they would have headed off to the park like that if they had seen their grandmother being bludgeoned to death in front of them. If they did, they showed no signs of concern as they were leaving.

The second possible timeframe was between 6.53 p.m. and when Gus left three minutes later.

Mr Orange's final suggestion was that Patricia was killed sometime after Gus left the house and 9.04 p.m., when everyone returned from the park.

If Kieran was the only one with blood on his hands, Mr Orange asked the jurors to consider at what stage Stephanie became aware that her grandmother was dead. He strongly suggested that if she only found out she was dead when she returned to the house with the others, then she would have had very little time to process everything before supposedly emerging from the house in disguise.

On that point, Mr Orange again warned the men and women of the jury to be wary of the 'frailties of the CCTV at the front', because it didn't cover the porch. He also criticised Ms Lacey for her comments in relation to Patricia's stature. The prosecuting barrister had suggested that Patricia was heavier than the person seen walking down the steps at 9.34 p.m., but Mr Orange said her remark ignored the evidence of her son, who described his mother as 'stocky'. He suggested the build of the figure was very much open to interpretation.

Mr Orange also claimed that his client knew Mr Lin's cameras covered their back garden, and he criticised the prosecution for not revealing that in evidence. If she knew about the camera, he wondered why she would have allowed herself to be viewed walking in the back door carrying the very same prop that had been used to set up the charade in the first place.

'How convenient of her to drop the ball in such spectacular fashion,' he said.

To cover all bases before he concluded, Mr Orange had to address the possibility that the jury believed the figure was Stephanie. If that was the case, he asked them to consider whether she in fact knew that Kieran had killed her grandmother.

'Could she have known?' he asked. 'Is there any evidence that she even saw the body? She was just nineteen. She described herself as an "airhead" in her interviews.

'Where would that information have come from? Kieran? If so, is it likely he told them as soon as they came back to the house? Is it more likely that he told them the same thing he told gardaí, that he killed her in self-defence?

'If she was working on the belief that Kieran was innocent in a criminal sense, then that must call into question what the prosecution wants you to believe in relation to the plot to cover it up.'

As if to muddy the waters even further, Mr Orange also asked the jurors to think about Gus. He asked them to question what compelled Gus and Louise to get involved, and he again reminded them of Stephanie's young age at the time, suggesting she would have been taking instructions from others.

To conclude, Mr Orange borrowed another very appropriate line from another famous novel. This time, Harper Lee's *To Kill a Mockingbird*. 'You never really understand a person until you consider things from his point of view ... until you climb into his skin and walk around in it.'

Mr Orange told the jurors that was the essence of his case *if* they believed the figure on the steps was Stephanie.

'You must consider her state of mind at the time, and look at what she was, and wasn't, aware of,' he said, before passing the baton to Louise's barrister, Mr Bowman.

Mr Bowman is one of the most successful criminal barristers in the country, and it's easy to see why. The skill set required to prosecute a case is clearly very different from that needed to defend one, and only the best of the best are equipped to handle both corners effectively.

Mr Bowman has an affable way of presenting a case that puts witnesses at ease and endears him to jurors. As the lead prosecutor in the high-profile 'Mr Moonlight' trial of 2019, he gave a masterclass in how to successfully prosecute complex cases where the only available evidence is circumstantial. The trial, which led to Tipperary farmer Patrick Quirke being found guilty of murdering his former lover's boyfriend, a local DJ called Bobby 'Mr Moonlight' Ryan, was at that time the longest murder trial in the history of the State. Mr Bowman's performance throughout the thirteen-week trial was even more impressive given the strength of the defence team fighting Mr Quirke's corner.

His friendly and good-natured manner extends beyond the floor of the courtroom, but underestimate his tenacity as a defence barrister at your peril. He is forensic in his approach to evidence, and if the need arises, his cross-examination of key witnesses can be brutal.

To open his final pitch on behalf of Louise, Mr Bowman asked the jurors to exercise great caution in their approach to the evidence relating to her. He described it as 'very different' from the cases faced by the others, in that it all came down to interpretation. He said the case against her could be 'straightforward or very complex', depending on how you looked at it. He remarked on how little time Ms Lacey spent summing up her case against Louise. Fifteen minutes, according to his watch. He said that could be perceived in one of two ways. It was either a 'slam dunk' case for the prosecution that didn't need to be expanded any further, or the evidence simply wasn't there. He preferred the latter.

'There's no smoking gun or forensic evidence pointing to her guilt,' he reminded the jurors.

He described his client as a 'homeless mother of five, who suffers from Graves' disease', but he advised them to put their personal views to one side.

Before drilling into the evidence, he said that the prosecution's case was based on inferences, and he reminded the jurors that there was no room to speculate. He also reminded them that she had no case to answer *unless* they were satisfied that her daughter, Stephanie, was the hooded figure seen leaving 66 Mountain View Park at 9.34 p.m.

Louise was charged in circumstances whereby she knew, or believed, that the father of three of her children had murdered her mother.

'Mere presence is not enough,' he said. 'To convict her, you must be satisfied that she did something with intent, and without reasonable excuse, to impede the apprehension or prosecution of Kieran Greene, in that she agreed, or acquiesced, in her daughter engaging in this supposed ruse.'

In relation to his client, 29 May 2017 was 'the only date in town', according to Mr Bowman. He reminded them that Louise maintained that the first she learned of what had happened to her mother was when Kieran told her what he did just before he handed himself in on 12 June 2017. She said she 'collapsed in a heap' when he told her. Mr Bowman asked where was the evidence that she had prior knowledge?

'You're being asked by the prosecution to take a giant leap of faith. Don't rely on your gut.'

He then turned his attention to the CCTV evidence from the rear of the house, which he asked the jurors to examine closely. The prosecution claimed that the plan to disguise Stephanie as her grandmother was hatched during conversations between her and her mother in the back garden after they returned from the park. Ms Lacey had shown the jurors two clips, one at 9.04 p.m. and another longer one at 9.08 p.m.

Mr Bowman claimed that it was impossible even to make out whether Louise and Stephanie were talking to one another in the clips. He criticised the quality of the footage, and said one simply couldn't tell if either of their mouths were moving. In fact, the only way he could tell Louise was having a cigarette was the smoke billowing into the night sky, and even then he had to speed up the footage to see it. Louise told gardaí she'd often sit in silence outside on the swing in the back garden.

'Perhaps that's what's happening here,' suggested her barrister.

Mr Bowman questioned Richard's claim that his sister tried to dissuade him from reporting their mother as a missing person. She claimed that simply didn't happen. In Louise's mind, Richard blamed her for his mother's death. In Mr Bowman's words, he was also a 'tad judgemental' when she moved back to the house after the gardaí were finished with it. 'Where was a mother of five with no alternatives supposed to go?' he wondered. He also put forward the proposition that perhaps Richard allowed his view of Louise to influence what he said in the case. He clearly felt she should have moved out years ago to give their mother some peace.

In Kieran's renewed statement to gardaí from prison in December 2017, he implicated Louise in a number of ways. Not only did he say she knew what happened on the night, he even told them she directed him to get the body out of the house, and also helped him by cleaning up the bathroom where her mother was killed. Mr Bowman rubbished this statement as being motivated by 'paranoia and jealousy', and he urged the jurors not to let it contaminate their deliberations in relation to his client.

To conclude, he submitted to the eleven jurors who would ultimately decide Louise's fate that the pieces of circumstantial evidence in relation to the case against her might 'grind up' against their suspicions, but in his opinion, they could never get beyond the high standard of proof required. He suggested that they couldn't rely on the CCTV evidence taken from the back of the house. Focusing his attention to lies Louise had told gardaí, Mr Bowman said, 'lies can only help if you're satisfied they're told for no other purpose', and he wondered if there was possibly another explanation for the untruths she told. Perhaps she was trying to protect her daughter.

'You simply cannot be sure beyond a reasonable doubt,' he said with conviction, before urging them to acquit.

Keith Johnston's barrister, James Dwyer SC, had waited days for his opportunity to make his final submissions. Now was his chance. He began by saying that the case against his client was 'full of speculation'. By now, the jurors knew that 'speculation' was a bad word in criminal trials. To find his client guilty, the jurors would have to climb into his skin on 9 June 2017 and walk around in it. They would have to be satisfied, beyond a reasonable doubt, that he knew, or at least believed, what his friend had done, and what he planned to do.

'The truth is, we have no idea what he knew at the time. This is classic speculation,' Mr Dwyer said.

'What Kieran said in his interviews can't be used against my client. You can't consider his statements at all when considering the case against Keith Johnston. There might be a temptation to use them to fill in blanks, or as a framework to slot evidence against him into, but you must not do so,' he warned.

Like Mr Bowman before him, he sought to toss Kieran's December statement into the shredder. He pointed to the many holes in his renewed version of events, which placed his client as the central figure in the grisly dismemberment of Patricia O'Connor. For starters, Kieran said the motivation for his updated confession was the guardianship agreement that had been put in place with his mother. Mr Dwyer said that was agreed three months beforehand and suggested his excuse didn't hold water. He also believed that his actions were motivated by the fear that his client had renewed his relationship with the woman Kieran still referred to as his girl-friend. His first-ever girlfriend, at that.

Kieran also claimed that Keith had told him he'd have to take the blame because Keith had a 'background in drugs'. Mr Dwyer pointed out that his client didn't have a criminal record at all. He also told the jurors that Keith's mobile phone was pinging off a mast near his home at the time Kieran claimed he was hacking up a body in a field in County Wexford. Granted, the trusted handyman he was representing wasn't on trial for disposing of the body, but Mr Dwyer felt it was important to challenge Kieran's accusations, just in case they contaminated the jury's analysis of the evidence.

'When is he supposed to have learned of the killing?' Mr Dwyer asked. 'We don't have trial by telepathy. Keith Johnston says he found out on Monday, 12 June 2017 – the same time as everybody else, and there is no evidence to suggest otherwise.'

Of course, the prosecution was relying on that 'nagging thought' that Keith had while he was working on the bathroom. That wasn't enough to establish belief, according to his lawyer. In relation to the 'sneaky look around' the house that Keith admitted to taking after suddenly thinking he could be cleaning up a crime scene, Mr Dwyer suggested that wasn't the action of a man who knew, or believed, that a brutal murder had taken place, especially when the man now accused of doing it is still in the house.

In relation to the shopping spree on 9 June 2017, Mr Dwyer said his client could not have been more open about what was being bought in the various hardware stores. He even allowed himself to be recorded on CCTV. In Mr. Price, he didn't even put the purchased items into bags to hide them. The saws bought in B&Q were just carried out of the shop, again not hidden in bags.

Mr Dwyer said that much had been made of the fact that two of each item was bought, 'DIY's version of Noah's Ark,' as Ms Lacey put it, but he said the significance of that was lost on him. Perhaps it was being suggested that two people participated in the act of dismemberment, but again Mr Dwyer reminded the jury that there was no evidence of his client being in Wexford later that night. Also, Richard mentioned that axes were used to chop wood in the household. 'Maybe Keith thought that's what they were to be used for,' Mr Dwyer said.

He also rejected the claim that his client was acting in concert with the only one on trial for murder. He claimed the CCTV footage didn't support that because Kieran did all the purchasing, and he also went on to buy other things, such as gloves, without Keith. After he did so, he then removed the baby seat out of the back of Patricia's car, presumably to make room for the transportation of the body later. Again, this was done out of Keith's sight. Mr Dwyer urged the jurors to ask why, and offered them his own opinion:

'Keith didn't know, and Kieran didn't want him to know. He was kept in the dark about everything, including the clean-up. He simply didn't know what Kieran was planning on this gruesome trip,' he said.

According to Mr Dwyer, the prosecution's contention that Keith told lies to gardaí didn't hold water. He simply couldn't remember all the shops they went to when he gave his voluntary statement in June 2017. Not mentioning them was suspicious, but only significant if he knew what Kieran was planning to do with the axes and hacksaws he bought. Mr Dwyer claimed the prosecution accused his client of being 'silent as a tomb' on the issue after his arrest, but he insisted Keith was the one who said he went to Woodie's DIY and B&Q, without prompting. He 'volunteered' that information, according to the senior barrister.

To conclude, he implored the jury to look at the evidence dispassionately, and to only focus on the evidence relating to his client.

'This is a gruesome case,' he said. 'A gruesome crime was committed. An enormous investigation was launched. They cast their net wide, to all people connected with the house. Look at Keith's movements. Sure, you might think there is cause to be suspicious, but scrutinise the evidence. If you do, I believe you'll see the evidence just isn't there.'

With closing speeches now out of the way, all that was left to do was for Mr Justice McDermott to explain the relevant law to the jurors and summarise the facts of the case.

He told them they could consider whether self-defence was an issue in the case. In other words, if they believed Kieran's June version of events, they would have to consider if he *intended* to kill or cause serious harm. If they believed he used more force than was reasonably necessary, then, he said, they *must* find him guilty of murder. Manslaughter would only come into it if Kieran had used only the force necessary in the circumstances. Mr Justice McDermott said the issue of self-defence depended very much on their assessment of the statements made by Kieran Greene.

He warned them that Gus's admission at the beginning of the trial was totally irrelevant to them. Quite simply, it wasn't to be used as evidence in the case. He also warned them to treat each of the accused separately, and he reminded them that the case had been run as a joint trial, and that it was essentially four separate trials they were being asked to consider.

Again, he warned them against using something one accused said against another as evidence relating to that other defendant. This was particularly relevant to Kieran's statement from prison. It was a warning the jurors had been given repeatedly throughout the trial. He also echoed the words of each of the barristers in the case when he asked them to leave their emotions outside the jury room, and to just carry out a 'clinical analysis of the evidence, based solely on the evidence'.

The prosecution relied on lies told by each of the accused during their interviews, but Mr Justice McDermott told the jurors that people lie for all sorts of reasons, 'including shame, a desire to conceal disgraceful behaviour, or out of panic or confusion'. In order for it to stick, he said the prosecution had to prove there was no innocent explanation for the lie.

In Kieran's case, the judge said there were three potential verdicts available: he could be acquitted, found guilty of murder, or not guilty of murder but guilty of manslaughter.

In relation to the others, he said they could be either acquitted, found guilty of impeding Mr Greene's prosecution for murder, or guilty of impeding his prosecution for manslaughter.

And then, just like that, after three days of closing speeches on top of five weeks of evidence, the jurors retired to their jury room with the judge's final words ringing in their ears. The court registrar glanced at the clock as they shuffled out of the courtroom: 'The jury retires at 3.15 p.m.,' she announced.

Kieran raised his gaze from the floor to watch them leave. The others also followed their exit. All they could do now was wait.

16.

VERDICTS

Sitting through the harrowing evidence heard during the trial was extremely upsetting for Rita and Patricia's other siblings. They listened to excruciating detail about the unspeakable violence visited on their beloved sister; unspeakable violence that was given a voice in open court.

Listening to her sister's name being blackened throughout proceedings was distressing enough, but knowing who had spoken all those despicable lies kept Rita awake at night. Trisha was depicted as some sort of monster, a violent bully who smoked weed and terrorised everyone in that house, including her grandchildren, whom Rita knew she adored. The lies spewed out of the mouths of people who should have loved her and been grateful for all she did for them: even her own daughter, Louise, and the apple of her eye, Stephanie. Rita was sure they were all guilty. It was written all over their faces. She just hoped the jury had been convinced too.

Waiting for a jury to make up its mind is the most gruelling part of the process, not just for the ones whose freedom hangs in the balance, but for those seeking justice for loved ones from the public gallery. Richard was spared the opening weeks of the trial as he was forced to wait outside the courtroom until he had given his evidence. Experiencing the whole ordeal from the outside brought its own anguish, though. His wife, Martina, was a rock to him throughout. As they, like his aunts and uncles, waited for the white smoke, they comforted one another and tried to lift each other's spirits. Time moved slowly.

The jury returned to Court 13 at 4.53 p.m. on the first day of their deliberations, having spent just under one hour and forty minutes considering the evidence. They were asked if they had reached any verdicts in relation to any of the accused. The jury forewoman told the registrar they hadn't, so they were sent home for the evening with the familiar warning from Mr Justice McDermott not to discuss the case with anyone. The rules are clear: during this time, jurors can only talk to other jurors about the case. All discussions must take place in the privacy of the jury room and when all jurors are present. They may bring whatever notes or exhibits they require into the jury room, but whatever is said within those four walls must stay within those four walls.

The journey back to Kilkenny that evening was a quiet one. Everyone was exhausted, both mentally and physically.

The next day was equally draining. It was an odd adjustment. The courtroom was usually a buzz of activity, but time seemed to stand still now. The waiting game was tedious. Journalists took it in turns to keep watch. The aroma of strong coffee from the press bench filled the room. Kieran had to wait in his holding cell downstairs, but the others were free to mill around the building. They were told not to stray too far, though.

After a long day of hanging around, the jury returned to court at 4 p.m. The forewoman handed the issue paper to the registrar. By now, they'd been deliberating for just under four and a half hours, and they wanted to go home. Mr Justice McDermott thanked them for their work and asked them to return to court at 10.30 the following morning. Laptops and notepads were rammed back into briefcases as the press pack prepared to head home. The jurors were also getting up to leave when the registrar noticed that a count had been entered on one of the boxes on the issue paper, which lists all the charges faced by the accused. The judge called the jurors back and asked them to take their seats again.

The sound of laptop bags unzipping ripped around the court-room as the registrar asked the forewoman of the jury if they had reached a verdict, upon which they were all agreed, on any of the counts. To everyone's surprise, she nodded. 'Yes, we have,' she replied. Rita's husband squeezed her hand. Richard braced himself.

'You say that Kieran Greene is *guilty* of murder. Is this a verdict of you all?' she asked.

'Yes, it is,' was the reply.

Kieran Greene barely flinched. He looked just as glum and despondent as he had throughout the long trial. He must have known his fate had been sealed a long time ago. That said, it's not uncommon for a person to give little or no reaction when they're convicted of murder. In fact, most don't. Deep down, many are prepared for it; others go into shock.

Relief was clearly etched on the faces of Patricia's loyal son and her siblings. Much as they wanted to express their feelings, there were no whoops of delight. It wasn't the time or place. They all responded to the verdict with the same dignity with which they had carried themselves throughout. Rita cracked a smile. She was entitled to it. A little smile for Trisha. She had prayed so hard for justice. That's all she wanted. That's all they all wanted. Nothing would bring her back, but they wanted those responsible to pay for what they did.

The jury was sent home for the evening, but they still had plenty of work to do.

One down, three to go.

After convicting Kieran of murder, the jurors then turned their attention to the case against Stephanie O'Connor. Louise looked anxious throughout the day. Aside from being concerned about her daughter's fate, she knew the next decision made by the jury would greatly affect her own future. If her daughter was acquitted, she knew she'd walk free too. That afternoon, again just a few minutes after 4 p.m., the jury returned from its deliberations.

After eight hours and thirty-six minutes, they found Stephanie *guilty* of impeding the apprehension or prosecution of Kieran Greene, knowing or believing him to have murdered Patricia O'Connor on 29 May 2017. Clearly, they believed that she was the figure seen leaving the house disguised as her grandmother at 9.34 p.m. on the night of her murder. For the first time during the trial, Keith Johnston became visibly upset in the dock beside his daughter. Louise closed her eyes. Her jaw tightened. It was hard to know if she was more devastated at her daughter going to prison or at the prospect of potentially following her. The case against her was still very much live.

Mr Justice McDermott told the jury they could continue their deliberations that afternoon, but they wanted to go home.

There was no objection to Stephanie being remanded on continuing bail after she was convicted. A date had yet to be set for her sentence hearing – it was decided to wait until everyone had been dealt with before looking at dates. Bizarrely, she returned to court the following day. She seemed in high spirits too, laughing and joking outside the courtroom before the third day of deliberations got under way.

Louise didn't have long to wait. She was convicted for her role just two hours later, again by unanimous verdict. She barely blinked.

And then there was one.

After Louise's departure, Keith was left all on his own in the dock. His brother sat beside him after the jury went back out to decide his fate.

One of his lawyers, Kieran Kelly BL, made a last-ditch effort to have the jury discharged on the grounds that an article published the day after Kieran Greene's conviction was prejudicial to his client.

Ms Lacey disagreed. Having read the article, which reported that Kieran 'begged' neighbours for a saw shortly after Patricia's murder, Ms Lacey said there was no mention of Mr Johnston in the piece. She also said there was nothing in the case about what was contained in the article. She argued that the application was 'extreme' and insisted that the jury could be relied on to bring in an impartial verdict.

Mr Justice McDermott agreed with the prosecutor. The jury had been repeatedly warned that media coverage of the trial was irrelevant. Understandably, the case had attracted a lot of media attention, and the numbers on the press bench had increased as the weeks went by; but Mr Justice McDermott felt the coverage to date had been of 'the highest professional standing and accuracy'. In relation to the controversial article, he said there was no factual connection to be drawn between what was said in the article and what happened some nine days later in various shops in Tallaght.

Keith stayed where he was, but not for long. The jury convicted him the following morning. After deliberating for just over twelve hours, their work was finally done. Mr Justice McDermott thanked them for sitting through what he described as 'a difficult and long case'. He said it had been difficult in so many ways, and thanked them for their service, before excusing them from duty for the rest of their lives.

Patricia's sisters wiped away tears and embraced each other outside the courtroom after Keith was found guilty. It had been such a long road. There were plenty of whoops and cheers back at Beaumont Hospital too when news filtered through to Patricia's former colleagues. They were delighted. Maybe now she can finally rest in peace, Breda thought.

With all five now convicted, Rita and her sisters felt the shackles were off and they could finally voice the opinions they'd been sitting on since the day Valerie got the dreaded knock on the door.

In the middle of a little huddle in the heart of the great hall of the CCJ, Rita told a handful of reporters that it was 'disgusting' to think that someone could put down their own mother the way Louise had.

Her older sister, Anne O'Sullivan, said, 'Trisha was a country girl at heart. She wanted to move back to Kilkenny with us, but they wouldn't sell the house.'

Before they left, they handed over a brief statement to the gathered media. It read:

> Finally, justice has been served for our beautiful sister who met her demise through tragic circumstances. She was the most kind and caring and loving grandmother, sister and mother. She was a hardworking woman who loved to share her care and kindness with all. It has been a very tough seven weeks sitting in that courtroom looking at the people who took our sister for their own selfish reasons. The effect on the family who found the first body parts of Patricia – we are so sorry you had to endure part of our pain, and we thank you for co-operating and helping the guards in every way you could. All the legal teams and witnesses, guards, army and civil defence, we thank you for all your help and participation. We can't thank you enough.

And with that, they all made their way back to Kilkenny. Richard didn't say much as he left the courthouse. He wanted to wait until the sentence hearing to say his piece. They'd all be back for it in April, or so they thought.

• • •

The sentence hearing was set for 20 April 2020, but by then the country, and indeed the whole world, was in the grips of the

Covid-19 pandemic. On that date, Kieran appeared before Mr Justice McDermott via a live video link from prison. The four others, all of whom were still on bail, were excused from attending.

Mr Justice McDermott decided the court wasn't in a position to proceed with the sentence hearing. He felt it wasn't appropriate, given the circumstances, so it was adjourned for two months in the hope that some normality would have returned by then.

The coronavirus hadn't gone away by the time the sentence hearing came round on 22 June 2020, but arrangements were made to ensure that it could safely take place. An overflow court, in which thirteen of Patricia's family members took over the public gallery, was set up, with a live video and audio link to the main courtroom. Keith Johnston's family were huddled together at the back of the courtroom. A number of lawyers were peppered across the benches at a social distance from each other, while the media were spread out across the empty jury box. Richard and Martina took their place in the body of the main courtroom.

Keith was first in the dock. He arrived with Stephanie a few minutes before the hearing got under way. Her hair was now a deep purple. Some of Patricia's friends from Beaumont Hospital gathered outside the courthouse with a large memorial photo montage of old pictures of his mother at work, which they later presented to Richard. He was very grateful. He missed her smile.

Detective Inspector Brian O'Keeffe took the stand again to give the court a summary of the evidence heard during the trial. Old wounds were soon reopened. New wounds were inflicted too as Patricia's sisters heard the details of Gus's interviews with gardaí for the first time. They couldn't believe it. How could he not have called emergency services? How could he just go back to bed like that, knowing his wife had been killed downstairs? He could at least have saved her the indignity of what happened to her body afterwards. He could have saved a lot of heartache. She could have had a proper funeral. Rita became visibly upset listening to what he had said.

A number of reports and testimonials were prepared ahead of the sentence hearing. Inspector O'Keeffe said he was 'slightly confused' by what he read in Louise's probation report. On the one hand, she said she now accepted the jury's decision. That would work in her favour. But if that was the case, Inspector O'Keeffe wondered, why did the report also state that she blamed Kieran and her father for getting her daughter involved? That was the first he'd heard of that allegation, and it wasn't backed up by what Stephanie told her probation officer. What's more, Gus couldn't possibly have put her up to it. He didn't return to the house until 10.23 p.m. that night. By then, Stephanie was already back at home, having left in her disguise almost an hour earlier. It didn't make sense.

At this point, Richard was given an opportunity to tell the judge how he had been affected by his mother's brutal murder, and the attempted cover-up that followed. More often than not, a victim impact statement is read into the record by a prosecuting barrister or one of the investigating officers. But Richard wanted to deliver his statement himself. He approached from the back of the court and walked straight past the dock without looking at any of the accused. He unfolded his prepared statement, cleared his throat and leaned into the microphone.

Demented, heartbroken, disgusted and deceived – these are only a few words to describe how I've felt about the murder of my mam since the twenty-ninth of May 2017.

My ability to have trust in people has changed. To process the amount of lies told to me by those who were my close family has led to many sleepless nights. The constant questions I ask myself: Could I have presented this? Why didn't I see the deceit around me? How could people I called family do such an unspeakable act?

The revelation of how my mam was murdered, the brutality of the act, the cold-hearted way in which she was dismembered, the disgusting way it was covered up, and then to find out who was involved will stay with me for the rest of my life.

All the pent-up frustrations and anger about how his mother was portrayed during the trial finally came to a head as Richard sat in the raised witness box, his father and sister just a few steps away. He described their portrayal of her as 'despicable'. He assured everyone in the courtroom that his mother was not the horrible person they had tried to make her out to be. He knew better. So too did her brothers and sisters, and the many friends she made through her work at the hospital. He said he'd been contacted by some of her former colleagues, who had only nice things to say about her. The girls from Beaumont Hospital's catering department had written to him to pay their respects. The letter outlined how horrified they were by all the lies that were told about their friend. They also wanted him to know that everyone who knew her in the hospital loved her. They described her as 'kind, loving and caring' and a fun person to be around. One of them, Bernie Heavey, penned a poem, entitled 'Patricia', which described her as 'a ray of sunshine' and their 'hero'. Their kind words were of great comfort to Richard, whose mother was never far from his thoughts.

> To have her taken away from me so cruelly when she had so much life left to live has left me totally devastated. My mam was a kind, caring and loving person, always willing to help with anything. I think about her all of the time. Her love of gardening, art, baking and nature and how she can't continue to pass on her love and knowledge to my children. My children have lost their nana far too early, not due to ill health, but due to the disgusting acts and lies of others.

Richard had spoken with his mother about her joining his family on holiday, but that wasn't to be. He said she wanted to learn a new skill, but instead she found herself 'drained financially, and unable to focus on what she wanted or needed'.

> I ask myself why do parents feel obliged to help their adult children, even though it causes tension and distress. Why did my mam have to die due to the utter selfishness and laziness of others?

He described how emotionally and physically draining he had found the whole trial process, and thanked Martina and their children for helping him get through what he described as 'three years of turmoil'.

> I put all my trust in the gardaí, the DPP, the courts and ultimately the jury, who I hoped could find the truth in all of this. I have now come to the conclusion that I will never know the full truth. I thank everyone involved in getting justice for my mam for their excellent work and sacrifice.

Not having his aunts and uncles in the courtroom for support didn't seem to faze Richard. He was a pillar of strength throughout the whole process. During the more difficult days, he was supported by his loving wife. It seemed from his statement that he had inherited his mother's ability to say it as it is.

> I'm at a loss to understand why after my mam's murder, they tried to destroy her character. Throughout the trial, and even now, no compassion, no real emotion, no remorse has been shown or spoken of by those involved.

His speech was kind and compassionate in places too, another nod to how his mother raised him. He even spared a thought for all those who found his mother's remains, a horror he wouldn't wish on anyone. The enormous loss he now felt was clear for all to see, but he also sympathised with the wider family, who had been robbed of the chance to get to know her.

I think of the impact on the innocent people involved: my family, my children, my other nieces and nephews. I know my children and family have been told the truth as best I can, and I wonder were my nieces and nephews given the same opportunity to know what really happened.

The five people in the dock had stolen so much from Richard. They had also denied his children the opportunity to get to know, and learn from, their grandmother; and robbed him of the chance to see her face one last time to say goodbye, something he said he'd never forgive any of them for.

He finished his powerful address by saying that he hoped the sentences handed down reflected the roles each person played in what he described as 'this terrible crime'.

Just as Richard was pushing his chair back, Gus's barrister rose to his feet to ask a question. Victim impact statements are considered as evidence in a case, so defence barristers are entitled to question the author. It's rare, but it is allowed. Mícheál P. O'Higgins SC promised to be sensitive. The judge gave a nod of approval, and Richard sat back down.

'May I ask what effect has this matter, and your father's participation, had upon you?' Mr O'Higgins asked.

Richard didn't hesitate to answer.

'My father has lost everything,' he replied. 'He has always looked after us. We were always number one. Family is number one to him. Everything is gone now. Fifty years living in that community, all gone. He has tried to build himself as a certain type of man his whole life, and now everything is lost.'

Mr O'Higgins didn't probe any further.

Patricia's sister, Colette Barry, then bravely took the stand to deliver a victim impact statement on behalf of her brothers and sisters. She took a big gulp of water before she began. Rita and the rest of the clan watched on from the overflow courtroom. They were so proud of her. Delivering an emotional statement like that at the front of a room full of lawyers and journalists is no easy task. To do it with the man who murdered your sister sitting just over your shoulder beside your convicted brother-in-law, niece and grandniece must have made it even more daunting for her. She apologised to the judge for her little water break before she started, to the amusement of her sisters down the hall.

She told the court the family was still in disbelief. They simply couldn't believe how their sister was so cruelly and brutally murdered, and they were 'sickened' to find out who was involved.

> The lies that were told, the cruel cover-up. It has been shocking and utterly disgusting to sit throughout the seven-week trial, to see all of their faces with no emotion of any kind.

Just like Richard before her, she told the judge that she and her brothers and sisters were 'deeply hurt' by how Trisha's character had been 'so cruelly tarnished by their spiteful lies'.

> The people who truly knew her, her sisters, brothers, friends, work colleagues, her neighbours, will defend her kind, caring, loving nature. A jolly woman who sang out loud as she went about her day.

Clearly swept away by the emotion of the moment, Colette broke down and sobbed. She paused. Mr Justice McDermott gave her an encouraging smile, to let her know there was no rush. Colette wanted everyone to know how much they loved their sister. No amount of words would ever do it justice, but the tears she shed for her spoke volumes. She persevered.

> They can never take those precious memories away from us. We are still trying to come to terms with the brutal and violent way her life came to a very sad end. Trisha, we love you always.

After Colette had returned to her family, the defence teams were invited to make submissions on behalf of their clients, with a view to assisting the judge to construct appropriate sentences.

Mr Justice McDermott's hands were tied in relation to Kieran. He had been found guilty of murder. A mandatory life sentence would soon follow.

Each of the others faced a maximum penalty of ten years in prison.

Mr O'Higgins pleaded to the judge to be as lenient as possible when it came to sentencing his 76-year-old client. He said he accepted full responsibility for his actions. What he did was 'wrong without justification. His conduct is all the more inexplicable because he was a kind and loving husband to her. He was a supportive father and grandfather,' he submitted.

His instructions were that after Patricia left the house, Gus became 'the sole rearer' of their two children. He said his client felt he was taken advantage of and controlled by his daughter, whom he described as a 'demanding person'.

Perhaps conscious that it was beginning to sound as if Gus was the victim in all this, Mr O'Higgins explained that he was just trying to put some context to his client's actions. He described the situation in the house as 'toxic', especially after Louise's family grew and the kids got older. In relation to his inaction on the night of the murder itself, Mr O'Higgins said that his client got 'caught up in a horrific experience, that wasn't his making'. Sure, he should have called the guards, not left the others to deal with the situation. He said he wanted to protect his daughter and 'not cause a family feud'.

A forensic psychologist assessed Gus ahead of his sentence hearing and found him to be a 'vulnerable and highly suggestive individual, who doesn't cope well with negative feedback'. His overall cognitive ability was below average, and he was characterised as someone who shies away from confrontation and is easily controlled by others. When he realised his wife was dead, he told the psychologist, he went into shock and just froze. When asked about the traumatic events of that night, he struggled to recall them in any great detail. Perhaps he was telling the truth when he told gardaí that he had been the victim of elder abuse at the hands of his demanding and controlling daughter. The report certainly seemed to suggest that he was vulnerable to such abuse.

Mr O'Higgins asked the judge to consider his client's otherwise faultless background. He had a 'long and valued work record', according to the senior barrister, who felt there was little public interest in sending a man of his advanced years to prison.

He said his guilty plea and genuine remorse should count for a lot and suggested he had already been punished for what he done.

'He has lost his place in his community, and was wrongly accused of actually killing his wife, something that undoubtedly attracts additional damage to his reputation,' Mr O'Higgins submitted.

Some of Gus's neighbours from Mountain View Park penned letters of support for the judge to consider. In Mr O'Higgins's opinion, it was clear his client had done something appalling, but he suggested he wasn't psychologically equipped to deal with the situation, and he pleaded for leniency.

When Mr Bowman rose to put forward his submissions on Louise's behalf, he tried to shed some light on the concerns raised by Inspector O'Keeffe about the genuineness of his client's acceptance of what she had done. It appeared that she had kept him in the dark somewhat too. He said it was self-evident from the CCTV evidence that Gus wasn't there at the time the plan was formed, so he simply couldn't have been involved. Louise also told her probation officer that Gus prevented her from going upstairs that night. Mr Bowman told the court that she had instructed him to say that wasn't true. He said her account of what happened on 29 May 2017 was 'sometimes confusing and difficult to follow', but that his express instructions from her were that she did accept the verdict of the jury.

He read out a number of testimonials on her behalf. Her second-eldest daughter had written a letter for Mr Justice McDermott, describing her mother as 'a kind, warm-hearted person, who did her best to keep the family together through a difficult time'.

Mr Bowman said his client and her children became homeless after she was forced to leave the house at Mountain View Park. They ended up staying in a one-bedroom apartment in Dublin city centre. A social worker who checked in on the children regularly described Louise as a caring mother who always put her kids first. That was certainly something she and Patricia had in common. A doctor who examined her before the trial found her to be extremely anxious, especially in light of the upheaval of her family unit. Louise described her children as 'the centre of her world' and said she'd do anything to protect them. She now claimed that's why she had lied to gardaí about the identity of the figure captured leaving the house that night. As soon as she realised Stephanie had participated, she saw her family was at risk. Mr Bowman suggested she was motivated by this concern for her family.

He also claimed she was remorseful, and aware of the effect her actions had had on her brother and the wider family.

'This wasn't premeditated,' he said. 'It was never her intention to conceal a crime. She just got caught up in a set of circumstances that spun out of control, and she's genuinely upset and distraught by what happened to her mother.'

Mr Bowman also drew the judge's attention to an agreement between Louise and the local authority, who provided her with more suitable living arrangements in Dundrum four months before the trial got under way. He said she had signed an undertaking to give up her tenancy if she was found guilty. He said his instructions were that a conviction would compromise her ability to keep her family together. Mr Justice McDermott looked perplexed. A guilty plea at an early stage would have entitled Louise to an automatic discount on her sentence, but she chose to contest the charge, as is her right. The trial judge asked Mr Bowman if he was trying to say she didn't plead guilty at the outset because of the threat to her home?

'Yes, is the answer to that question,' Mr Bowman sheepishly replied. Those were his instructions.

Keith Johnston's barrister, Mr Dwyer, reminded the judge of his client's role in the attempted cover-up. Despite what Kieran said about him, it wasn't the prosecution's case that he had anything to do with the dismemberment of Patricia O'Connor. It was never admitted in evidence, so he submitted that Keith's offence was towards the lower end of the scale of seriousness. Also contrary to what Kieran said in his statement from prison in December 2017, Mr Dwyer confirmed that his client didn't have a previous criminal record. He described him as a strong family man, who was 'devoted' to his children and took his parental responsibilities very seriously. He, like Mr Bowman before him, said his client acknowledged the devastation caused to the deceased and her family, and he too pleaded for leniency.

The mother of the young autistic boy who Stephanie befriended paid a glowing tribute to her in one of the many testimonial letters handed into the court on her behalf by her barrister, Mr Orange. He told the court that his young client had been on anti-depressants since her grandmother's murder. He said her age was of note: she was 22 years old now, but just 19 at the time. He walked the court through the findings of her probation report, highlighting the fact that she was considered to be in the low-risk group in terms of reoffending. Mr Orange described her as an 'impressive and intelligent young woman', who didn't drink or take drugs. He also pointed to one of the report's conclusions, which suggested probation services as an alternative to a custodial sentence.

Given the number of submissions made on behalf of Gus, Louise, Stephanie and Keith, Mr Justice McDermott decided to adjourn sentencing to a later date to allow him some time to consider appropriate sentences for each of them. However, he was conscious of the delay already imposed on all involved due to the Covid-19 pandemic, so he wouldn't leave them waiting for long. He told them he'd deliver his ruling at the end of the week.

There was no need to prolong Kieran's agony any longer. There was nothing left for the judge to decide. No submission or testimonial could alter his fate. He was asked to stand.

'Kieran Greene, you have been convicted by a jury of murder,' Mr Justice McDermott declared. 'As a matter of law, there's only one sentence that can be imposed, and that is life.'

17.

CARNATIONS AND MUMS

By the time it came to sentencing Kieran Greene and the others, the Victorian People's Flower Gardens in the Phoenix Park were in full bloom. Pristinely kept flowerbeds, dotted across the long, manicured greens, were bursting with the brightest of blossoms.

Friday, 26 June 2020 was a spectacular summer's day. From early morning, people flocked to the public garden to bask in the sunshine. Many of those attending court that day happily took the scenic route. It was a far cry from the dark, damp, cold surroundings of the courthouse when the trial opened five months beforehand.

Once again, Richard, his aunts and uncles made the trip to the Criminal Courts of Justice. For the last time, they hoped. Breda took the morning off work to be there too. Richard was one of the first into Court 6, where Mr Justice McDermott was sitting. The others assumed their positions in the overflow court. Some of them wore colourful summer dresses. Trisha would have approved.

Louise and Stephanie were first into the dock. Stephanie had a backpack with her, clearly not expecting to be going home afterwards. Her father joined them a few moments later, while Gus took his seat at the back of the courtroom to allow for social distancing. He seemed pleased with the arrangement.

Once everyone was in place, Mr Justice McDermott made his entrance. Light filtered into the courtroom through an external bronze screen, drenching the walnut furniture and fittings in glorious sunshine. From behind a recently fitted Perspex screen, he began by making some general observations in relation to the offences. To begin with, he reminded everyone that the maximum penalty available to him for the crimes committed by the four remaining accused was ten years in prison.

He chose not to go into the now well-worn details of how Patricia was killed, save to say that what happened to her was 'simply appalling'. The facts spoke for themselves.

'The most shocking aspect of the case, and the one which has attracted considerable attention, is the dismemberment of her remains afterwards,' he said.

That said, when it came to sentencing, he pointed out, he could only consider the offences of which those before him were found guilty. In other words, he couldn't punish them for the heinous acts of Kieran Greene. Those in the public gallery wondered if he was trying to manage their expectations.

'There are aspects of this case which rightly deserve condemnation and give rise to high emotion on the parts of those related to and friendly with the late Mrs O'Connor, and indeed amongst people at large,' he added.

He then explained that it was the court's function to assess the wrongdoing of each offender, and to *solely* look at what they were responsible for. He couldn't look beyond that.

Mr Justice McDermott is resolute when it comes to ensuring a person's right to a fair trial is maintained throughout the process. He, like the eleven jurors who ultimately sealed the fate of Kieran and the others, must leave emotion to one side and remain impartial to the core. But now that guilty verdicts had been delivered, he was free to let his opinions on certain matters be known.

He spoke about the devastating effect Patricia's gruesome death had had on her 'immediate and caring family', as set out in the victim impact statements delivered by Richard and Colette earlier in the week.

One of the most important things for those who truly cared for Trisha was that her good name would be restored. Mr Justice McDermott assisted them on that front by saying:

'The picture of Mrs O'Connor presented to me was one of a retired lady, who had worked hard all her life for her family and children, and for her grandchildren.

'She was a lady who was set to enjoy her retirement, if that were available to her. She wished only to get on with her retirement, if that were available to her, and wished just to get on with what was left of her life.'

He described the way Richard spoke about his mother as 'eloquent', and in a really classy touch, he reminded everyone gathered in the two courtrooms of the real reason they were there:

'Patricia O'Connor was the focus of attention to this court,' he said. 'She was the victim of this dreadful crime. She had a life and a future, until it was ended by the murder committed by Kieran Greene.'

Before moving on to sentencing, he also commended the gardaí for their 'painstaking' work in resolving this difficult case. He paid particular tribute to all those who trawled through the tough terrain of the Wicklow Mountains for the remains of Mrs O'Connor.

Then he turned his attention to Gus. He described his reaction to learning that his wife had been killed as 'appalling'.

'He didn't seem very interested or concerned that his wife was dead, instead he simply suggested that someone call the gardaí and retired to bed.

'He behaved disgracefully. He betrayed his wife. He refused to give her all the dignity and respect she was due.'

Despite his lawyer's pleas earlier in the week, Mr Justice McDermott refused to accept that Gus's offending was at the lower end of the scale of seriousness.

'It's appalling to think his suggestion that gardaí be called was rejected, and he still did nothing about it. CCTV evidence shows him up and about. I am satisfied he knew Kieran Greene moved and dismembered his wife's body before he made the false report.'

He criticised Gus for keeping up the charade even after Patricia's remains were found in the mountains. He described it as yet another 'gross betrayal' of his wife. He also chastised him for not telling Richard the truth, and for allowing him to believe his mother was missing at a time when he knew she was dead.

Mr Justice McDermott noted Gus's remorse, but accused him

of having no appreciation of the significance of not giving Richard, and others, an honest account of why he did what he did. He accepted all the mitigating factors put forward by Mr O'Higgins. He said he was conscious that a custodial sentence was 'a serious matter' for a 76-year-old man, but he also felt he *had* to serve some time in prison for what he did. All things considered, he decided eighteen months was appropriate. Gus's barrister jumped to his feet, pleading with the judge to consider suspending part or all of the sentence. His dramatic plea was met with a chorus of tut-tuts from the public gallery. In a last-ditch effort to get the judge to change his mind, Mr O'Higgins even submitted that his elderly client was very vulnerable to Covid-19, suggesting prison wouldn't be a safe environment for him. The judge wasn't for turning, though.

Next, Louise and Stephanie found themselves in the judge's crosshairs. Mr Justice McDermott told them their ruse was 'clearly contrived and adopted to avoid the consequences of [Patricia's] murder'.

'You allowed him the space that he needed to cover up what he did and dispose of the body. There was no attempt to call emergency services or a neighbour.'

He described their reactions as 'shocking and callous' and a 'gross betrayal' of their mother, grandmother, brother, uncle, family and friends. Louise bowed her head as he took aim at her specifically. He told her that she bore the greater degree of responsibility because of her 'dominant role' in the household. She was supposed to be the adult.

'Your behaviour allowed Kieran Greene to take whatever steps he needed to avoid detection,' he said.

Mr Justice McDermott said he still wasn't satisfied that either of them had provided a full and true account of their involvement. In the immediate aftermath of being convicted, Louise repeatedly implicated her own father, claiming he was the one behind the ruse. Stephanie blamed Kieran – she said he gave her €20 to do it. In any event, the judge accepted that Stephanie had played a lesser role in what he described as 'the horrible pretence'.

Before passing sentence, he said he was mindful of the knock-on effect a custodial sentence would have on Louise's other four children, especially with Kieran in prison too. He noted that she had been described as 'a caring and loving mother' by the family's social worker. That depiction was met with more tut-tuts. He spoke about the possibility of them losing their home if Louise were sent to prison, and for a moment everyone thought he was going to look at an alternative to a custodial sentence. However, given the gravity of the offence and her quasi-acceptance of her role in it, he felt he was left with no choice but to jail the mother of five. He handed down a three-year sentence, but suspended the final six months. Stephanie was jailed for one and a half years.

Keith Johnston was the last to feel the judge's carefully considered and measured wrath. Mr Justice McDermott described the very thought of dismembering Patricia's remains as 'grotesque'.

'It was clear her remains were never to be found, or if found, more difficult to identify,' he said. 'It was an important element in trying to hide the murder. He must have been mindful that if the body was never found, she would never get a proper burial, thereby causing even more distress to her family and friends.'

He scolded him for becoming a 'willing participant in a very cruel deception of her son, who was trying to find her'.

Again, he reminded those gathered that he could only sentence Keith for the offence he was convicted of. Despite what Kieran said, Keith wasn't accused of dismembering Patricia.

The judge accepted that he was a hardworking man, who showed 'a positive strength of character' to overcome a drug problem in his teenage years. He noted that he had provided considerable assistance, both practical and financial, to the O'Connor family down through the years, and that his offending behaviour was a 'serious deviation' from his otherwise positive character traits, but again he felt he had to mark what he had done with a custodial sentence. The so-called 'trusted handyman' was jailed for three years.

Flanked by his wife, Martina, his aunts, uncles and friends, Richard came outside afterwards to address the media. They all wore flowers to signify their loss. It was also a fitting tribute to Patricia's love of gardening. They chose carnations and chrysanthemums – 'mums', as Trisha used to call them. She definitely would have approved of those.

Richard wanted to thank everyone who had helped to secure the guilty verdicts for those involved in his mother's murder and the cover-up that followed. He also thanked all the soldiers and members of the public who had found her remains scattered across the Wicklow Mountains. He took a moment to compose himself before delivering his final message from the steps of the courthouse:

My mam was a kind and loving person. She was a mother, a sister and a grandmother, who had many years left to live that were so cruelly taken from her. The sentences given today we feel is not enough, but no length of time is long enough for the crimes they have committed. May they live with this on their consciences for the rest of their lives.

When he had finished, Richard stepped back into the embrace of his loved ones. It had been a long, hard road for them all, but they had walked every step of the journey together. That's what family is all about. They'd hoped for longer sentences, but no amount of punishment would bring Trisha back. Justice had been served. Those responsible were behind bars. The ones who really loved her could finally give her a proper send-off.

As they prepared to leave, a lovely framed photo of Trisha danced around the crowd. Her big smile was there for all to see.

Be happy, keep smiling.

ACKNOWLEDGEMENTS

First, I would like to thank Sarah Liddy, Commissioning Editor at Gill Books, for giving me a platform to tell Patricia's story. After one cup of coffee with Sarah, I knew Gill Books was a good fit for me. I didn't want to just retell a gruesome murder story for the sake of it, and thankfully Sarah shared my vision for the book. She understood how important it was to me to put Patricia centre-stage, and to have her voice heard after so many lies were told about her during the trial. It was a great comfort to know that Sarah was always there if I needed advice. She is a true professional who really cares about what she does, and she was a joy to work with.

I would also like to offer my sincere thanks to all of Patricia's family members, friends and former colleagues who helped me to tell her story. Some of those who contributed didn't want to be named, but I'm so grateful for their help in giving me a much deeper and better understanding of who Patricia really was. Special thanks to her sisters Rita and Kathleen for giving up so much of their time, during what could only have been the most difficult of times for them both. Their strength and dedication to their beloved sister truly inspired me and kept me motivated. It was a real joy to hear about Patricia through the stories of her friends and former colleagues at Beaumont Hospital, especially Breda Wosser, Sandra Flynn and Josie Dunne. We are often judged by the company we keep, and it's fair to say that Patricia surrounded herself with the kindest, funniest and most loving bunch of friends you could ask for. Breda deserves particular praise for all her contributions. It was clear from the first of our many chats that Patricia was a very dear friend of hers and she, like the others, just wanted the world to know what an amazing person she was. They all spoke so fondly of Patricia and I hope I did their accounts and memories of her justice.

Many thanks to the rest of the team at Gill Books who worked on this project, especially my editor Aoibheann Molumby, whose golden fingerprints are all over the finished product. Aoibheann is a workhorse and, lucky for me, she is a master of her craft. Her attention to detail is second to none. I really couldn't have asked for a better guide throughout the whole process. Special thanks too to Laura King, who had the tough task of sourcing photographs for the book, and to all the designers, proofreaders, typesetters and printers who helped bring the book to life. Much praise is also due to Avril Cannon, Publicity Executive, and Teresa Daly, Marketing and Communications Manager, for all their work in promoting the book.

Thanks to my esteemed colleagues and friends, Alison O'Riordan, Ireland International News Agency; Andrew Phelan, *The Herald* and the *Irish Independent*; Deborah Naylor, Virgin Media News; Barry Cummins, RTÉ; and Sue Nunn from KCLR 96FM for all their help. Thank you also to Sinéad Spain, Group Head of News at Communicorp Media, for her unrivalled support in everything I do, and to *The Pat Kenny Show* on Newstalk and

Today FM's *The Last Word with Matt Cooper* for giving me the airtime to bring detailed updates from the Central Criminal Court to our listeners on a daily basis.

And on a personal note, I would like to thank my dear friend David Fitzpatrick and the whole team at BóTOWN for keeping the show on the road while I worked on the book. As my deadline loomed, David shielded me from the day-to-day distractions of running a busy restaurant so I could focus solely on getting it across the line. He is the ultimate business partner and friend. You really couldn't ask for a better person to be in your corner, particularly when the going gets tough. Our lifelong friendship means the world to me and I'm eternally grateful for everything he has done for me.

I would also like to thank my family. They are my greatest source of strength and encouragement. Thanks to my mum Noreen, brother John, sisters Gertrude and Eileen, brother-in-law Julien and nephew Jack for all their love and support. I'll keep a special copy for my biggest fan, my father John, to whom this book is dedicated. He passed away in 2018, but is never far from my thoughts and was with me all the way through this. He was my sole companion on all those long, lonely, sleepless nights as I put the book to bed. He's the reason I do what I do. Thanks, Pops.

A final nod to a very special person, who will remain nameless. You know who you are. Thank you for being my confidant and for keeping my secret project to yourself.